# Lecture Notes in Artificial Intelligence 1712

Subseries of Lecture Notes in Computer Science
Edited by J. G. Carbonell and J. Siekmann

## Lecture Notes in Computer Science

Edited by G. Goos, J. Hartmanis and J. van Leeuwen

W0042643

# Springer

*Berlin*
*Heidelberg*
*New York*
*Barcelona*
*Hong Kong*
*London*
*Milan*
*Paris*
*Singapore*
*Tokyo*

Harold Boley

# A Tight, Practical Integration of Relations and Functions

 Springer

Series Editors

Jaime G. Carbonell, Carnegie Mellon University, Pittsburgh, PA, USA
Jörg Siekmann, University of Saarland, Saarbrücken, Germany

Author

Harold Boley
Stanford Medical Informatics
251 Campus Drive, Stanford, CA 94305-5479, USA
E-mail: boley@SMI.Stanford.EDU

Cataloging-in-Publication data applied for

**Die Deutsche Bibliothek - CIP-Einheitsaufnahme**

**Boley, Harold:**
A tight, practical integration of relations and functions / Harold Boley. -
Berlin ; Heidelberg ; New York ; Barcelona ; Hong Kong ; London ; Milan ; Paris
; Singapore ; Toyko : Springer, 1999
 (Lecture notes in computer science ; 1712 : Lecture notes in artificial
intelligence)
 ISBN 3-540-66644-3

CR Subject Classification (1998): I.2, F.4, F.3, D.3

ISBN 3-540-66644-3 Springer-Verlag Berlin Heidelberg New York

© Springer-Verlag Berlin Heidelberg 1999
Printed in Germany

Typesetting: Camera-ready by author
SPIN 10705076    06/3142 – 5 4 3 2 1 0    Printed on acid-free paper

# Preface

As in other fields, in computer science certain objects of study can be synthesized from different basic elements, in different ways, and with different resulting stabilities. In subfields such as artificial intelligence, computational logic, and programming languages various relational and functional ingredients and techniques have been tried for the synthesis of declarative programs. This text considers the notions of relations, as found in logic programming or in relational databases, and of functions, as found in functional programming or in equational languages. We study a declarative integration which is tight, because it takes place right at the level of these notions, and which is still practical because it preserves the advantages of the widely used relational and functional languages PROLOG and LISP. The resulting relational-functional language, RELFUN, will be used here for exemplifying all integration principles.

Part of the unique attraction of computer science stems from the fact that most of its notions permit a multitude of simultaneous perspectives, connecting form and content, theory and practice, etc. Thus, the study of programming involves syntax, semantics, and pragmatics: Syntactically, a program can be specified by grammar formalisms on several levels. Semantically, a program can be characterized as a static entity such as a mathematical model and by dynamic computations such as derivation traces. Pragmatically, a program can be run by an interpreter, in an abstract machine, and as native code of a real computer. In order to obtain insights into new programming paradigms one can start off from either of these ends or from somewhere in the middle. The texts treats most of these perspectives for the RELFUN integration, whose development started at the practical ends, later tailored theoretical ones for them, and now is proceeding in both directions:* In chapter 2.6. the PROLOG-like user syntax is specified by an EBNF grammar. In chapter 3 the semantics is founded equivalently on Herbrand models and on SLD-resolution. In chapter 5 the pragmatics is implemented via the Warren Abstract Machine. For further summaries we refer to the reader's guide at the end of the overview chapter 1 and to the synopses at the beginning of all five chapters.

---

*This research was supported by the Univ. Kaiserslautern, the SFB 314, and the BMBF under the DFKI Grants ITW 8902 C4 and 413-5839-ITW9304/3.

Here we summarize our contributions to the theory and practice of tight relational-functional integration:

- The relational notions of non-ground terms and (don't-know) non-determinism were integrated with the functional notions of application values and higher-order functions into a minimal kernel system (chapter 1).

- This was extended by 'first-class' finite domains and exclusions (chapter 4), sort hierarchies, 'single-cut' determinism specification (chapter 2), etc.

- Encapsulated partial (non-ground) data structures were transferred to the functional paradigm even for computations with ground I/O (chapter 2).

- The semantics of first-order functions was founded on the same model-theoretic level as that of relations (chapter 3).

- Relational-functional transformers, compilers, and abstract machines were developed in LISP (chapter 5).

- Using these, application studies were conducted about declarative programming in engineering domains (chapter 1).

- The reusability of concepts, techniques, and source programs was shown with the languages COLAB (BMBF project ARC-TEC) and DRL (BMBF project VEGA).

My thanks go first to Michael M. Richter for having set standards in combining theory and practice, for discussions concerning Horn-logic and higher-order functional programming, for many suggestions with respect to succinct formulation, for his encouragement during this entire work, as well as for establishing the DFKI department of Intelligent Engineering Systems. And I want to thank all 'IIS' colleagues at the DFKI for their patience in times when I was preoccupied with this work. In particular, in the ARC-TEC knowledge-compilation group, Philipp Hanschke, Knut Hinkelmann, and Manfred Meyer provided input that helped me improve things. More recently, in VEGA, Andreas Abecker, Otto Kühn, and Holger Wache have also given me important feedback on the use and presentation of RELFUN. In particular, in the DRL and RFM groups we have been discussing issues of declarative representation languages and relational-functional machines. Thanks to Panagiotis Tsarchopoulos for joining us for a while. On this occasion I want to acknowledge the software contributions to the defining RELFUN interpreter by the (former) students Simone Andel, Michael Christen, Klaus Elsbernd, Andreas Gilbert, Victoria Hall, Hans-Günther Hein, Michael Herfert, Thomas Labisch, Markus Perling, Ralph Scheubrein, Michael Sintek, Werner Stein, and Stefan Steinacker. Additional special thanks go to Markus Perling and Michael Sintek for their key contributions to the compiler/emulator system and to most of the other RELFUN components as well as for their careful proof-reading of several drafts of this text. Many other people at the Fachbereich Informatik and the DFKI of the University of Kaiserslautern have helped me in important ways, and I want to thank you all.

As this text is a revision of my Habilitationsschrift at the Fachbereich Informatik of the Universität Kaiserslautern, I also want to acknowledge my referees Wolfram-M. Lippe (Institut für Informatik, Universität Münster), Otto Mayer, and Michael M. Richter, as well as the head of my Habilitation committee, Stefan Heinrich. Furthermore, I am thankful to Burckhard Strehl and his colleagues and students from the Fachbereich Mathematik of the Universität Kaiserslautern for their help with our RELFUN-based ontology for the Mathematics International study program. I am also grateful to Andreas Dengel and his collaborators from DFKI's Information Management and Document Analysis lab for providing an environment that permitted the development of Web-oriented REL-FUN enhancements such as ONTOFILE. Moreover, my thanks extend to Mark Musen and his collaborators at Stanford Medical Informatics for giving me the opportunity to explore cross-fertilizations of RELFUN and PROTEGE axiom languages. Finally, I appreciate the advice of Ralf Kleinfeld from infoTex Kaiserslautern about setting up the RELFUN Web domain http://www.relfun.org/.

Kaiserslautern and Stanford, July 1999                      Harold Boley

# Contents

# Chapter 1

# An Overview of the Relational-Functional Language RELFUN

This overview considers research and development in integrated declarative programming based on the design, semantics, implementation, and use of the RELFUN (RELational-FUNctional) language. RELFUN reciprocally extends Horn relations and call-by-value (eager) functions just enough to yield a unified operator concept. Relations acquire application nesting and higher-order notation; functions acquire nongroundness and non-determinism. Relations are defined by Horn-like clauses implicitly returning true; functions are defined by rules with an additional returned-value premise. This minimal relational-functional kernel then provides a platform for common extensions such as finite domains, avoiding their duplication as separate features of logic and functional languages. Operational (interpreter in pure LISP), procedural (SLV-resolution), fixpoint, and model-theoretic semantics were developed for pure RELFUN. The compiler system has a layered structure, ranging from source-to-source transformers to a declarative classifier, to a code generator for the WAM (Warren Abstract Machine). Applications include a library of declarative (hyper)graph operations, a CAD-to-NC transformer of geometry/plan terms, as well as sharable knowledge bases on materials science and engineering.

## 1.1 Declarative Merger via Minimal Extensions

The aim of *declarative programming* is separating user-oriented knowledge and problem specification (the 'what') from machine-oriented data representation and execution control (the 'how'), permitting to focus the former by mechanizing the latter. The two classical declarative paradigms are applicative (functional) programming in the tradition of pure LISP and logic (relational) programming following pure PROLOG. Moves towards "declarativeness in the large" were quite successful with modern functional (e.g., Haskell [FHPJW92]) and relational (e.g., Gödel [HL94]) programming. However, the intuitive basic communalities between functional and relational languages have led to increasing efforts at their integration in search of a unified declarative paradigm variously called 'functional-logic', 'relational-functional', etc. (in fact, there is now an integrated Gödel-successor language, Escher [Llo94], and a standardization proposal, Curry [Han97]). The present work approaches central issues of such an integration with an emphasis on syntactic and semantic simplicity as called for by practical use. The discussion is based on our experience with the design, semantics, implementation, and use of the RELFUN (RELational-FUNctional) language [Bol99a].

RELFUN can be viewed as a 'minimal commitment' interchange format for declarative programming: PROLOG **and** LISP programs can be generated from a neutral specification, which can also be executed directly. This is analogous to the generation of HTML **and** LaTeX from SGML. Running the RELFUN interpreter and compiler, users can rapidly prototype, test, apply, and maintain relational-functional programs in a high-level, neutral format; employing the translator from a RELFUN to an ISO PROLOG subset (`rfp2pl`, based on `relationalize` of section 1.4) and that from a RELFUN to an ANSI COMMON LISP subset (`deta` of [Sin95]), users can also deliver many programs in these existing relational and functional standards. (Translators to further relational, functional, and relational-functional languages can benefit from available modules, as did our translator to a KIF [GF91] subset.) Keeping within our relational-functional interchange subset, users will thus be able to build up a declarative library, distributed via the WWW [Bol96], without committing to any one of the languages reachable by a translator. Besides this direct, 'object-level' Web use of RELFUN, we also conceived an indirect, 'meta-level' Web application, ONTOFILE [Bol99b], sketched in section 1.5. On the basis of REL-FUN and XML a Relational-Functional Markup Language (RFML) can thus be realized.

Let us first consider characteristics of PROLOG-like relational programming and LISP-like functional programming wrt relational-functional cross-extension and integration. The resulting relational-functional language design, kernel RELFUN, then provides a platform for the study of further useful extensions preserving uniformity.

More precisely, we have followed a two-stage strategy for developing a tightly integrated, practically oriented declarative language:

1. Find initial *minimal* extensions sufficient to integrate the essential relational and functional notions of PROLOG and LISP, which have shown their usefulness over the longest period of time.

2. Find further *common* extensions of the integrated relational-functional language needed in practice and implementable efficiently, thus avoiding later efforts of integrating separate extensions (from further declarative constructs to graphical interfaces).

The RELFUN language, studied in this work, is an instance of such a development:

1. Kernel RELFUN integrates the kernels of PROLOG ('sequentialized Horn clauses') and LISP ('named `lambda` expressions') via *operators*, which constitute the 'least general generalization' of PROLOG relations and LISP functions via four essential cross-extensions (detailed below).

2. Pure RELFUN extends this integrated kernel (i.e., relations *and* functions) mainly by constructors and operators of *varying arities*, a 'first-class' reconstruction of the practically established *finite domains* (and the complementary, new *finite exclusions*), and *order-sorted logics*; full RELFUN again extends the pure sublanguage by 'single-cut' determinism specification for operator definitions, relational-functional meta-calls, (graphical) I/O, debugging tools, etc.

This development strategy was prototypically confirmed by the ease with which it was possible to extend our already integrated relational-functional language by finite domains and exclusions, thus avoiding separate relational and functional extensions, and the difficulties of their later integration.

Our rationale for striving for minimality of the integrated declarative kernel language can be summarized as follows:

1. Minimality helps to keep integrative notions clearly separate from various additional features. In a very large relational-functional language kernel the essential integrative aspect would become lost among all the other aspects.

2. An integration achieved through a smaller kernel is stronger than one achieved through a larger kernel because it has to fuse the relational and functional notions more thoroughly.

3. Teaching of declarative programming is easier when using a smaller set of integrated relational-functional notions.

4. Industrial acceptance of a declarative language will be more likely with a simple kernel than with a complicated one.

5. If the declarative kernel is large already, the full language in practice is even larger. This entails a number of general disadvantages, some of which have been often discussed in connection with large imperative programming languages such as PL/1, ADA, and C++ (the latter compared to Java). Let us just mention two:

    (a) Large applications, in particular data bases and knowledge bases, can be developed and maintained more easily in a small language.

    (b) The language itself is easier to use and maintain if it is smaller.

6. The smaller we can keep the relational-functional kernel, the more design economy we can gain through *common extensions* benefiting both the integrated language and its two sublanguages.

7. There is also an aesthetic appeal in attempting to achieve an integration with minimal conceptional overhead.

Thus, our primary concern is *minimal integrative extensions* of both declarative programming paradigms wrt fusion into the desired relational-functional kernel. For this, two prominent relational essentials, (R1) and (R2), are mapped to corresponding extensions of functional programming, and two prominent functional essentials, (F1) and (F2), are similarly transferred to the relational paradigm:

**(R1)** The relational essential of permitting first-order *non-ground terms* (terms being or containing free logic variables, which may become bound by calls) will be transferred to functional programming in the following way: a function can take non-ground terms as arguments by using (two-sided) unification instead of (one-sided) matching, and similarly can return non-ground terms as values. With call-by-value evaluation of functional applications this will lead to innermost conditional narowing [Fri85].

**(R2)** Since a non-ground (e.g., inverse) function call may deliver several 'solution values', this also entails a transfer of the relational essential of *(don't-know) non-determinism* (solution search, implemented by backtracking enumeration as in PROLOG) to functional programming. Historically, however, non-ground functional programming was proposed as a result of relational-functional integrations [DL86], while non-deterministic functional programming was first introduced as a purely functional generalization [Hen80].

**(F1)** The functional essential of *application values* (function applications return value terms, hence can be nested into 'functional compositions') will be transferred to relational programming as follows: a relation that holds (its call succeeds) always returns the value `true` in the manner of a characteristic function, besides possibly binding variables. On the other hand, each argument of a relation call may be the value returned by an application rather than a directly specified term. Hence, (passive, instantiated) structures are explicitly distinguished from (active, evaluated) applications by transferring a version of LISP's `backquote` on function arguments to PROLOG's relation arguments; RELFUN's PROLOG-like syntax marks instantiation vs. evaluation by square brackets vs. round parentheses, while the logical semantics further sharpens the distinction via disjoint alphabets of (uninterpreted) constructor and (defined) function symbols.

**(F2)** The functional characteristic of *higher-order functions* is more problematic. For instance, the survey [Han94] does not treat the integration of higher-order functions into logic programming but considers it as interesting for future work. The fundamental difficulty here is that an adequate common denotational semantics for full logic-plus-functional programming would have to bridge an increased gap [Ric93]: logic programming is based on Horn logic, a fragment of first-order predicate logic, while functional programming is based on recursion theory, dealing with full-fledged higher-order functions. Rather than abandoning Herbrand models [Llo87] in favor of, say, Henkin models [Llo94], our functional sublanguage thus only permits functions named by terms (constants or structures), not anonymous (lambda) functions, because named functions are computationally complete (already with a fixed set of 'combinators', but we allow them to be user-defined), predominant in practice, and easier to integrate with relations (avoiding the issue of lambda variables vs. logic variables, and the undecidability of higher-order unification). The functional essential of *higher-order functions over named functions* (named functions as functional arguments and values) will then be transferred to relational programming: a relation can take named relations as arguments (an operator returning a relation as its value is again a function).[1]

## 1.2 From Relations and Functions to Operators

Reciprocally extending relations and functions, the RELFUN notion of *operators* covers an area spanned by two orthogonal dimensions, (non-)truth-valuedness and (non-)determinism: varying the **type** of values, an operator can be specified to return only truth-values (as an unmixed relation does), to return both truth-values and general values (as a mixed relational-functional operator does), or to return only non-truth-values (as an unmixed function does); independently varying the **number** of solutions, an operator can be specified to deliver exactly one solution (being deterministic like a classical function) or to deliver zero or more solutions (being non-deterministic like a classical relation).

More precisely, kernel RELFUN's operators extend pure PROLOG's relations towards the functional essentials, (F1) and (F2), of section 1.1 by making them *(three-valued) characteristic functions* on success returning true (instead of just printing yes), on failure yielding unknown (instead of printing no), and for explicitly available negative information returning false. They extend LISP's functions by enabling the relational essentials of section 1.1: (R1) *non-ground*

---

[1] Conversely, our relational sublanguage permits logic variables also in the relation position of queries and definitions ('predicate variables'), introducing some syntax of *second-order predicate logic*. This will be transferred to functional programming ('function variables'). The higher-order functions and relations permitted here, although practically very useful, embody just conservative, syntactic extensions that can be reduced to equivalent first-order versions by introducing a dummy operator. For the resulting first-order relational-functional language a common (Herbrand-)model-theoretic semantics will be introduced.

*functions* with free logic variables as/in arguments (which may become bound through calls) and as/in values; (R2) *non-deterministic functions*, enumerating any number of zero (i.e., failure or unknown) or more values. These individual extensions are just sufficient for being integrated into our uniform operator concept: generally, RELFUN's operators can take ground or non-ground arguments; they always either fail with unknown (permitting no variable bindings) or enumerate one or more truth-values, true or false, or any other ground or non-ground values (along with possible bindings of argument variables).

Such an operator is defined by a system ('procedure') of *valued clauses*, which – as a simple extension to PROLOG's Horn-clause top-level syntax – can let the new infix "&" precede an explicit *foot* expression that evaluates to the returned clause values. Semantically, valued clauses can be ordered wrt expressive power as follows, where *extra-variables*, not occurring in a clause head $op(arg_1, ...)$, are permitted in all clause premises – both in body conditions $cnd_i$ and as/in a foot expression $exp$:

(1) *Unit clauses* (facts) $op(arg_1, ...)^2$ for extensional relation definitions are implicitly true-valued.

(2) *Unconditional directed equations* $op(arg_1, ...)$ :& $exp$ for operator (normally, function) definitions whose case distinctions are made only via unification of left-hand sides (written as clause heads) return an explicit right-hand-side (rhs) expression value.

(3) *Non-unit clauses* (rules) $op(arg_1, ...)$ :- $cnd_1, ..., cnd_M$ for relation definitions whose case distinctions require conditions (written as clause premises, also used for accumulating partial results in extra-variables) are implicitly true-valued.

(4) *Conditional directed equations* $op(arg_1, ...)$ :- $cnd_1, ..., cnd_M$ & $exp$ for operator (normally, function) definitions whose case distinctions require conditions, as in (3), again return an explicit rhs expression value, as in (2).

Note that the unconditional definitions (1) and (2) are listed before the more expressive conditional definitions (3) and (4). Further, the true-valued definitions (1) and (3) stand before the more expressive arbitrary-valued definitions (2) and (4), respectively: a function's explicit value may happen to be true. In particular, a Horn rule of the form (3) can be regarded as a true-valued conditional directed equation $op(arg_1, ...)$ :- $cnd_1, ..., cnd_M$ & true specializing (4). Similarly, (1) may be seen as the specialization $op(arg_1, ...)$ :& true of (2), with a constantly true rhs expression, or as the specialization $op(arg_1, ...)$ :- true of (3), with a constantly true condition; both in turn can be seen as the specialization $op(arg_1, ...)$ :- true & true of (4), with a constantly true condition and expression.

---

[2]For clauses written as part of text lines or semantic models, the PROLOG dot terminator "." will always be elided.

We may thus view RELFUN operator definitions as Horn clauses equipped with a truth-value convention, as in (1) and (3), or generalized by a value-returning specification, as in (2) and (4); we may simultaneously view them as directed equations understood to have a constantly true rhs, as in (1) and (3), or having an arbitrary rhs, as in (2) and (4). In both of these views the "&"-symbol precedes expression premises, while the ":-"-symbol precedes condition premises. Alternatively, the RELFUN notation would support a chiefly functional perspective, where the ":&"-symbol precedes all kinds of premises: an ordinary ","-conjunction can be parenthesized into a truth-functional expression $(cnd_1, \ldots, cnd_M)$ – which returns just a truth-value – in the (3)-equivalent $op(arg_1, \ldots)$ :& $(cnd_1, \ldots, cnd_M)$ acting as the rhs of the directed equation infix ":&"; a valued "&"-conjunction can be parenthesized into a conditional expression $(cnd_1, \ldots, cnd_M \ \& \ exp)$ – which returns an arbitrary value – in the (4)-equivalent $op(arg_1, \ldots)$ :& $(cnd_1, \ldots, cnd_M \ \& \ exp)$ acting as the rhs of ":&". The ordinary notation for conditional equations, $op(arg_1, \ldots) = exp$ if $cnd_1, \ldots, cnd_M$, whose "if"-clause always qualifies the "="-infixed equation, would not support reinterpreting $(exp$ if $cnd_1, \ldots, cnd_M)$ as a self-contained construct.

Summarizing, valued clauses integrate Horn-logic facts (1) and rules (3), as well as unconditional (2) and conditional directed equations (4), possibly with extra-variables, into one kind of axiom. This tight integration of Horn clauses and directed equations will be anchored in the model theory (as indicated in section 1.4) and distinguishes RELFUN from all those functional-logic languages that employ an explicit equality **predicate** and are based on *Horn logic with equality* (an example will be discussed in section 1.6).

As in PROLOG, the premises of a valued clause are conveniently processed from left to right, the clauses of a procedure in an analogous textual top-down manner. Operator definitions not making unique case distinctions (e.g., through pairwise disjoint clause heads) give rise to non-deterministic search realized depth-first, by backtracking. In the relational-functional semantics (cf. section 1.4), this 'AND/OR-sequentialism' conceptually becomes 'AND/OR-parallelism'.

Full-RELFUN operator definitions augment this by 'single-cut' determinism specifications in valued clauses, restricting the cut ("!") use of PROLOG: there is at most a single "!" per clause, which is syntactically regarded as a separator, not as a parameterless pseudo-goal, to emphasize the departure from a pure-RELFUN clause.[3] Also, an n-ary once built-in is provided to avoid intra-clause determinism specification via "!". Because of RELFUN's integrated notion of operators, new methods of (avoiding) determinism specification will immediately benefit both its relations and functions.

---

[3]Thus, full RELFUN's OR-sequential single-cut separator "!" would correspond to an (optional) OR-parallel commit operator "|" in (extended) committed-choice languages.

# 1.3  PROLOG-LISP-RELFUN Comparison

Some of our relational-functional notions will now be exemplified by developing RELFUN higher-order operators from a corresponding PROLOG relation somepro and LISP function somelsp. These generalize the well-known member predicate (function), replacing its equality test by the application of an arbitrary testing predicate: if it succeeds on a list element, the relational versions just answer affirmatively, whereas the functional versions return the list starting with the successful element (i.e., what LISP calls a "useful non-nil value", truth-functionally equivalent to true); after the first success, the relational versions can be restarted for finding further successful elements (non-determinism), whereas the functional versions just stop (determinism). The following table contrasts the some definitions, incidentally exemplifying how RELFUN's *interchangable PROLOG-like and LISP-like syntax* attempts to bridge an old syntactic schism:[4]

| | |
|---|---|
| **PROLOG source:**<br><br>`somepro(P,[F|R]) :- G =.. [P,F],`<br>`                     call(G).`<br>`somepro(P,[F|R]) :- somepro(P,R).` | **RELFUN representations:**<br>PROLOG-like syntax:<br><br>`somer(P,[F|R]) :- P(F).`<br>`somer(P,[F|R]) :- somer(P,R).`<br><br>LISP-like syntax:<br><br>`(hn (somer _p (tup _f | _r)) (_p _f))`<br>`(hn (somer _p (tup _f | _r))`<br>`    (somer _p _r))` |
| **LISP source:**<br><br>`(defun somelsp (p l)`<br>`  (cond ((null l) nil)`<br>`        ((funcall p (first l)) l)`<br>`        (t (somelsp p (rest l)))))` | **RELFUN representations:**<br>PROLOG-like syntax:<br><br>`somef(P,[]) :& false.`<br>`somef(P,[F|R]) :- P(F) !& [F|R].`<br>`somef(P,[F|R]) :& somef(P,R).`<br><br>LISP-like syntax:<br><br>`(ft (somef _p (tup)) false)`<br>`(ft (somef _p (tup _f | _r)) (_p _f)`<br>`    ! '(tup _f | _r))`<br>`(ft (somef _p (tup _f | _r))`<br>`    (somef _p _r))` |

---

[4]On the top-level, ":-"-clauses are mapped to "hn"-lists, ":-...&"-clauses become "ft"-lists. Bidirectional PROLOG-LISP-syntax translation [Her92] is an integral part of RELFUN's programming environment.

While the PROLOG version somepro requires the extra-logical "=.." (univ) and meta-logical call built-ins for applying its predicate argument P to the first list element F, the corresponding RELFUN version somer just employs the second-order logic notation P(F). While the LISP version somelsp uses a conditional for branching on its three cases, the corresponding RELFUN version somef employs three clauses, explicating LISP's cond determinism by a single-cut;[5] LISP's list selectors first and rest are replaced by unification, as in PROLOG (RELFUN's lists are written with an n-ary tuple constructor, implicit in its PROLOG-like "[...]"-syntax); since RELFUN's variables are syntactically marked off from (operator) constants (by a leading underscore or capital letter), COMMON LISP's (funcall p (first l)), via SCHEME's/EULISP's (p (first l)), can be cleanly replaced by (_p _f) or P(F); LISP's identification of false with nil (RELFUN's "(tup)" or "[]") is abolished.

Given facts woman(linda), woman(mary), and man(john), a list of persons can be checked for "Some woman to the right of some man?" by a function-in-relation nesting like somer(woman,somef(man,[linda,john,mary])), which via somer(woman,[john,mary]) returns true. All versions but somelsp can be called with non-ground arguments ('symbolically'), as for constructing "A list of men" by somer(man,L), which returns true and binds L to a non-ground list of the form [john|R] (non-determinism will be exemplified below); somef(man,_) instead returns the non-ground list as its value (PROLOG's anonymous variable "_" suppresses the binding).

Bringing together the non-determinism of PROLOG and value returning of LISP, we can join somer and somef to somerf, our actually proposed RELFUN version (again transformable into a relational RELFUN version somerfr):

| RELational-FUNctional proposal: | Relational RELFUN transform: |
|---|---|
| somerf[P]([F\|R]) :- P(F) & [F\|R]. <br> somerf[P]([F\|R]) :& somerf[P](R). | somerfr[P]([F\|R],[F\|R]) :- P(F). <br> somerfr[P]([F\|R],V) :- <br>                      somerfr[P](R,V). |

In essence, somerf makes somer's clauses list-valued or, omits somef's determinism (cut) and false specifications. Thus, somerf becomes a generator applying the testing predicate P to successive list elements and enumerating P-

---

[5] Usually, cond's virtual 'cutting' of the condition-action clauses following the first clause with a non-nil condition is not considered as compromising functional (globally deterministic) declarativeness; a similar view may be possible for the transcription of cond clauses into single-cut (locally deterministic) pattern-action clauses of a (globally non-deterministic) declarative language. Anyway, the current "!"-use saves a negated repetition of P(F) in the third clause and could again be encapsulated into a relational-functional if...then...else... built-in, but a more pure and concise non-deterministic solution will be suggested as the final version somerf below.

headed sublists as returned values, while for no (more) such sublists yielding unknown. In addition, for permitting 'partial applications', also possible with Currying, somerf employs P as a parameter indexing the operator name, so that the list is left as the single argument.

Modifying an earlier example, the call somerf[man]([linda,john,mary]) is deterministic, returning the list that starts from the only man, [john,mary]. The call somerf[woman]([linda,john,mary]) is non-deterministic, enumeratively returning the lists that start from each woman, [linda,john,mary] and [mary]. This non-deterministic function call can be nested into another somerf call, somerf[man](somerf[woman] ([linda,john,mary])), deterministically returning [john,mary], since the second attempted outer call, somerf[man]([mary]), fails with unknown. The non-ground call somerf[woman](L) alternates infinitely many returned values of the forms [linda|R] and [mary|R], with corresponding bindings of L to [...,linda|R] and [...,mary|R]. Using the parameterized somerf[man] itself as the somerf parameter, somerf[somerf[man]]([[linda,mary],[linda,john,mary],[john]]) interprets the list values of the two successful sublist calls relationally as true, so the main call non-deterministically enumerates the two returned values [[linda,john,mary],[john]] and [[john]].[6]

Finally, somerfr, a 'relationalized' version of the somerf function (compare the definitions in the table above), employs an extra argument for representing the returned value, like the translation of unconditionally defined first-order functions in [Kow83]. However, since this returned value originated from somef's "useful non-nil value" for a relation (somer), we would not normally make it an additional argument just for reformulating the somerf function as a relation (somerfr) again. In fact, somerf appears to be the 'local optimum' in our relational-functional derivation series. It exhibits a principal advantage of functions, namely that their nestings can be analyzed and transformed more easily than corresponding relational conjunctions. For example, a program optimization eliminating redundant operator calls and duplicate backtracking solutions may collapse somerf nestings using the same predicate parameter P, because besides backtracking somerf acts like the list identity if the first list element

---

[6]Certain such parameterizations may deserve a name. In LISP, numberlist, member, and other specialized functions could be defined on the basis of somelsp, perhaps using an anonymous lambda expression:

```
(defun numblsp (l) (somelsp #'numberp l))
(defun memblsp (x l) (somelsp #'(lambda (e) (equal x e)) l))
```

RELFUN permits corresponding definitions on the basis of the general somerf, instead of the anonymous lambda expression employing a generally useful unary eq1 operator (if the visibility of eq1 outside the membrf definition is not desired, the membrf body could encapsulate the eq1 clause into an implicational goal of the RELFUN extension discussed in [Her95]):

```
numbrf(L) :& somerf[numberp](L).
membrf[X](L) :& somerf[eq1[X]](L).
eq1[C](A) :- equal(C,A).
```

With these, membrf[john]([linda,john,mary]) via somerf[eq1[john]]([linda,john,mary]) returns [john,mary]; somerf[membrf[john]]([[linda,mary],[linda,john,mary],[john]]) acts, non-deterministically, like the above somerf self-parameterization. Similarly for numbrf.

satisfies P (also, for the empty list, the unknown signal is preserved). For the functional version we could thus use a concise, general static transformation rule:

```
somerf[P](somerf[P](L)) --> somerf[P](L)
```

The relational `somerfr` counterpart would instead have to transform conjunctions by a rule needing a contextual application condition to prevent further occurrences of the required intermediate-result variable (a more general version would also have to permit non-adjacent or even permuted `somerfr` calls):

```
somerfr[P](L,M), somerfr[P](M,N) --> somerfr[P](L,N)
   if M doesn't occur elsewhere in the conjunction
```

## 1.4 Semantics and Implementation

The semantics of the first-order-reduced RELFUN kernel is formalized by equivalent *procedural*, *fixpoint*, and *model-theoretic* means, extending those of logic programming [Llo87]. In particular, the procedural SLD-resolution for Horn-clause programs is extended to *SLV-resolution* for valued-clause programs, e.g. accomodating value returning and operator nesting. Simultaneously, the underlying Herbrand (base) models, containing ground 'atoms' (flat relationships), are extended to *Herbrand cross models*, containing ground 'molecules' (flat function applications asymmetrically ":&"-paired with terms). Instead of all ground term equations in the Herbrand base for models of logics with (e.g., symmetry-axiomatized) equality [Fri84], the Herbrand base for cross models thus contains all ground 'innermost' defined-function applications associated with all ground terms, denoting their ultimate computation values (just as the usual Herbrand base contains all ground relation applications, denoting their ultimate truth). For integrated relational-functional programs, such models become united to *Herbrand crossbase models*, containing both atoms and molecules.

As an illustration, the middle row of the table below gives RELFUN definitions of corresponding non-deterministic relational and functional programs for computing partof relations and functions over materials. The table's upper row shows their least models, which are finite since the programs are confined to constructorless relational (DATALOG) and functional (DATAFUN) language subsets. The entire middle row can also be regarded as a single relational-functional program, whose least crossbase model is the union of the columns of the upper row.

Knowledge implicit in the programs is made explicit by the models, here containing the reflexive-transitive closure of the main and auxiliary part relations/functions (e.g. giving all parts of ferroconcrete). For fixed input-output modes of the relations, here to be declared as partr(in,out), `mainpartr(in,out)`, and `auxipartr(in,out)`, the ground atoms of the Herbrand model are in a one-to-one correspondence to the ground molecules of the Herbrand cross model. However, the left-to-right direction of molecules extensionally formalizes the semantics of (directed) functions via 'pointwise' argument-value definitions; this mode-like information is lost in atoms, extensionally formalizing (undirected) relations. Thus, without separate mode declarations the `partr` relation does not distinguish the 'whole-part' direction of the `partf` function from the 'part-whole' direction of a possible inverse. Note that molecule directedness does not affect the non-deterministic semantics of functions such as `partf`, which is formalized by two molecules such as $partf(ferroconcrete)$ :& $concrete$ and $partf(ferroconcrete)$ :& $steel$ having the same argument but different values. SLV-resolution, provably equivalent to the models, can be used to obtain all possible answers from the programs; e.g. `partr(ferroconcrete,X)` via five relational SLV-refutations non-deterministically binds X to `ferroconcrete`, `concrete`, `steel`, `iron`, and `carbon`, while `partf(ferroconcrete)` via five functional SLV-refutations non-deterministically returns these values. SLV-resolution is realized in pure LISP as part of an interpreter that provides both an operational semantics and an implementation of full RELFUN.

The implementation of RELFUN generally rests on a *definitional interpreter* for operationally specifying the language, *compilers/emulators that extend the WAM (Warren Abstract Machine)* for executing it efficiently, and *source-to-source transformers* for reducing language extensions or preparing programs to source-to-instruction compilation. Normally, there are alternative paths for efficiently running a RELFUN program. Most naturally, the first-order-reduced RELFUN kernel can be either transformed to PROLOG via the `relationalize` algorithm (e.g. rewriting a function like `partf` to a relation like `partr`) or, compiled to the extended WAM via its nesting-`flattening` phase (e.g. transforming the nesting `partf(mainpartf(W))` to the conjunction `_1 .= mainpartf(W)`, `partf(_1)`, with the new variable `_1` bound by a generalized is-primitive, ".="), not needing its `extra-argument-inserting` phase (illustrated by the `somerf-somerfr` transition in section 1.3). Our WAM emulators, based on [War83, AK91], reuse the first argument register in a new way, namely for value returning, giving rise to a natural optimization, namely unary-function nesting without register transfer.

To illustrate, the lower row of the table gives the extended WAM code of the `partr` and `partf` programs along with their `auxipartr` and `auxipartf` subprograms (the elided `mainpartr` and `mainpartf` subprograms being similar). Even without going into details, the juxtaposition of corresponding relational and functional WAM instructions shows the optimization of the nestings `partf(mainpartf(W))` and `partf(auxipartf(W))`: relational register transfers via `get` and `put` instructions become unnecessary in the functional version since `mainpartf/1` and `auxipartf/1` return their values to the X1 register, where they are needed by the `partf/1` recursions.

| Least Herbrand (base) model: | Least Herbrand cross model: |
|---|---|
| $\{partr(ferroconcrete, ferroconcrete),$ | $\{partf(ferroconcrete) : \& \ ferroconcrete,$ |
| $partr(concrete, concrete),$ | $partf(concrete) : \& \ concrete,$ |
| $partr(steel, steel),$ | $partf(steel) : \& \ steel,$ |
| $partr(iron, iron),$ | $partf(iron) : \& \ iron,$ |
| $partr(carbon, carbon),$ | $partf(carbon) : \& \ carbon,$ |
| $partr(ferroconcrete, concrete),$ | $partf(ferroconcrete) : \& \ concrete,$ |
| $partr(ferroconcrete, steel),$ | $partf(ferroconcrete) : \& \ steel,$ |
| $partr(ferroconcrete, iron),$ | $partf(ferroconcrete) : \& \ iron,$ |
| $partr(ferroconcrete, carbon),$ | $partf(ferroconcrete) : \& \ carbon,$ |
| $partr(steel, iron),$ | $partf(steel) : \& \ iron,$ |
| $partr(steel, carbon),$ | $partf(steel) : \& \ carbon,$ |
| $mainpartr(ferroconcrete, concrete),$ | $mainpartf(ferroconcrete) : \& \ concrete,$ |
| $mainpartr(ferroconcrete, steel),$ | $mainpartf(ferroconcrete) : \& \ steel,$ |
| $mainpartr(steel, iron),$ | $mainpartf(steel) : \& \ iron,$ |
| $auxipartr(steel, carbon)\}$ | $auxipartf(steel) : \& \ carbon\}$ |

## Relational program:

```
partr(W,W).
partr(W,P) :- mainpartr(W,I),
              partr(I,P).
partr(W,P) :- auxipartr(W,I),
              partr(I,P).
mainpartr(ferroconcrete,concrete).
mainpartr(ferroconcrete,steel).
mainpartr(steel,iron).
auxipartr(steel,carbon).
```

## Functional program:

```
partf(W)  :& W.
partf(W)  :& partf(mainpartf(W)).

partf(W)  :& partf(auxipartf(W)).

mainpartf(ferroconcrete) :& concrete.
mainpartf(ferroconcrete) :& steel.
mainpartf(steel) :& iron.
auxipartf(steel) :& carbon.
```

## Relational WAM code:

```
partr/2: try_me_else p2, 2
         get_x_value X1, X2
         proctrue
p2:      retry_me_else p3
         allocate
         get_y_variable P, X2
         put_y_variable I, X2
         call mainpartr/2, 2
         put_unsafe_value I, X1
         put_y_value P, X2
         deallocate
         execute partr/2
p3:      trust_me_else_fail
         allocate
         get_y_variable P, X2
         put_y_variable I, X2
         call auxipartr/2, 2
         put_unsafe_value I, X1
         put_y_value P, X2
         deallocate
         execute partr/2
. . .
auxipartr/2: get_constant steel,X1
             get_constant carbon,X2
             proctrue
```

## Functional WAM code:

```
partf/1: try_me_else p2, 1

         proceed
p2:      retry_me_else p3
         allocate



         call mainpartf/1, 0


         deallocate
         execute partf/1
p3:      trust_me_else_fail
         allocate



         call auxipartf/1, 0


         deallocate
         execute partf/1
. . .
auxipartf/1: get_constant steel,X1
             put_constant carbon,X1
             proceed
```

We think the WAM-extension path is important to obtain a direct relational-functional language implementation avoiding dependency on PROLOG compilers. Also, a `relationalized` RELFUN program has sacrificed the functional style, is harder to read and use, and is statically longer than its (relational-) functional source; so it cannot substitute the source, but still debugging tools would operate on this too low, `relationalized` level. Moreover, most pure-RELFUN extensions of kernel RELFUN (e.g. finite domains and exclusions) also affect the relational sublanguage, but are not available in normal PRO-LOG compilers. As an alternative to transforming RELFUN subsets to PRO-LOG, they can be transformed to LISP; the FLIP work [Sin95] couples one of our WAM emulators with an abstract functional stack machine that provides better-than-WAM efficiency for emulating deterministic functions.

Altogether, the table gives a top-down illustration of the scope of our concerns wrt relational-functional programs (middle row), extending from model-theoretic semantics (upper row) to compilative implementation (lower row).

## 1.5 Applications

Besides the exemplary RELFUN definitions small enough to be discussed in this work, some quite realistic RELFUN programs were written (for examples of increasing size also see the collection in [Bol93a]; further examples are online[7]). Five such RELFUN applications will be sketched here: A library of declarative graph and hypergraph operations, a CAD-to-NC transformer of declarative geometries and plans, sharable knowledge bases on elementary materials science and production/recycling materials engineering, a relational-functional genetic algorithm for approximations to traveling-salesman problems, as well as a language for modeling exterior and interior ontologies of File/HTTP URLs. Our initial focus has been on the representation of engineering knowledge, supporting its evolutionary maintenance and inferential use [ABH+95]. This has later been broadened to include, e.g., Web applications [Bol96].

**1. Declarative (hyper)graph representation and processing:** Directed recursive labelnode hypergraphs, which generalize directed labeled graphs with regards to more natural modeling of multi-level structures and n-ary relationships, were embedded into RELFUN [Bol92a]. Operations on such (generalized) graphs are specified in a declarative fashion to enhance readability and maintainability. For this, graphs are represented as nested RELFUN terms kept in a normal form by rules associated directly with their constructors. Certain kinds of sharing in graph diagrams are mirrored by binding common subterms to logical variables. Apart from these, declarative graph processing makes a mostly functional use of RELFUN: graph terms become the arguments and returned

---

[7]The RELFUN homepage at the URL `http://www.dfki.uni-kl.de/~vega/relfun.html` contains sample sources and dialogs as well as documents on applications.

values of functions. The package includes generalized set operations, structure-reducing operations, and extended path searching.

**2. Generation of abstract NC programs from CAD-like geometries:** In our COLAB suite of experimental NC-program generators for lathe turning of rotational-symmetric workpieces [BHH+91, BHHM95], one version was written entirely in RELFUN [Sin91, BPS97]. This mainly functional program consists of three principal transformation components, which can be used individually and in combination. First, a term representation of the CAD-like geometrical raw data is parsed into a recursively classified workpiece, exhibiting production-relevant workpiece features (e.g. 'grooves' and 'shoulders') as a nested term. From this, a skeletal production-plan term is created by mapping features to sequential, commutative, and alternative subplans (ultimately, lathe actions). Finally, the abstract NC program is generated as a list of actions via a qualitative simulation 'executing' the plan in order to fix alternative subplans and sequentialize commutative ones.

**3. Sharable knowledge bases for materials science and engineering:** Physical/chemical properties of the elements and their groupings (ELEMENTS) [SSB93] as well as engineering properties of certain plastics pertaining to production/recycling (RTPLAST) [Buh94, BBK94] have been provided as sharable RELFUN knowledge bases. The ELEMENTS knowledge base represents the period system of the elements by a nested relational fact for each element (e.g. specifying the atomic weight, a ternary electron-configuration structure, and a varying-arity structure of possible oxidations) and functions for computing atom groups and tables. The RTPLAST knowledge base represents the family of recyclable thermoplastics (e.g., polyolefines subsuming polypropylenes) as a lattice of second-order subsumption relations between predicates or sorts, and their engineering properties (e.g., density, hardness, and additives) as facts centered around such order-sorted first arguments. Knowledge concerning production and recycling is represented by relational-functional rules (e.g., certain additives enforce recycling in closed circles). RTPLAST thus permits interactive and embedded queries for selecting thermoplastics with given combinations of properties (e.g., reflecting production/recycling requirements).

**4. A genetic algorithm for the traveling-salesman problem:** The GeneTS study showed how a relational-functional language can be used for specifying and running genetic algorithms [Per97]: informal descriptions of the traveling-salesman problem (TSP) and its genetic solution strategy are systematically developed into an executable RELFUN specification. This application achieves good approximations to optimal TSP solutions by employing a genetic-algorithm variant with TSP-tailored chromosome representations and genetic operators (mainly mutation and crossover). The genetic TSP algorithm requires about 240 lines of RELFUN source, a program-size reduction by a factor of 4 to 5 compared to a similar C implementation. On the other hand, the efficiency of the GeneTS specification is not comparable to that of a genetic TSP implementation in C, because of its list rather than array realization of chromosomes. GeneTS thus necessitates using the C-based RAWAM [Per98], RELFUN's fastest compiler-emulator combination.

**5. A conceptual-modeling language for file/HTTP ontologies:** To cope with the ontological complexity of (distributed) file systems, the ONTOFILE language was introduced [Bol99b]. On the basis of RELFUN and the metadata-element set Dublin Core, it describes files by exterior and interior ontologies for the respective structuring of their manifest and underlying features. These declarative representations are subdivided into manifest file designators, attributes, and relations as well as underlying file entities and properties. Exterior designators are RELFUN terms uniformly used to name local and global files by URLs of schemes `file` and `http`, respectively. Exterior attributes and relations are refined by parameters; single-valued and multiple-valued attributes are represented, respectively, by deterministic and non-deterministic functions. Interior entites and properties are modeled by subsumption heterarchies; property-to-entity applications return the files in which they hold. An interior ontology can be employed at the same time, like in fact retrieval, as a knowledge base formally summarizing the content of files and, like in document retrieval, as an index for the names of files containing detailed information. Besides retrieval, interior heterarchies permit two kinds of inference, inheritance and expansion.

While all five applications employ both relations and functions, RELFUN's functional style is emphasized in 1., 2., and 4., while its relational style is stressed in 3.; application 5. gives equal weight to relations and functions. This relational-functional composition has changed during the development of some of these applications, reflecting moving problem specifications and various programmer preferences; smooth shifts between both styles were possible because of the natural transformations between RELFUN relations and functions, both manual and automatic. Also, RELFUN's single-cut is used frequently by applications 1. and 5., employed sparingly by application 4., avoided via a top-level once by 2., and not required by 3. As expected, the single-cut is used mostly as a determinism-specification device for functions. Actually, the experience with applications 1. and 2. motivated the inclusion of a single-cut operator into the full-RELFUN system. On the other hand, we have kept the development of application 3. confined to the cutless relational-functional style.

## 1.6   Related Work

Here we compare our integration of relational and functional programming with three other recent languages, namely LIFE, ALF, and HiLog, representing typical current proposals in the field of extended declarative programming. The BABEL-like integration of lazy evaluation (call-by-need) with backtracking can only be mentioned here, as it is orthogonal to the issues studied with our minimal extensions and entails a further layer of advantages and disadvantages [HLW92]. Since there is still some lack of reports on applications of relational-functional languages (comparable to the RELFUN applications sketched in section 1.5), this aspect will not appear here.

**Sorts and constraints:** LIFE (Logic, Inheritance, Functions, Equations) [AKP93] generalizes first-order constructor terms to $\psi$-terms, built from sorts with an unordered, varying-length attachment of features (attributes); these are unified during relation calls in a special manner, involving the computation of the greatest lower bound (glb) in an explicit sort lattice. RELFUN keeps ordered constructors, which, however, can have varying lengths; it has 'first-class' sorts unifying via LIFE-like glb computation; there is also an extension, ORF (Object-centered RelFun) [Sin93b], which is based on 'facts' whose unordered unary-constructor-term arguments are used as attributes ('positionalized' to ordinary facts), and which permits 'parallel' inheritance (realized via rules). LIFE keeps ground, deterministic functions, whose calls are matched by defining rules as soon as they become ground (non-ground calls 'residuate') in the fashion of constraint-logic programming. RELFUN permits non-ground, non-deterministic function calls, integrating them with relations, but also permits relational-functional determinism (not: groundness) specifications affecting calls, clauses, or procedures; 'first-class' finite domains and exclusions permit 'residuationless' constraint propagation. While LIFE deliberately separates relations (unification) and functions (matching), RELFUN emphasizes their integration, from non-deterministic relations via non-deterministic functions to deterministic functions.

**Equations and rewriting:** ALF (Algebraic Logic Functional language) [Han91] consists of Horn clauses for user-defined relations and (conditional) equations for user-defined functions; RELFUN's valued clauses encompass both kinds of definition, replacing the equality predicate "=" of an equation by ":-...&", where "..." stands for zero or more conditions, whose "="- become ".="-calls. For example, if appfun is defined as the list-concatenation function, in ALF the conditional equation (with extra-variables L1 and E)

```
last(L) = E  <-  appfun(L1,[E]) = L
```

can be employed to define the function last; the equivalent RELFUN definition consists of the valued clause (which uses the extra-variable E first in the result-accumulating condition and then in the value-returning position)

```
last(L)  :-  L .= appfun(L1,[E]) & E.
```

Note that the ALF definition embeds the function application of last into the "="-predicate of the head equation, whereas the RELFUN definition employs the function application (just like a relation application) directly as the clause head: while ALF avoids regarding relations as boolean functions, REL-FUN wishes to put relations and functions on the same (top-)level of clauses. The declarative semantics of ALF is that of Horn-clause logic with equality;

for RELFUN a model-theoretic semantics for first-order functions was developed directly on the level of the usual Herbrand models for Horn relations. The operational semantics of ALF is based on SLD-resolution for relations and rewriting and innermost basic narrowing for functions; for RELFUN's valued clauses SLV-resolution was developed to encompass relations and functions, corresponding to innermost narrowing. The efficiency-enhancing inference rule of rewriting used in ALF could be adapted for optimizing REL-FUN programs with deterministic functions (with a confluent rewriting system). ALF has a many-sorted type structure and a (parameterized) module system, used by a preprocessor; RELFUN employs order-sorted unification and modules/files managed like the workspace. The implementation of both languages uses an extended WAM: ALF has integrated deterministic rewriting into the WAM; RELFUN uses a WAM-coupled abstract stack machine for deterministic functions [Sin95] (non-deterministic functions being WAM-integrated).

**Higher-order notation:** HiLog [CKW93] extends Horn clauses by a higher-order syntax and allows arbitrary terms in places where constructors (functors) and relation names occur in predicate calculus. The same is true for RELFUN. For instance, a *variable* used as a *constructor* permits elegant structure traversal in both HiLog and RELFUN. Similarly, the earlier RELFUN higher-order relation somer (cf. section 1.3), using a *variable* in the place of a *relation name*, is also a well-formed HiLog definition. In addition, "database schema browsing" rules in HiLog can use the *structure* relations(Obj) as a (parameterized) *relation name*:

```
relations(Obj)(R)   <-   R(Obj,Arg2).
relations(Obj)(R)   <-   R(Arg1,Obj).
```

An equivalent RELFUN definition marks off the structure with square brackets:

```
relations[Obj](R)   :-   R(Obj,Arg2).
relations[Obj](R)   :-   R(Arg1,Obj).
```

The relational query relations[john](X) binds X to the names of all binary relations (a tuple of which) containing john. Unlike HiLog, RELFUN may reformulate this higher-order relation using a syntax for higher-order functions, where the structure's passive functor use becomes a defined-function application and the output argument R becomes its returned value:

```
relations(Obj)   :-   R(Obj,Arg2)   &   R.
relations(Obj)   :-   R(Arg1,Obj)   &   R.
```

The functional query relations(john) returns all binary relation names containing john. This example also shows a difference in the interpretation of variables used as premises (here, the returned value R): while HiLog would impose a kind of implicit metacall, RELFUN just returns the value unless evaluation is enforced by its explicit meta-operator `ecal` (from LISP's `eval` and PROLOG's `call`). Generally, while HiLog evaluates variables (only) in places of atomic formulas, RELFUN instantiates variables (uniformly) in the top-level and in subterms. In both languages, the higher-order syntax, although very useful, can be reduced to a first-order (Horn-logic) semantics by introducing an `apply` dummy operator [War82]. Problems of its (more direct) WAM implementation are discussed in [CKW93] as well as chapter 5.

## 1.7  Reader's Guide

After this overview, constituting chapter 1, an extended relational-functional style is developed in chapter 2, the model-theoretic semantics of a pure RELFUN is given in chapter 3, first-class finite domains and exclusions are incorporated in chapter 4, and the WAM compilation of a multiple-valued RELFUN is dealt with in chapter 5.

The following chapter 2, a completely revised version of [Bol92b], develops extended relational-functional programming in RELFUN. First, relations are extended to an open-world semantics as well as to varying-arity and higher-order operators. Second, DATALOG relations are 'directed' to DATAFUN functions, thus deriving the constructorless subset of RELFUN, including non-groundness and non-determinism; full RELFUN is introduced via functions defining self-normalizing data structures; higher-order functions follow naturally. Third, the relational-functional style is demonstrated in use via Warren's serialise program, the Wang algorithm, and McCarthy's eval function. Further, the EBNF syntax of full RELFUN is specified.

Chapter 3, an update of [Bol93b], gives a model-theoretic characterization of a pure RELational-FUNctional language. Herbrand crossbase models are introduced to capture the semantics of both relations (as sets of undirected ground atoms) and functions (as sets of directed ground 'molecules', i.e. calls paired with values). SLD-resolution for definite (relational) clauses is extended to SLV-resolution for valued (functional) clauses, obtaining a top-down relational-functional proof procedure. The soundness of SLV-resolution wrt our crossbase models is shown. Then the fixpoint characterization of least Herbrand models is extended to least Herbrand crossbase models, obtaining a bottom-up relational-functional enumeration procedure. Using this operator, the completeness of SLV-resolution is shown.

In chapter 4, a slightly adapted version of [Bol94], finite domains and finite exclusions are incorporated into the integrated relational-functional language as first-class citizens. Our domains/exclusions are structures prescribing one/forbidding all of their finite number of argument constants. As terms, they can be used in relational queries and definitions to obtain increased efficiency and readability. In functional programming they also permit 'closed non-deterministic' and 'negative' answers as returned values. Unification is extended to treat the pairing of domains, exclusions, and other terms (e.g. as the membership of a constant in a domain or the intersection of two domains). Dually, domain/exclusion anti-unification is introduced (e.g. as the union of two domains) to permit clause generalizations.

Finally, chapter 5, a replacement of [Bol90], deals with multiple-valued functions and the WAM compilation of (multiple-valued) RELFUN. The first part introduces multiple-valuedness (e.g. the quotient-and-remainder sequence of a division function), as opposed to non-determinism (e.g. the enumeration of the positive and negative solutions of a square-root function). Variations of a palindrome example are used to discuss single-valued and multiple-valued RELFUN. The second part presents the phases of our compilation strategy: Source-to-source transformers normalize multiple values that are active calls into a 'denotative' version, 'flatten' (possibly non-deterministic) function nestings, and reduce higher-order operators to a 'constant-operator' form. A source-to-instruction translator generates code for the WAM by functionally extending the use of X-registers and 'put'/'get' instructions.

# Chapter 2

# Extended Logic-plus-Functional Programming

Extensions of logic and functional programming are integrated in RELFUN. Its valued clauses comprise Horn clauses ('true'-valued) and clauses with a distinguished 'foot' premise (returning arbitrary values). Both the logic and functional components permit LISP-like varying-arity and higher-order operators. The DATAFUN sublanguage of the functional component is shown to be preferable to relational encodings of functions in DATALOG. RELFUN permits non-ground, non-deterministic functions, hence certain functions can be inverted using a ".="-primitive generalizing the 'is' of PROLOG. For function nestings a strict call-by-value strategy is employed. The reduction of these extensions to a relational sublanguage is discussed and their WAM compilation is sketched. Three examples ('serialise', 'wang', and 'eval') demonstrate the relational/functional style in use. The list expressions of RELFUN's LISP implementation are presented in an extended PROLOG-like syntax.

## 2.1 Introduction

Many approaches are possible for combining logic and functional programming, as illustrated by the collection [DL86]. These can be preclassified in two principal dimensions. (1) The combination may start with a model-theoretic semantics which is then refined (via proof theory) for practical programming or, it may start with an implemented operational semantics which is tuned in practice and then abstracted for model-theoretic foundation. (2) A quite separate distinction is whether one is interested in a loosely coupled hybrid system or, whether one strives for a tightly integrated logic/functional language.

With RELFUN we have been pursuing the latter alternatives of these dimensions: it was first operationally defined as a highly integrated language (cf. [Bol86]), which was later endowed with a model-theoretic semantics capturing the essence of the integration (cf. chapter 3).

The language's operational side stems from its origin as a pure-LISP-based interpreter. Also the present version is both implemented in, and can access precoded functionality from (a subset of) COMMON LISP. Besides the definitional interpreter this implementation consists of a WAM compiler/emulator system. The RELFUN-in-LISP implementation runs all the examples to be presented here, where the speed is acceptable except, understandably, for the LISP-in-RELFUN example.

RELFUN's integrating concept is valued clauses, encompassing both PROLOG-style Horn clauses (for defining relations) and directed conditional equations (for defining functions). While the former start off from Horn logic, the idea for the latter is to regard a function definition like

$$ signum(x) = \begin{cases} -1 & if \quad x < 0 \\ 0 & if \quad x = 0 \\ 1 & if \quad x > 0 \end{cases} $$

not as clauses of a logic with **equality** (shown on the left) but as clauses that **return** the right-hand sides of the directed equations via a ("&"-marked) premise following after possible conditions (shown on the right):

```
eq(signum(X),-1) :- X < 0.        signum(X) :- X < 0 & -1.
eq(signum(0),0).                  signum(0) :- & 0.
eq(signum(X),1)  :- X > 0.        signum(X) :- X > 0 & 1.
```

Hence, function calls need not be embedded into eq calls with auxiliary request variables, as in eq(signum(-2.7),SignumA), eq(signum(3.1),SignumB), SignumA < SignumB, but can be written directly, as in signum(-2.7) < signum(3.1). We then interpret value-returning premises (after the ampersand) as generalized Horn-rule premises: apart from being terms like -1 they may be calls like *(-1,X) or member(X,[-1,-3,-5]) and nestings like +(*(-1,X),3) or member(X,rest([-1,-3,-5])). Nestings are evaluated strictly call-by-value, as, classically, in FP [Bac78].[1]

---

[1](Nested) function calls will be written with (round) parentheses, while [embedded] structures or lists will be distinguished by [square] brackets. Since in the above eq definition signum can be seen as the constructor of a structure, this version can be simulated in RELFUN, too. Since RELFUN employs a LISP-like prefix notation also for builtin relations such as < and >, the runnable RELFUN forms of the two versions are

```
eq(signum[X],-1) :- <(X,0).        signum(X) :- <(X,0) & -1.
eq(signum[0],0).                   signum(0) :- & 0.
eq(signum[X],1)  :- >(X,0).        signum(X) :- >(X,0) & 1.
```

The RELFUN notions of *relation* and *function* are amalgamated to an abstract *operator* concept: functions are generalized to non-ground, non-deterministic operators, hence relations can be viewed as characteristic functions. Our notion of relations as true-valued functions is like in SLOG [Fri85], except that RELFUN's valued facts return true implicitly. Another amalgamating notion is akin to LISP's "useful non-nil values": relation-like operators may on success return a value more informative than true (e.g., we can let member return the list starting from the element found). All kinds of RELFUN operators can be applied in generalized Horn-rule premises, which are usable uniformly to the left as well as to the right of the "&"-separator. Actually, such premises constitute a kind of (variable-sharing) conditional expression or *valued conjunction*, also permitted as a top-level query (e.g., member(X,L) & member(X,M), with L and M bound but X free, non-deterministically binds X to common elements of L and M and returns X-headed rest lists of M). A special valued conjunction calling only relations to the left of "&" and having a single variable to its right (e.g., country(X), between(X,atlantic,pacific) & X) can be viewed as an indefinite description or $\eta$-expression (e.g., $\eta(x)[country(x) \land between(x, atlantic, pacific)]$), also provided in other relational/functional amalgamations (see [PS91]).

Certain RELFUN functions can be inverted by calling them non-ground (by-value) on the right-hand side (rhs) of a generalized PROLOG is-primitive, ".=", mimicking relations (incl. the above eq predicate). RELFUN thus provides a version of *innermost* conditional narowing [Fri85]. Its operational semantics *flattens* functional nestings to relational conjunctions, thus inherits the search-space reduction of SLD-resolution [BGM88]. Hence, a WAM implementation of (first-order) RELFUN can catch up the speed of PROLOG (see chapter 5).

Besides its attempt at integrating basic notions of PROLOG and LISP, many of RELFUN's extended concepts can also be transferred to relational and functional programming individually. In the following section (2.2) the extended relational component will be treated, including higher-order relations. The next section (2.3) will augment this by the extended functional component and discuss its benefits. Then, the section (2.4) before the conclusions (2.5) will give three sample uses of the relational/functional style. Finally, the appendix (2.6) will specify the common syntax.

## 2.2 Relations Defined by Hornish Clauses

### 2.2.1 Open-World DATALOG

First we consider DATALOG i.e., PROLOG without structures (constructor symbols applied to arguments). This 'simple-domain' language of (normalized) relational databases is also a subset of RELFUN. DATALOG clauses have identical syntax[2] and equivalent semantics in PROLOG and RELFUN. Queries to RELFUN differ only as follows: they **return** the truth-value **true** instead of **printing** the answer **yes**; they signal failure by yielding the truth-value **unknown** instead of printing **no**.

When we stay in the relational realm of RELFUN this makes not much of a difference since **true** can be mapped to **yes** and **unknown** can be mapped to **no**. However, when proceeding to RELFUN's functional realm, queries will be able to return the third truth-value **false**: this is to be mapped to those of PROLOG's **no** answers for which the closed-world assumption is justified. In general, however, RELFUN does not make the closed-world assumption, and in the absence of explicit negative information modestly yields **unknown** instead of 'omnisciently' answering **no**.

For example, given the DATALOG knowledge base

```
subfield(architecture,bridgebuilding).
applicable(pharmacy,medicine).
applicable(computerscience,bridgebuilding).
applicable(computerscience,computerscience).
applicable(Tool,Field) :- subfield(Field,Sub),
                          applicable(Tool,Sub).
```

a successful query like `applicable(computerscience,architecture)` returns **true** in RELFUN and prints **yes** in PROLOG; however, a failing query like `applicable(computerscience,agriculture)` yields **unknown** in RELFUN but prints **no** in PROLOG. As with most real-life knowledge, what we know about computer-science applications is inherently open-ended; RELFUN's **unknown** reply agrees to the required open-world semantics.

Later, in DATAFUN, certain relations such as `subfield` will be reformulated as functions (cf. section 2.3.1). This will also have consequences for 'Horn' rules such as the `applicable` rule which still define a relation but call a sub**function**, e.g., in a ".="-rhs: `applicable(Tool,Field) :- Sub .= subfield(Field), applicable(Tool,Sub)`. To accomodate such functional (and ".="-'equational') extensions in relational rules, we speak of *hornish rules* or, generally, *hornish clauses*.

Two further extensions of DATALOG, varying-arity DATALOG and higher-order DATALOG, will be treated implicitly in the corresponding full-PROLOG extensions (see subsections 2.2.4 and 2.2.5).

---

[2]The syntax shown for full RELFUN will continue to be PROLOG-like (cf. appendix 2.6). In the implementation it becomes equivalent LISP-like list expressions. Although the (older) LISP-like syntax will not be shown here, some users still prefer it to the (newer) PROLOG-like syntax. RELFUN has been given two syntaxes to facilitate communication between users from the LISP and PROLOG communities.

## 2.2.2  PROLOG-like Structures and Lists

Let us now proceed to PROLOG with *structures* and its RELFUN extensions. PROLOG has only constructor symbols and no defined function symbols; arguments to PROLOG relations must always be (passive) structures and can never be (active) calls. RELFUN, on the other hand, does support both of these categories, hence has a notational need to distinguish between them.

First consider the more basic distinction of relations on the one hand, and constructors and defined functions on the other hand: while mathematical accounts of first-order logic express the distinction by disjoint sets of relation (predicate) and function symbols, PROLOG just distinguishes predicate (top-level) and functor (sublevel) **uses** of these symbols, and permits the same symbol to occur as a predicate and as a functor. This permits metalogical reinterpretations of certain structures as goals (via `call`).

In the same interactive-programming spirit RELFUN does not distinguish active and passive functor **symbols** but just active and passive functor **uses**. For this we note that all functor uses take the form of applications, which we write with round parentheses for 'active' operator calls and with square brackets for 'passive' structured terms. In the relational part of RELFUN this means that only top-level relation calls are written with parentheses, PROLOG-like structures are written with brackets. (In the functional part both top-level and nested function calls will be parenthesized, too.)

Consider the successor constructor s, often used together with 0 for specifying invertible operations on natural numbers. Thus, while in PROLOG the structure corresponding to 2 is s(s(0)), in RELFUN it is s[s[0]]. For instance, the RELFUN lesseq relation definition

```
lesseq(0,N).
lesseq(s[M],s[N]) :- lesseq(M,N).
```

permits the call lesseq(X,s[s[0]]) to generate the X-values 0, s[0], or s[s[0]].

N-element RELFUN *lists*, as in LISP and PROLOG, can be regarded as a short-hand for nested binary structures (we use the distinguished constructor "cns" instead of the usual "."). For example, the (non-ground) list [s[s[0]],[E,F],s[0]] reduces to the nesting cns[s[s[0]],cns[cns[E,cns[F,nil]],cns[s[0],nil]]]. A vertical bar in lists causes their cns-reduction to end with the element after the "|" (usually a variable) rather than with the distinguished constant nil. Thus, [X,Y|Z] reduces to cns[X,cns[Y,Z]]. This "lists-to-structures" transformation is used both for WAM compilation and mathematical formalization. Note that the sorted relation definition in PROLOG/RELFUN

```
sorted([]).
sorted([X]).
sorted([X,Y|Z]) :- lesseq(X,Y), sorted([Y|Z]).
```

and its cns-reduced form in RELFUN

```
sorted(nil).
sorted(cns[X,nil]).
sorted(cns[X,cns[Y,Z]]) :- lesseq(X,Y), sorted(cns[Y,Z]).
```

consistently employ square brackets to indicate the 'passiveness' of lists and structures, while in PROLOG the cns-reduced form would employ round parentheses.

### 2.2.3  Varying-Arity Structures

Lists can also be given a direct N-element interpretation because RELFUN permits *varying-arity structures* i.e., structures containing a vertical bar. Like cns was used as a binary list constructor we use tup as an N-ary list constructor $(N \geq 0)$. That is, [...] should be regarded as an abbreviation for tup[...]. This convention holds even if [...] contains a "|". So, the earlier lists really stand for tup[s[s[0]],tup[E,F],s[0]] and tup[X,Y|Z]. Such tup structures can again be viewed as nested cns structures as shown for lists above.

Varying arities are also permitted for all other RELFUN constructors. This can be used for reinterprating many 'untyped' list representations as constructor-'tagged' structures. For instance, unbounded staples and dumps of elements can be written as varying-arity structures staple[...] and dump[...], whose constructors distinguish the two 'types' of element collections. The unification of RELFUN structures containing a "|" generates a **list** value for a variable after the "|", as if the "|" would appear in a list context. Similarly, lists constitute the only structures to be spliced into other structures after the "|". Lists are thus the 'neutral' data structure for transporting the "|"-remainders of varying-arity structures.

For example, staple[book,folder,folder|Rest] represents a staple with a book followed by two folders on the top, and some unspecified remainder Rest. When unified with staple[book,Y,Y,paper,Z,paper], Y is bound to folder and Rest to the list [paper,Z,paper]. This list can again be spliced into, say, a dump beginning with a book, dump[book|Rest], resulting in dump[book,paper,Z,paper].

Unlike PROLOG we permit the vertical bar to follow directly after an opening square bracket, both in lists and in (other) structures. For any list X, the list [|X] is the same as X; additionally given a constructor c, the structure c[|X] exclusively uses the elements of the list X as its arguments. Thus with the Rest binding [paper,Z,paper], dump[|Rest] is equivalent to dump[paper,Z,paper].

It is now possible to define elementwise equality of staples and dumps using the facts

```
argumenteq(staple[|Args],dump[|Args]).
argumenteq(dump[|Args],staple[|Args]).
```

where the two Args occurrences of each fact will be bound to unifying lists of elements. Thus, while staple[book,X,X] and dump[Y,paper,paper] would not unify, the call argumenteq(staple[book,X,X],dump[Y,paper,paper]) succeeds.

Another use of varying-arity structures is the term representation of clauses themselves. In PROLOG ":-" can be regarded as a binary functor whose arguments are the clause head and a nesting of binary "','"-conjunctions for the body; in RELFUN it is reinterpreted more concisely as an N-ary constructor (N $\geq$ 1) whose first argument is the head and whose remaining arguments make up the body conjuncts. The rule of the DATALOG example in subsection 2.2.1 thus becomes the PROLOG structure

```
:-(applicable(Tool,Field),
   ','(subfield(Field,Subfield),applicable(Tool,Subfield)))
```

and the RELFUN structure

```
:-[applicable[Tool,Field],subfield[Field,Subfield],
                    applicable[Tool,Subfield]]
```

The use of lists to treat "|" in all contexts suggests a technique for reducing varying-arity structures to fixed-arity ones. Each varying-arity c[x1,...,xN|X] could be replaced by the unary c[[x1,...,xN|X]], where the single argument is a list containing the original c arguments as elements. However, this naive method introduces unnecessary bracketing (which could be hidden to the user) and hinders *intrastructure WAM indexing* [Sin93a] with respect to a structure's top-level arguments (which become 'neutralized' to a tup or cns constructor). Instead of listifying all c arguments, a 'semi-listifying' method might keep a fixed number, $K \leq N$, of initial arguments and only listify the remaining ones, resulting in the (K+1)-ary c[x1,...,xK,[xK+1,...,xN|X]]. However, even if global static analysis is used to find the smallest K such that a vertical bar or a closing square bracket is used after the Kth argument of c (for K = 0 leading back to the naive method), an interactive user could employ c[a1,...,aI|R] with I < K. In certain queries such a structure could be pretranslated to c[a1,...,aI,R1,...,RJ,R*], with I+J = K, by 'unrolling' the variable R used after the "|" i.e., generating new variables R1, ..., RJ and R*, and on success binding R to [R1,...,RJ|R*]. In general, it is hard to avoid making possible query patterns statically known to the global analyzer.

## 2.2.4 Varying-Arity Relationships

Proceeding from constructor terms to atomic formulas, we come to the LISP-inspired PROLOG extension of *varying-arity relation applications* i.e., clause heads and bodies directly containing a "|". Thus, both structures and applications can be ended by a vertical bar followed by an ordinary variable; equivalently, they could be ended by a "sequence variable" as used in KIF [GF91]. Varying-arity applications give argument sequences the flavor of an implicit list data structure. For instance, the N-ary version ($N \geq 0$) of the sorted relation

```
sorted().
sorted(X).
sorted(X,Y|Z) :- lesseq(X,Y), sorted(Y|Z).
```

permits calls like sorted(0,W,s[s[0]],s[s[s[0]]]), binding W to 0, s[0], or s[s[0]].

As in LISP, this N-ary, 'polyadic', flexibility gained can be used, among other things, to flatten nestings of binary associative operators like + and append. Their output cannot go to the (usual) last argument position because of the asymmetry of "|"-list-splicing; the only uniformly usable output argument is the first one.

For example, while ordinary PROLOGs' ternary append relation is already quite flexible, LM-PROLOG [CK85] defines a natural N-ary extension ($N > 0$), which in RELFUN is rewritten as

```
append([]).
append(Total,[]|Back) :- append(Total|Back).
append([First|Total],[First|Front]|Back) :-
                              append(Total,Front|Back).
```

It 'contains' LISP's unary null predicate, a list-typed PROLOG-like binary "=" relation, and a permuted, list-typed version of PROLOG's ternary append relation (append(1,[],1) won't succeed), but is actually a varying-arity relation, which can be used in surprisingly diverse ways. Two samples are append([a,b,c],L1,...,Lm), splitting a given list into arbitrarily many lists, and append([a,b,a,b,a,b],Leftcontext,[a,b,a],Rightcontext), unifying symmetric list segments.

Of course, a simple transformer can put the varying number of arguments of such relations into a single list. For sorted the additional brackets would lead back to the original definition; for append, with its distinguished first argument, however, they would become a syntactic burden. Also, the transformation can result in serious problems for even the standard WAM-indexing scheme because the first (and only) relation argument becomes of type list indiscriminately. This could be remedied by a version of the semi-listifying arity-fixing technique sketched for structures in subsection 2.2.3 (e.g., listifying only the N-1 input lists of append).

## 2.2.5 Higher-Order Constructors and Relations

While PROLOG restricts constructors and relations to constants, RELFUN also permits them to be variables or structures. This enables a restricted kind of *higher-order operators*, syntactically reducible to first-order operators, but more expressive and cleaner than PROLOG's use of extralogical builtins like functor, "=..", and metacall as higher-order substitutes. Higher-order **unification** of the kind studied with λProlog [NM90], however, is orthogonal to the extensions in RELFUN, which for simplicity and efficiency lives without anonymous λ-expressions (thus avoiding problems with λ-variables [Bac78]) and 'semantic' extensions of Robinson unification.

*Constructor variables* can be used to abstract from, or force equality of, the 'type' of structures, as encoded by their constructor. For example, the unification of staple[book,X,X] and F[Y,paper,paper] succeeds, binding F to the constructor staple. Also, the argumenteq definition of subsection 2.2.3 can be generalized to arbitrary constructors, using a single fact:

argumenteq(F[|Args],G[|Args]).

A converse definition, of constructoreq,

constructoreq(F[|Args1],F[|Args2]).

may be used to check equality of only the 'types' of two structures, as in the successful constructoreq(staple[paper,book],staple[book,folder,X]). For PROLOG's structures constructoreq could be simulated by two calls of the functor builtin.

*Constructor structures* embody parameterized constructors such as stack[integer], which are themselves applicable to arguments as in stack[integer][3,1,2]. The above constructoreq fact can thus be refined to a conspareq definition, succeeding for equally parameterized constructor applications such as a stack and a heap of integers:

```
conspareq(F[Argtype][|Args1],G[Argtype][|Args2]).
```

The variables F and G stand here for constructors, e.g. stack and heap, of constructor structures, whose single Argtype parameters must be equal.

*Relation variables in queries* enable to find all relationships between given arguments. In the DATALOG knowledge base (cf. subsection 2.2.1) the query R(X,bridgebuilding) needs only fact retrieval for binding R to the relation subfield and X to the object architecture or, R to applicable and X to computerscience; the query R(computerscience,architecture) requires rule deduction for binding R to applicable. Later, using footed clauses (section 2.3), relations found in this way will become returnable values, as in R(X,X) & self[R][X], returning self[applicable][computerscience], where the R-value is part of a constructor structure. Note that the R's employed here are 'relation-request' variables, free at the time of invoking the queries. More usual (mainly in LISP-based PROLOGs) is to permit variables in relation position only if they are always bound at the time of the call, as in the example of the next paragraph.

*Relation variables in clauses* permit the use of higher-order facts (recognized as such by the context) like virtue(supports), virtue(protects), etc. to abstract rules like

```
honorable(X) :- supports(X,Y).
honorable(X) :- protects(X,Y).
```

etc. to the single rule ("Honorable is who has a virtuous relationship to someone")

```
honorable(X) :- virtue(R), R(X,Y).
```

Here we apply virtue as a unary second-order relation over binary relations, but more general higher-order relations can be useful.

*Relation structures* can be employed for defining operations on relations. For example, the relational product can be defined using the structure relproduct[R,S] as a relation, which permits relational square to be defined with just a fact that uses a relproduct structure as its second argument:

```
relproduct[R,S](X,Z) :- S(X,Y), R(Y,Z).
relsquare(R,relproduct[R,R]).
```

While the structure relproduct[...] can be (higher-order-)called directly, as in relproduct[fathrel,mothrel](john,W), the constant relsquare is (first-order-)called to bind a variable, which is then used as a structure-valued relation variable, as in relsquare(fathrel,T), T(john,W).

As discussed in chapter 5, higher-order relations of this form are not easily compiled into the WAM, which collects all clauses with the same **constant** relation name and arity into a procedure. However, relation variables and structures can be eliminated by simply introducing an `apply` relation constant as in [War82], which we shorten to ap: hor(...) is replaced by ap(hor,...) in all heads and bodies, moving the higher-order relation hor to the first argument position. The last example thus becomes

```
ap(relproduct[R,S],X,Z) :- ap(S,X,Y), ap(R,Y,Z).
ap(relsquare,R,relproduct[R,R]).
```

and can be queried by, e.g., ap(relsquare,father,T), ap(T,john,W). Note that the relsquare clause and goal would not have needed the ap dummy because the relsquare relation is a constant. However, even if all calls to a relation in a program can be found to be first-order by static analysis, the user could still issue relation-variable queries like P(R,relproduct[R,R]). In the WAM these would only work in the form ap(P,R,relproduct[R,R]), and presuppose that the relsquare clauses are ap-transformed, like all other ones. Consider the effect of having all clauses collected into ap/i procedures, whose first arguments always are the former relation names (hence, i > 0). The discriminating effect of calling differently named procedures is lost, but is simulated by the usual first-argument indexing, loosing of course the refined discrimination of non-ap first-argument indexing. Fortunately, in our WAM we can index on all arguments (to the left of "|"), thus regaining full discriminative power for ap-reduced clauses.

For constructor variables and structures an analogous first-order reduction is possible using a dummy constructor, which should again be ap in order to permit metacalls for reduced clauses. As for earlier reductions this will affect WAM indexing: (top-level) structure's constructors are all mapped to the same dummy constant, loosing the constructors' indexing power, which could be regained by also indexing on their first arguments.

# 2.3   Functions Defined by Footed Clauses

## 2.3.1   DATAFUN as a Functional Database Language

We now proceed to functions, first considering DATAFUN, the functional subset of RELFUN corresponding to PROLOG's DATALOG subset.

### 2.3.1.1   Molecular Rules and Non-ground Functions

Let us consider the database example in [WPP77], containing the following DATALOG facts about country areas (given in thousands of square miles):

```
area(china,3380).
area(india,1139).
area(ussr, 8708).
area(usa,  3609).
```

Although these binary relations would permit requests like `area(Cntry,8708)`, their normal use direction is of the kind `area(ussr,Area)`: the large value range of possible areas makes it unlikely that a user ask for a country with a precisely given thousands-of-square-miles area such as 8708 (the problem would become even more noticeable if the exact areas were stored, perhaps as real numbers, with rounding problems etc.) Therefore[3], in our opinion this 'historical' DATA-LOG example should be rewritten functionally, as already implied in [GM84]. For this we extract the second argument from the DATALOG facts and use it as the so-called *foot* after a "`:&`"-infix (contracting the mixfix "`:- &`" to the size of PROLOG's neck symbol "`:-`" [Bol97]):

```
area(china) :& 3380.
area(india) :& 1139.
area(ussr)  :& 8708.
area(usa)   :& 3609.
```

The resulting special DATAFUN clauses are called *molecular rules*, here used for the pointwise definition of the RELFUN function `area` mapping from country names to natural numbers. The definition emphasizes the natural `area` use direction, as in `area(ussr)`, a function call **returning** the value 8708.

The main advantage of distinguishing an 'output' argument of a relation as the returned value of a corresponding function is the possibility of *nested calls* such as

```
+(area(china),area(india),area(usa))
```

where the parenthesized inner applications are (not passive structures but) active function calls that return their values to the ternary + use (cf. section 2.2.2); for reasons of conciseness, program analysis, and variable elimination this is preferable to flat relational conjunctions such as

```
area(china,A1), area(india,A2), area(usa,A3), +(Area,A1,A2,A3)
```

The main disadvantage lies in the issue of *inverted calls*, which are easier and sometimes more logically complete for 'usage-neutral' relations: a functional

---

[3]We do not make use of the argument that *area : Cntry* $\longrightarrow$ *Area* is a mapping (or 'functional' in, e.g., the relational database sense) while its inverse is not (some small countries' areas coincide if rounded to 1000 sq. mi.), because RELFUN does allow non-deterministic functions, as will be shown shortly.

non-termination problem is illustrated in [Fri84]. However, RELFUN's inversion method for functions appears quite natural, and for its DATAFUN subset completeness problems do not arise. A generalized form of PROLOG's is-primitive is employed to unify the values of a free function call with the value to be used as the argument of the inverse function, where a call is *free* if all its (actual!) arguments are different free variables. More generally, DATAFUN (RELFUN) permits *non-ground* function calls which like DATALOG (PROLOG) goals may contain repeated logical variables (non-ground terms).

As a simple example with just one free variable consider 8708 .= area(Cntry), the inverse function call corresponding to the above-discussed relational inversion area(Cntry,8708). Independently from the context (e.g., in a ".="-rhs) the free call area(Cntry) non-deterministically returns the values 3380, 1139, 8708, or 3609, at the same time binding Cntry to china, india, ussr, or usa, respectively, in the textual order of the area molecular rules in the knowledge base. Within the above ".="-call only the third of the returned values unifies with the left-hand side (lhs), so the inversion correctly binds Cntry to ussr.

Other operators such as the exponentiation relation may be hardly or impossibly inverted, which again suggests to rewrite them as 'directed' functions, leading from non-ground facts like

```
exp(X,0,1).
exp(X,1,X).
```

to *non-ground molecular rules* like

```
exp(X,0) :& 1.
exp(X,1) :& X.
```

Here, the first clause has a ground foot, 1, while the second one has a *non-ground foot*, X (in DATAFUN this must be a variable). Non-ground foots can yield both ground and non-ground values, as in exp(2,1), returning 2, and exp(Y,1), returning Y, respectively.

### 2.3.1.2   Footed Rules and the density Example

In [WPP77] there are also DATALOG Horn facts about population (in millions), which we think should be 'functionalized' to DATAFUN molecular rules as demonstrated for area. On this basis the paper supplies the population density (per square mile) of a country, using the DATALOG rule (somewhat extralogical because of the ".="-call for D)

```
density(C,D) :- pop(C,P), area(C,A), D .= (P*1000)/A.
```

This can be mimicked by the equivalent DATAFUN rule (with ".="-calls for P and A)[4]

```
density(C)   :-  P .= pop(C), A .= area(C)  &  /(*(P,1000),A).
```

which may be condensed to the DATAFUN rule (without ".="-calls or auxiliary variables)

```
density(C)   :&  /(*(pop(C),1000),area(C)).
```

Generally, rules containing an "&" separator are called *footed rules*. The rule premises to the left of "&" are called *body premises* and act exactly like the premises of a hornish rule. The premise to the right of "&" is called a *foot premise* and differs from the other premises only in that its value becomes the value of the entire rule. Together, these premises form a *valued conjunction*, which like an "&"-less conjunction can also be used directly as a query. Molecular rules are special footed rules with an empty conjunction of body premises (the separator sequence ":- &" is normally joined to ":&") and a foot premise which just is a term (denoting a value without evaluation). So, unlike the footed area rules in subsection 2.3.1.1, the shortened footed density rule above is not a molecular rule since its foot evaluates an expression. The most natural use of the DATAFUN database would be functional calls like density(usa), returning the density value for usa. However, these rule formulations could also be inverted or even be called freely to enumerate all country/density pairs as in the relational call density(Cntry,Dnsty) (delivering both countries and their densities as bindings) or the functional call density(Cntry) (delivering countries as bindings with their densities as values).

To conclude the density example of [WPP77], PROLOG's "database query" rule

```
ans(C1,D1,C2,D2) :- density(C1,D1), density(C2,D2),
                    D1 > D2, 20*D1 < 21*D2.
```

and request ans(C1,D1,C2,D2) for finding countries whose population density differs by less than 5%, in RELFUN could be mimicked directly but can also be rewritten as a single valued conjunction

```
D1 .= density(C1),  D2 .= density(C2),
>(D1,D2),  <(*(20,D1),*(21,D2))      &  ans[C1,D1,C2,D2]
```

where the auxiliary global ans relation transmutes to a temporary ans constructor.

---

[4]Following LISP, RELFUN currently does not distinguish arithmetic operators as infixes, but like all other operators applies them as prefixes.

### 2.3.1.3 Non-determinism, DATALOG Relationalizing, and WAM Compilation

While free **calls** for the inversion of the area and density functions produce non-deterministic results, the **area** and **density definitions** themselves are deterministic. In RELFUN *non-deterministic function definitions* are also allowed, which return more than one value even for ground calls.

For instance, the subfield relation of the DATALOG example in section 2.2.1 could be extended non-deterministically, expanded by a transitive-closure version subclosure, and transcribed into a function definition, as in the following DATAFUN example:

```
subfield(engineering) :& mechanics.
subfield(engineering) :& architecture.
subfield(architecture) :& bridgebuilding.
subclosure(Field) :& subfield(Field).
subclosure(Field) :& subclosure(subfield(Field)).
applicable(pharmacy,medicine).
applicable(computerscience,bridgebuilding).
applicable(computerscience,computerscience).
applicable(Tool,Field) :- applicable(Tool,subclosure(Field)).
```

In this knowledge base the ground call subfield(engineering) non-deterministically returns the values mechanics or architecture; finding a subfield path from engineering to bridgebuilding, applicable(computerscience,engineering) returns true. Note that the operator applicable itself is left a relation but its former Horn rule using a flat relational conjunction became a hornish rule that nests the (non-deterministic!) subclosure function into the recursive call. The original relational form could again be mimicked using a ".="-call, leading to

```
applicable(Tool,Field) :- Sub .= subclosure(Field),
                          applicable(Tool,Sub).
```

This *flattening* of the applicable definition exemplifies the first step of RELFUN's *relationalize* transformation, a varying-arity version of the function-to-relation translation in [Kow83], leading from DATAFUN clauses to DATALOG clauses. The second step introduces *extra arguments* for values returned in a ".="-rhs or in the foot, where new **first** (not: last) arguments are used to cope with varying-arity DATAFUN ("|"-calls); denotative foots directly become the extra argument of the conclusion while evaluative foots generate a new variable (from _1, _2, ...) used as the extra argument of both the foot and the conclusion. Thus, the relationalized form of the above DATAFUN example is

```
subfield(mechanics,engineering).
subfield(architecture,engineering).
subfield(bridgebuilding,architecture).
subclosure(_1,Field) :- subfield(_1,Field).
subclosure(_2,Field) :- subfield(_1,Field), subclosure(_2,_1).
applicable(pharmacy,medicine).
applicable(computerscience,bridgebuilding).
applicable(computerscience,computerscience).
applicable(Tool,Field) :- subclosure(_1,Field),
                          applicable(Tool,_1).
```

Besides this kind of RELFUN-to-PROLOG translation we have implemented a more direct WAM compilation of non-deterministic, non-ground functions (see chapter 5): the WAM temporary register X1 (identical to the argument register A1) is also used for passing returned values, so that first-argument nestings need not be flattened because the caller directly finds the returned value of the first callee in argument register X1.

## 2.3.2 Full RELFUN Exemplified by "Self"-Functions

When enriching DATAFUN with structures and lists we arrive at full RELFUN (we will immediately transfer the relational varying-arity extensions). Returning to successor structures for natural numbers, one should first note that it is illegal to nest active calls into passive structures like this: s[+(M,N)]. The usual equational definition of binary addition could still be transcribed by employing a ".="-call for +'s recursion:

```
+(0,N) :& N.
+(s[M],N) :- A .= +(M,N) & s[A].      (or   +(s[M],N) :& +(M,s[N]).)
```

However, we prefer another method, relying on functions defined to simply return "their own call as a structure". Since the same functor can be a constructor and a defined function, we can define, e.g., s and tup as the following *self-passivating functions*:

```
s(M) :& s[M].
tup(|Z) :& tup[|Z].   (or   tup(|Z) :& [|Z].   or   tup(|Z) :& Z.)
```

Now, s and tup may also be called as active functions, evaluating their arguments in the usual call-by-value manner and returning passive structures that use the evaluated arguments as their arguments and the respective function names as their constructors.

For example, the call tup(subfield(engineering),s(s(0))) non-deterministically returns the lists [mechanics,s[s[0]]] or

[architecture,s[s[0]]]; the LISP-cons-like tup-"|"-use tup(s(0)|[0])
returns [s[0],0]; the COMMON LISP-list*-like tup-"|"-use
tup(a,b,c|[d,e]) returns [a,b,c,d,e]. Moreover, the s definition ena-
bles a direct analogue to equational addition:

```
+(0,N) :& N.
+(s[M],N) :& s(+(M,N)).
```

It should also be noted here that RELFUN definitions obey the "constructor
discipline" [O'D85], which with our notation amounts to saying simply that
"clause heads must not have embedded parenthesized expressions". This would
be violated by the eq-nested signum calls shown in the introduction.

The earlier relation-to-function transcriptions (e.g., for the subfield operator) decreased the arity by one because one relation argument was distinguished
as the function value. Alternatively, relations can often be refined to functions
of the same arity returning an additional useful value. One class of functions
generated in this way is *filter functions* i.e., functions acting as the identity for
certain arguments or argument combinations, and failing for other ones. For
instance, the sorted relation on lists of section 2.2.2 can be refined to the follo-
wing filter function, whose recursive call is nested after the "|" into a cons-like
tup call:

```
sorted([]) :& [].
sorted([X]) :& [X].
sorted([X,Y|Z]) :- lesseq(X,Y) & tup(X|sorted([Y|Z])).
```

This sorted function returns sorted lists unchanged (for non-ground
ones like [s[0],E,s[s[0]]] enumerating their correct instantiations, here
[s[0],s[0],s[s[0]]] and [s[0],s[s[0]],s[s[0]]]), and fails for unsorted
lists (such as the non-ground [s[s[0]],E,s[0]]).

Below, a sample sorted call is given, which occurs in an (internally non-
ground and non-deterministic) functional version of the well-known relational
slow-sort program [Llo87]. This sort definition also exemplifies an essential
use of non-ground function calls: since such calls both bind request variables
and return a value, they can be used to split results into bindings, for the calls
occurring somewhere above or after them, and a value, for the caller nested
directly above them.

```
sort(X) :& sorted(perm(X)).

perm([]) :& [].
perm([X|Y]) :& tup(U|perm(delete(U,[X|Y]))).

delete(X,[X|Y]) :& Y.
delete(X,[Y|Z]) :& tup(Y|delete(X,Z)).
```

Let us consider this bottom-up. The auxiliary function delete non-deterministically removes occurrences of its first argument from the list in its second argument. The permutation function can then use a non-ground delete call for result splitting: it non-deterministically binds U to arbitrary list elements, for the cons-like tup call, and returns U-less lists, for the recursive perm call. Finally, the sort main function calls the above sorted filter on the non-deterministic permutations of its argument. Note that this functional sort version specifies a computationally preferable (nesting) sequence by calling perm before sorted. In the relational sort specification commutativity of conjunction appears to permit calling sorted before perm, which, however, would not run in normal PROLOGs, as discussed in [Llo87]. A related benefit of the functional formulation is that the computationally less meaningful sort use for 'unsorting' a given sorted list is syntactically marked by a ".="-call over a free sort call, whereas the relational version employs symmetrically-looking non-ground sort calls for both use modes, that would suggest "equality of rights".

A variant of filters is *self-testing functions*, which can also be viewed as self-passivating functions that yield unknown for an argument (sequence) considered "ill-formed". For example, the varying-arity sorted relation of section 2.2.4 can be refined to a self-testing function that fails for unsorted argument sequences:

```
sorted() :& sorted[].
sorted(X) :& sorted[X].
sorted(X,Y|Z) :- lesseq(X,Y), sorted[|W] .= sorted(Y|Z) &
                                              sorted[X|W].
```

Now, the non-ground call sorted(s(0),E,s(s[0])) returns the correct instantiations of sorted[s[0],E,s[s[0]]], while sorted(s(s[0]),E,s(0)) yields unknown.

Concluding the series of "self"-functions, let us proceed to *self-normalizing functions*, a variant of self-testing functions performing argument normalization. For instance, the previous list sort function can be used to define bag as a varying-arity function that returns a bag structure of the sorted arguments i.e., a normalized multiset:

```
bag(|X) :- W .= sort(X) & bag[|W].
```

Now, the call bag(s[s[0]],0,s(s[0]),s(0)) returns bag[0,s[0],s[s[0]],s[s[0]]]. Recalling the discussion in section 2.2.2, it should be clear that even for a defined function (e.g., bag) no evaluation (e.g., normalization) will happen if it is applied with square brackets: tup(bag(s[0],0),bag[s[0],0]) returns [bag[0,s[0]],bag[s[0],0]].

The flattening, extra-arguments, and relationalize transformations from DATAFUN to DATALOG in subsection 2.3.1.3 are easily generalized to corresponding RELFUN-to-PROLOG transformations. For example, the above varying-arity bag function becomes a relation which must bind normal forms to a request variable (the extra first argument) instead of just returning them: bag(bag[|W]|X) :- sort(W,X). However, self-normalizing functions constitute a paradigmatic class of operators for which a relational reformulation seems not practically useful: a concise functional nesting like set(bag(s[0],0),bag[0,s[0]]) would become the relational conjunction bag(B,s[0],0), set(S,B,bag[0,s[0]]), treating the active and passive bags completely differently, even though they both evaluate to (equal) structures for the set. Again recalling subsection 2.3.1.3, the X1-reuse for value returning in the WAM also supports full RELFUN because X1 can point to structured return values on the heap just as it points to structured variable values.

## 2.3.3   Higher-Order Constructors and Functions

Our derivation of functional programming extensions now arrives at variables and structures used as constructors or functions, and at their combination with non-ground and non-deterministic calls.

*Constructor variables and structures*, introduced in a relational context (section 2.2.5), are also useful in a functional setting. For instance, a function genints enumerates the integers in the alternating order 0, ±1, ±2, ..., returned as the infinitely non-deterministic values 0 or s[0] or p[0] or s[s[0]] or p[p[0]] or ... Its definition employs a constructor variable, Sign, for building up a homogeneous, 'absolute' nesting before binding the structure's "neutral signs" (equal in all levels!) to either the successor or predecessor constructor. Instead of using the constants s and p, we could also apply as constructors the defined functions 1+ and 1-[5] or structures like inc[1] and inc[-1].

```
genints()     :& 0.
genints()     :& genints(Sign[0]).
genints(Sign[N]) :- Sign .= s & Sign[N].
genints(Sign[N]) :- Sign .= p & Sign[N].
genints(Sign[N]) :& genints(Sign[Sign[N]]).
```

While the main **nullary** genints/0 generates all integers, the auxiliary **unary** genints/1 can also be called as genints(Sign[...Sign[0]...]) to generate the integers whose absolute value is not less than the 'absolute' argument, as genints(s[0]) to generate the positive integers, as genints(p[0]) to generate the negative integers, and in other meaningful ways.

---

[5]RELFUN accesses a selected subset of COMMON LISP functions as builtins. Unusually named examples are the numeric successor and predecessor functions 1+ and 1-, whose application to an argument, say 6, in mathematical or PROLOG syntax becomes 1+(6) and 1-(6), returning 7 and 5, respectively. RELFUN's **ecal** primitive, a combination of LISP's **eval** and PROLOG's metacall, permits the activation of structures, as in ecal(1-[1-[0]]), returning -2.

*Function variables in queries* can be utilized much like the corresponding relation variables (see section 2.2.5). For example, given the DATAFUN version of the density database (cf. subsection 2.3.1.2), the query F(china) asks for all unary properties of china, enumerating the attribute F = area with the returned value 3380, the attribute F = pop with its value, etc.

*Function variables in clauses* give us the abstraction power of functional arguments in the fashion of functional programming. Thus, revise is a ternary function applying any unary function F to the Nth element of a list (for N greater than the list length or N less than 1 it returns the list unchanged):

```
revise(F,N,[]) :& [].
revise(F,1,[H|T]) :& tup(F(H)|T).
revise(F,N,[H|T]) :& tup(H|revise(F,1-(N),T)).
```

Similarly, the sort function could be parameterized by a Compare relation to be handed to the sorted filter, which would abstract from the specific lesseq relation (in particular, from the representation of naturals as s structures). Of course, this "functional style" of universally quantified operator variables, occurring on both sides of definitions, is also useful in purely relational examples. Conversely, the "relational style" of existentially quantified operator variables, occurring only on the rhs of definitions, would also be useful in purely functional examples. Thus, the earlier function-variable query about china could be further abstracted for use in the rhs of a rule returning attribute/value pairs of an object. The below attval function employs both the rhs-only variable Attribute and an lhs/rhs variable Valfilter (bound, e.g., to numfilter) for filtering the values returned by Attribute:

```
attval(Obj,Valfilter) :& tup(Attribute,Valfilter(Attribute(Obj))).
numfilter(X) :- numberp(X) & X.
```

Note that the free variable Attribute in the first tup position becomes bound by its application in the second tup position before the tup actually returns the pair.

*Function structures* can be employed like "function-forming operators" in FP [Bac78]. Bringing the relational-product example in section 2.2.5 back to functional programming, functional composition can be defined by using the structure compose[F,G] as a function, which permits twice to be defined as a compose-structure-valued molecular rule:

```
compose[F,G](X) :& F(G(X)).
twice(F) :& compose[F,F].
```

Again, while the structure compose[...] can be (higher-order-)called directly, as in compose[fathfun,mothfun](john), the constant twice is rather (first-order-)called in function position to return an applicable function structure, as in `twice(fathfun)(john)`.

Let us now turn to the combination of higher-order operators with non-ground and non-deterministic calls.

For example, $F^{-1}$, the inversion of a unary function F, can be defined as a function structure `inv[F]` which calls F freely within a ".="-call only accepting F values that match the argument V of $F^{-1}$ (for an N-ary F we just add a "|"):

`inv[F](V) :- V .= F(X) & X.`   (N-ary   `inv[F](V) :- V .= F(|X) & X.`)

Thus, `inv[area](1139)` calls `1139 .= area(X)`, hence returns india or other countries for which `area` returns 1139 (the general `inv` for N-ary F's would also work, returning `[india]` or other country singleton lists).

Another example, a version of the $\mu$-operator, additionally employs a result-splitting-like technique (used in the `sort` definition) to fork the entire result of a call into both the binding of a request variable and the returned value. First, we define a non-deterministic generator `naturals`, enumerating the naturals from an initialization given in the first argument, where the next natural is always both bound to the second argument and returned.

```
naturals(N,N) :& N.
naturals(N,V) :& naturals(1+(N),V).
```

For instance, `naturals(3,V)` binds V to 3 or 4 or ...; at the same time it returns each of these values. This then permits to concisely define a non-deterministic `mu` higher-order function taking unary functions over the naturals as its argument and returning **their** smallest argument for which they return 0, then their second-smallest argument, etc., diverging if there is none (left[6]):

```
mu(F) :- 0 .= F(naturals(0,V)) & V.
```

The `ap` reduction of higher-order relations in section 2.2.5 directly transfers to function variables and structures. For instance, the above rule could be reduced to

```
ap(mu,F) :- 0 .= ap(F,ap(naturals,0,V)) & V.
```

---

[6]RELFUN's `once` primitive (or "!" symbol) could be employed above (or after) the ".="-call to prevent the possibly diverging search for further solutions when the first solution is found, thus simulating the usual – unbounded – minimalization of unary functions [for (1+N)-ary functions "|" can be used to minimalize over the first argument, making `mu[F]` a function structure, as shown in square brackets]:

```
mu(F) :- once(0 .= F(naturals(0,V))) & V.     (or   mu(F) :- 0 .= F(...) ! & V.)
[mu[F](|Nargs) :- once(0 .= F(...|Nargs)) & V.]
```

changing F from a function variable into an argument variable. The effects on the WAM implementation are the same as discussed for higher-order relations.

## 2.4   The Logic/Functional Style in Use

Several RELFUN projects have explored the use of relational/functional programming for non-toy problems: the language has been evaluated and tuned by programs for realistic tasks such as hypergraph processing [Bol92a], NC-program generation [BHH⁺91, BPS97], and materials engineering [BBK94]. In order to facilitate comparison with other languages, this section gives versions of three well-known non-trivial programs in RELFUN's logic/functional style (not all features of RELFUN will be needed in these examples).

### 2.4.1   serialise: Inplace Specialization of Structures

After the `density` database, the second practical PROLOG example given in [WPP77] is the relational `serialise` program. Its task is to transform a list of items into a corresponding list of their alphabetic serial numbers; e.g., [p,r,o,l,o,g] should become [4,5,3,2,3,1].

The subrelations of `serialise` demonstrate the use of the "logical" variable: first `pairlists` binds a request variable to a non-ground list of free variables (the prospective answer list), e.g. [Y1,Y2,Y3,Y4,Y5,Y6], and another request variable to a corresponding list of non-ground structures, e.g. [pair[p,Y1],pair[r,Y2],pair[o,Y3],pair[l,Y4],pair[o,Y5], pair[g,Y6]], thus generating two variable-coupled "incomplete data structures" (now often called "partial data structures"); then `arrange` (quick)sorts the list of `pairs` into a binary tree, calling a `partition` relation that uses the items in the first `pair` arguments for (string) comparison (unifiable non-ground terms are considered as duplicates to be identified by the first `partition` clause, e.g. joining pair[o,Y3] and pair[o,Y5] via Y5 = Y3); now numbered can count the ascending items, left to right, at the fringe of the tree and note the resulting serial numbers by "inplace updates" (more precisely, "inplace specializations") in the second `pair` arguments, which by logical-variable equality instantiate `pairlists`' prospective answer list to the final, ground result.

Although this binary serialise relation can be called like serialise([p,r,o,l,o,g], [4,5,3,2,3,1]), to check the relationship, and like serialise([p,r,o,l,o,g], S), to generate the list of serial numbers, it cannot be called like serialise(I, [4,5,3,2,3,1]), to generate all item lists mapping to given serial numbers (the comparison relation, e.g. the string< builtin below, expects constant items): the main serialise algorithm just employs a relational syntax to express a non-invertible function from item lists to serial-number lists, while it does make an essential, "two-results" use of the subrelation `partition` and of intermediate non-ground terms.

Therefore it appears natural to reformulate `serialise` in RELFUN's non-ground functional style, keeping the `partition` relation and intermediate non-ground returned values[7]. Relationship-checking calls will then look like `[4,5,3,2,3,1] .= serialise([p,r,o,l,o,g])`, a ".="-call containing a ground function call for serial-number generation as its rhs. The above explanation for the relational version can be transferred to this functional one by noting that the "principal result" is now always returned as a value instead of being bound to a request variable: the `pairlists` non-ground function only binds its prospective-answer result for use as `serialise`'s foot premise R, but directly returns the list of pairs to the `arrange` function, which again returns its non-ground tree to the first argument of the self-nested `numbered` function.

```
serialise(L) :- numbered(arrange(pairlists(L,R)),1) & R.

pairlists([X|L],[Y|R]) :& tup(pair[X,Y]|pairlists(L,R)).
pairlists([],[]) :& [].

arrange([X|L]) :-
    partition(L,X,L1,L2),
    T1 .= arrange(L1),
    T2 .= arrange(L2) &
    tree[T1,X,T2].
arrange([]) :& void.

partition([X|L],X,L1,L2) :- partition(L,X,L1,L2).
partition([X|L],Y,[X|L1],L2) :-
    before(X,Y), partition(L,Y,L1,L2).
partition([X|L],Y,L1,[X|L2]) :-
    before(Y,X), partition(L,Y,L1,L2).
partition([],Y,[],[]).

before(pair[X1,Y1],pair[X2,Y2]) :- string<(X1,X2).

numbered(tree[T1,pair[X,N1],T2],N0) :&
    numbered(T2,1+(N1 .= numbered(T1,N0))).
numbered(void,N) :& N.
```

Note that the body of the first `arrange` clause can be simplified to

---

[7]While the need for non-ground terms is self-evident in relational programming (ground relational programming isn't very useful), they require some justification in functional programming. The `serialise` example shows how non-ground terms can be useful internally in a computation even if its external input/output is ground terms. This is analogous to an internal use of **complex** numbers in computing **real** results.

partition(L,X,L1,L2) & tree(arrange(L1),X,arrange(L2)) if tree is defined as a self-passivating function or, similarly, if 3-tups are used instead of
labeled binary trees (cf. section 2.3.2). Also notice that numbered 'updates'
the pair structures at the roots of the tree structures by ".="-binding the unavoidable logical variable N1 to the recursion result obtained from traversing the
left subtree T1, a value which is incremented by 1+ for use in traversing the right
subtree T2. This works since RELFUN's ".="-builtin both binds and returns
the value of its rhs.

Moreover, we can extract a reusable, parameterized sorting specification from
the serialise program, thus simplifying the remaining specification. For this,
the quicksort function qsort on lists is made generic wrt list-element types
through an element-comparison relation Cr used as parameter. Applied to a
non-empty list, arrange returns the value of a labeled binary tree construc-
tor/function call, while qsort returns the value of our functional list concate-
nator appfun (incidentally, some clause orders and variable names as well as
partition's argument sequence are changed):

```
qsort[Cr]([]) :& [].
qsort[Cr]([X|Y]) :- partition[Cr](X,Y,Sm,Gr) &
    appfun(qsort[Cr](Sm),tup(X|qsort[Cr](Gr))).


partition[Cr](X,[Y|Z],[Y|Sm],Gr) :-
            Cr(Y,X),  partition[Cr](X,Z,Sm,Gr).
partition[Cr](X,[Y|Z],Sm,[Y|Gr]) :-
            Cr(X,Y),  partition[Cr](X,Z,Sm,Gr).
partition[Cr](X,[X|Z],Sm,Gr) :- partition[Cr](X,Z,Sm,Gr).
partition[Cr](X,[],[],[]).
```

With qsort "modularized out" in this higher-order manner (Cr = before),
serialise becomes a very concise function:

```
serialise(L) :-
  numbered(qsort[before](pairlists(L,R)),1) &
  R.

pairlists([],[]) :& [].
pairlists([X|L],[Y|R]) :& tup([X,Y]|pairlists(L,R)).

before([X1,Y1],[X2,Y2]) :- string<(X1,X2).

numbered([],N).
numbered([[X,N]|R],N) :- numbered(R,1+(N)).
```

It is now most easily observed that an external ground call
such as serialise([d,a,l,l,a,s]), via the internal non-ground

call (with numbered operating here on qsort's list-of-lists value) numbered([[a,Y2],[d,Y1],[1,Y3],[s,Y6]],1) & [Y1,Y2,Y3,Y3,Y2,Y6], externally returns the ground value [2,1,3,3,1,4].

Finally, the relation before, needed to compare or identify non-ground *partial data structures* such as (the pair structures in [WPP77] as well as) the two-element lists in our above version, only checks their first elements, hence defines a non-linear *partial order* on their ground-term instantiations. E.g., [a,Y2] and [a,Y5] become identified but [a,1] and [a,2] are incomparable. With such a partial-order comparison relation (the earlier arrange relation as well as) the above partition relation become *partial operators* in the sense that they yield unknown for lists with incomparable elements.[8] Although in serialise ground terms are never used as before arguments, in general partition could be made a total operator by treating Cr(X,Y) and incomparable elements together, as the catch-all case of a nested if...then...else...:

```
partition[Cr](X,[Y|Z],Small,Great) :-
   partition[Cr](X,Z,Sm,Gr),
   if Cr(Y,X) then Small .= [Y|Sm], Great .= Gr
            else if Y .= X then Small .= Sm, Great .= Gr
                         else Small .= Sm, Great .= [Y|Gr].
partition[Cr](X,[],[],[]).
```

## 2.4.2 wang: On-the-Fly Construction of Proof Trees

Since its pure LISP description in [MAE+62], Wang's proof algorithm for the propositional calculus has often been reformulated to demonstrate the use of declarative languages. The algorithm applies reduction rules to a sequent representation of propositional formulas until an atomic formula occurs in both the antecedent and consequent of all derived sequents, reporting true, or no more rule is applicable to a sequent, reporting false. [PS91] gives a version with an extra relation argument for constructing a proof tree "on-the-fly", whose size can be computed by an invertible function.

Here we give a RELFUN version that returns the trees of successful proofs, where subtrees are built and their roots labeled "on-the-fly" by a constructor and two self-passivating functions: the constructor indicates that an atomic formula occurs on both sequent sides and the self-passivating functions exhibit the reduction of a formula on the right (consequent) or on the left (antecedent) side.

---

[8]The ensuing ground-partialness of qsort[before] was noticed by Philip Wadler within the context of a Curry-mailing-list discussion about programming in a functional-logic (narrowing) versus a functional-only (rewriting) style (http://www-i2.informatik.rwth-aachen.de/~hanus/curry/listarchive/0076.html).

For example, `wang([],[impl[and[p,and[q,r]],and[and[p,q],r]]])` returns the and-associativity proof tree

```
right[
  impl[and[p,and[q,r]],and[and[p,q],r]],
  right[
    and[and[p,q],r],
    right[
      and[p,q],
      left[
        and[p,and[q,r]],
        left[and[q,r],both[p,wang[[r,q,p],[p]]]] ],
      left[
        and[p,and[q,r]],
        left[and[q,r],both[q,wang[[r,q,p],[q]]]] ] ],
    left[and[p,and[q,r]],left[and[q,r],both[r,wang[[r,q,p],[r]]]]] ] ]
```

The main wang function's first clause initializes with [] two auxiliary (atomic formula) arguments of a workhorse function that either returns a proof tree, or yields unknown. In the former case, wang commits to the tree value by employing a 'sole' cut ("! ." or "!.", instead of only ".", as the footed-clause terminator). In the latter case the second wang clause returns false, thus implementing a procedure-specific closed-world assumption for the wang operator. The work function realizes the usual reduction rules deterministically, employing 'ankle' cuts ("! &" or "!&" instead of just a "&" separator) for committing to each rule before its foot is reached. In most work clauses no body premises are needed between the conclusion and the foot, hence their ankle cut coincides with a 'neck' cut (":- !" is joined to "!-", ":- !&" or ":& !" to "!&")[9].

```
wang(L,R) :& work(L,R,[],[])!.   (or  wang(L,R)   :&  if W .=
                                       work(L,R,[],[]) then W
wang(L,R) :& false.                                 else false.)
```

---

[9]RELFUN only permits a single cut per clause, so premises to the left of "!" can be interpreted, during clause invocation, as the arguments of an implicit once operator followed by a neck cut. Also, as a "single-cut language", it is akin to a committed-choice language (CCL), obtainable by (1) restricting the left-"!" premises to 'guards' and by (2) parallelizing clause invocation. Like for PROLOG, a cut(-avoidance) discussion will be necessary for relational/functional languages. For example, wang's sole cut can be encapsulated into an if...then...else... (as shown in parentheses), a valued version of PROLOG's ...->...;..., but this entails a ".="-variable to avoid recomputation of the entire work. Although some relational/functional cuts may be justified by the determinism of many functions, the question of better ways of determinism specification remains. For instance, one could **declare** the work procedure as deterministic in one place instead of using a "!" in each of its clauses (in the final clause, just for uniformity and CCL kinship). Note, however, that RELFUN employs "!" as **part of the clause syntax**, like CCLs use "|", not as an "extra-logical goal"; unlike in CCLs, for a neck cut the syntax "!-" or "!&" is as concise as PROLOG's cutless neck symbol ":-" [Bol97]. In work this syntax acts like clause-oriented determinism annotations (for a non-neck cut also specifying a clause's "commit point"), from which a declaration for the entire procedure could be extracted.

```
work([],[],A,B) :- member(X,A), member(X,B) !&
    both[X,wang[A,B]].
work([X|L],R,A,B) :- atomic(X) !&
    work(L,R,[X|A],B).
work(L,[X|R],A,B) :- atomic(X) !&
    work(L,R,A,[X|B]).
work(L,[not[P]|R],A,B) !&
    right(not[P],work([P|L],R,A,B)).
work([not[P]|L],R,A,B) !&
    left(not[P],work(L,[P|R],A,B)).
work(L,[and[P,Q]|R],A,B) !&
    right(and[P,Q],work(L,[P|R],A,B),work(L,[Q|R],A,B)).
work([and[P,Q]|L],R,A,B) !&
    left(and[P,Q],work([P,Q|L],R,A,B)).
work(L,[or[P,Q]|R],A,B) !&
    right(or[P,Q],work(L,[P,Q|R],A,B)).
work([or[P,Q]|L],R,A,B) !&
    left(or[P,Q],work([P|L],R,A,B),work([Q|L],R,A,B)).
work(L,[impl[P,Q]|R],A,B) !&
    right(impl[P,Q],work([P|L],[Q|R],A,B)).
work([impl[P,Q]|L],R,A,B) !&
    left(impl[P,Q],work([Q|L],R,A,B),work(L,[P|R],A,B)).
work(L,[equiv[P,Q]|R],A,B) !&
    right(equiv[P,Q],work([P|L],[Q|R],A,B),work([Q|L],[P|R],A,B)).
work([equiv[P,Q]|L],R,A,B) !&
    left(equiv[P,Q],work([P,Q|L],R,A,B),work(L,[P,Q|R],A,B)).

left(|R)  :& left[|R].
right(|R) :& right[|R].

member(X,[X|R]).                  (or    member(X,[X|R]) :& [X|R].)
member(X,[Y|R]) :- member(X,R).   (or    member(X,[Y|R]) :&
                                                member(X,R).)
atomic(F[|R]) !- unknown.
atomic(X).
```

The alternative member definition (using both parenthesized clauses) is the LISP-like version mentioned in the introduction. (Using the first parenthesized clause and the second unparenthesized clause gives a definition returning [X|R] instead of true only for an X occurring as the **first** element of the **original** list.) Our functional **wang** algorithm could again be degenerated to a non-tree-building relational algorithm by just omitting **all** "&"-separators; the resulting hornish clauses could then be simplified, mainly by bringing the work recursions to the top-level.

## 2.4.3   eval: Interpreting a LISP Subset in RELFUN

Most LISP-in-LISP metainterpreters descended from the metacircular eval/apply specification of LISP 1.5 [MAE[+]62]. The operational semantics of pure LISP was later transcribed to a concise pure PROLOG **relation** eval [PP82]. The below deterministic RELFUN **function** eval, corecursive with apply, defines, without concern for efficiency, a non-trivial LISP subset including closures, macros, and an object-level eval[10].

LISP lists (and function calls) are represented as RELFUN lists (with distinguished first elements). As usual, lists with first element lambda are interpreted as temporary, anonymous functions. Permanent, named functions (and macros) become relational defun (and defmacro) facts from which calls extract lambda functions.

For instance, defun(ff,[x],[cond,[[atom,x],x],[t,[ff,[car,x]]]]), asserted as a fact into the main knowledge base, can be called as in eval([ff,[list,[cdr,[quote,[a,[[b,c],d]]]],2,3]],[]), returning the atom b.

```
eval([],A) !& [].
eval(t,A) !& t.
eval(E,A) :- numberp(E) !& E.
eval(E,A) :- atom(E) ! [_,V] .= assoc(E,A) & V.

eval([quote,Exp],A) !& Exp.
eval([function,Fn],A) !& [closure,Fn,A].

eval([cond],A) !& [].
eval([cond,[P,Q]|R],A) :- [] .= eval(P,A) !& eval([cond|R],A).
eval([cond,[P,Q]|R],A) !& eval(Q,A).

eval([Fn|Exps],A) :-
    atom(Fn),
    defmacro(Fn,Args,Body) !&
    eval(apply([lambda,Args,Body],Exps,A),A).

eval([Fn|Exps],A) :& apply(Fn,evlis(Exps,A),A).
```

---

[10]We do not try here to capture the LISP subset in RELFUN which is required for our implementation of RELFUN in LISP; it would need some profane features for reading/printing etc., but could avoid the advanced features mentioned. This would provide a 'codefinition' of RELFUN and LISP, like the one proposed for PROLOG and LISP in Kenneth M. Kahn's "Pure Prolog in Pure Lisp" response (Logic Programming Newsletter 5, Winter 83/84) to the "Pure Lisp in Pure Prolog" [PP82] paper. A direct definition of RELFUN in RELFUN has been prepared by reducing it to a meaning-preserving sublanguage (via flattening or relationalizing), for which a PROLOG-like (vanilla) metainterpreter can be given.

```
apply(Fn,Vals,A) :-
    atom(Fn),
    defun(Fn,Args,Body) !&
    apply([lambda,Args,Body],Vals,A).

apply(car,[[Hd|Tl]],A) !& Hd.
apply(cdr,[[Hd|Tl]],A) !& Tl.
apply(cons,[Hd,Tl],A) !& [Hd|Tl].
apply(atom,[Val],A) !& lispatom(Val).
apply(eq,[Val1,Val2],A) !& lispeq(Val1,Val2).

apply(add1,[Val],A) !& 1+(Val).
apply(sub1,[Val],A) !& 1-(Val).

apply(list,Vals,A) !& Vals.
apply(eval,[Val],A) !& eval(Val,A).

apply([lambda,[],Body],[],A) !& eval(Body,A).
apply([lambda,[Arg|Rargs],Body],[Val|Rvals],A) !&
    apply([lambda,Rargs,Body],Rvals,[[Arg,Val]|A]).

apply([closure,Fn,Env],Vals,A) !& apply(Fn,Vals,Env).

apply(Fn,Vals,A) :& apply(eval(Fn,A),Vals,A).

evlis([],A) :& [].
evlis([E|Re],A) :& tup(eval(E,A)|evlis(Re,A)).

assoc(N,[]) :& [].
assoc(N,[[N,V]|Ar]) !& [N,V].
assoc(N,[_|Ar]) :& assoc(N,Ar).


lispatom([Hd|Tl]) !& [].
lispatom(X) :& t.

lispeq(X,X) :& t .= lispatom(X)!.
lispeq(X,Y) :& [].
```

This LISP interpreter performs more well-formedness checks than most LISP-based ones: the correct number and structure of arguments is verified by unification (e.g., quote should have exactly one argument), yielding unknown for ill-formed expressions. The eval function corecurses with the usual evlis auxiliary to evaluate actual arguments; for uniformity, even arguments of special forms and macros are submitted to evlis (in the final eval clause) iff their function is itself the result of an evaluation (in the final apply clause). The specification has no need for the usual pairlis auxiliary because a lambda application leads to an apply recursion through the lambda-argument and actual-value lists; that the Arg/Val pairs thus extend the environment, A, in reversed order does not matter for legal LISP operators, having no duplicate lambda variables (as usual, our interpreter does not prevent formal-argument repetitions; however, by reversing the pair order in the A-list it effects LISP's normal left-to-right evaluation even on lambda binding).

## 2.5   Conclusions

The RELFUN research attempts to combine and extend programming concepts and techniques that have accumulated in the relational (principally, PROLOG) and functional (prototypically, LISP) communities.

A comprehensive subset of PROLOG is kept as a sublanguage with little syntactic modification (structures written with square brackets instead of parentheses, cut used as a separator instead of a goal). This basis is then systematically extended by advanced relational notions, a rich set of functional notions, and a combination of both.

The functional sublanguage of RELFUN is much influenced by the implementation language LISP. But as in newer functional languages, like ML and MIRANDA, a function is defined by "pattern→action" clauses instead of a conditional expression. Generalizing pattern matching to unification, RELFUN permits non-ground functions, as allowed in other logic/functional integrations [DL86]. This also leads to non-deterministic functions, enumerating finitely or infinitely many values via backtracking.

The relational/functional integration entails a continuing cross-fertilization of the two language styles. For instance, relational (logical) variables are reused for enabling the non-ground function arguments and values; also, the relational (extra-logical) once/"!" is reused for making function calls/definitions deterministic. In RELFUN these constructs are employed in the same fashion for relations and functions. Conversely, varying-arity and certain higher-order operators are transferred from the functional to the relational world. Again, the cross-fertilization leads to a uniform use of such operators in both sublanguages.

In fact, some operators can play the role of both functions and relations. For example, the concise pair of clauses

```
disj[Op|Ops](|Args) :& Op(|Args).
disj[Op|Ops](|Args) :& disj[|Ops](|Args).
```

defines disj as a varying-arity, higher-order, non-ground, non-deterministic

**function** structure that recursively applies its operator parameters op1, ... (one or more relations or functions) to zero or more (possibly non-ground) arguments arg1,..., enumerating the (possibly non-ground) values of op1(arg1,...), ... A disj call fails if none of these operator calls successfully returns a value, hence we have at the same time defined a disjunction **relation** of 'success'/'failure' logic. (A cut ending the first clause would prevent functional value enumeration as well as relational truth multiplicity after the first success.)

Summarizing, RELFUN provides a tunable system of relational/functional language extensions, which can be used in isolation and in free combination. In particular, this holds for the orthogonal functional, varying-arity, higher-order, and cut extensions of the pure-PROLOG-like Horn language. Several other extensions of pure PROLOG/LISP, e.g. finite domains (see chapter 4) and sort lattices (see [Hal95]), being quite independent from the ones in the RELational/FUNctional kernel, were added in a uniform fashion, e.g. leading to domain values as well as arguments. Further extensions, e.g. modules [Her95], may follow in a similar manner.

Besides the 'dynamic' interplay between our language extensions, there are 'static' reduction possibilities for several of them. Most notably, the functional sublanguage can be relationalized and the higher-order part can be reduced to the first-order part. While with these reductions RELFUN's semantics is indirectly founded on the usual Herbrand models for Horn clauses, there is also a more direct characterization of RELFUN's first-order hornish and footed clauses (see chapter 3), using functionally extended Herbrand models (instead of distinguishing an equality relation). The 'horizontal' transformations of the full language into a sublanguage are also important in preparation for RELFUN's 'vertical' WAM compilation. While the complete language is implemented as an interpreter, a slightly restricted version is also realized as a compiler/emulator (see chapter 5 and [Sin95]). The RELFUN sources are available in (a portable subset of) COMMON LISP along with programming examples,[11] e.g. the ones that were discussed here.

In our hybrid expert-system shell, COLAB, RELFUN's backward rules were augmented by forward rules, taxonomies, and constraints [BHHM95]. Problems of realistic size have been solved by RELFUN [Bol92a, BBK94] and RELFUN/COLAB [BHH+91] programs.

---

[11] The RELFUN homepage, which can be found in the World Wide Web at the URL address http://www.dfki.uni-kl.de/~vega/relfun.html, provides a complete release.

# 2.6  Appendix: The RELFUN Syntax

The following EBNF rules specify the PROLOG-like syntax of full RELFUN, revising the formalization without cuts in [Her92]. By using start symbol *clause*, one obtains full RELFUN, permitting single-cut and cutless clauses; instead using *valued_clause* (*cut_valued_clause*), one obtains the cutless (single-cut) REL-FUN subset only. Note that the non-terminal *hornish_fact* (*cut_hornish_fact*) just abbreviates the non-terminal *hornish_rule* (*cut_hornish_rule*) for empty *expr_seq* strings. Under the same condition *footed_rule* (*cut_footed_rule*) can be abbreviated to *footed_bodiless* (*cut_footed_bodiless*). Then, in *cut_hornish_rule* and *cut_footed_bodiless*, the neck symbol '!-' and '!&' similarly abbreviates derivations of ':-' '!' and ':&' '!', respectively. For uniformity, *cut_footed_rule* is permitted to derive the equivalent subsequences '!' '&' and '&' '!'; however, the body-side abbreviation '!&', like the corresponding neck symbol, is only allowed in this 'cut-return' ordering. Finally note that, to support semantic aspects, the grammar does not strive for minimality: calls of builtins and special operators could also be derived via expression applications to arguments.

| | | |
|---|---|---|
| *clause* | ::= | *cut_valued_clause* \| *valued_clause* . |
| | | |
| *cut_valued_clause* | ::= | *cut_hornish_clause* \| *cut_footed_clause* . |
| *cut_hornish_clause* | ::= | *cut_hornish_fact* \| *cut_hornish_rule* . |
| *cut_footed_clause* | ::= | *cut_footed_bodiless* \| *cut_footed_rule* . |
| *cut_hornish_fact* | ::= | *head* '!.' . |
| *cut_hornish_rule* | ::= | *head* ('!-' *expr_seq* \| ':-' *cut_body_prem*) '.'. |
| *cut_footed_bodiless* | ::= | *head* ('!&' *expr* \| ':&' *cut_foot_prem*) '.'. |
| *cut_footed_rule* | ::= | *head* ':-' (*expr_seq* '!&' *expr* |
| | | \| *cut_body_prem* '&' *expr* |
| | | \| *expr_seq* '&' *cut_foot_prem*) '.'. |
| *cut_body_prem* | ::= | *expr_seq* '!' *expr_seq* . |
| *cut_foot_prem* | ::= | '!' *expr* \| *expr* '!' . |
| | | |
| *valued_clause* | ::= | *hornish_clause* \| *footed_clause* . |
| *hornish_clause* | ::= | *hornish_fact* \| *hornish_rule* . |
| *footed_clause* | ::= | *footed_bodiless* \| *footed_rule* . |
| *hornish_fact* | ::= | *head* '.' . |
| *hornish_rule* | ::= | *head* ':-' *expr_seq* '.' . |
| *footed_bodiless* | ::= | *head* ':&' *expr* '.'. |
| *footed_rule* | ::= | *head* ':-' *expr_seq* '&' *expr* '.'. |
| | | |
| *head* | ::= | *term* '(' *term_seq* ['\|' *variable*] ')' . |

| | | |
|---|---|---|
| *expr_seq* | ::= | [*expr* {',' *expr*}] . |
| *expr* | ::= | *expr args* |
| | | \| *primitive_call* |
| | | \| *term* . |
| *primitive_call* | ::= | *builtin args* |
| | | \| *special args* |
| | | \| *term* '.=' *expr* . |
| *args* | ::= | '(' *expr_seq* [ '\|' *expr* ] ')' . |
| | | |
| *builtin* | ::= | *builtin_function* \| *builtin_predicate* \| *builtin_extra* . |
| *builtin_function* | ::= | 'abs' \| '+' \| '-' \| '*' \| ... . |
| *builtin_predicate* | ::= | 'atom' \| '<' \| ... . |
| *builtin_extra* | ::= | 'readl' \| ... . |
| *special* | ::= | 'ecal' \| 'once' \| 'naf' \| 'tupof' . |
| | | |
| *term_seq* | ::= | [*term* {',' *term*}] . |
| *term* | ::= | *constant* \| *variable* \| *structure* \| *list* . |
| *constant* | ::= | *symbol* \| *string* \| *integer* \| *real* . |
| *variable* | ::= | *big_char* {*char*} \| '_' \| '_' (*small_char* \| *digit* ) {*char*} . |
| *structure* | ::= | *term list* . |
| *list* | ::= | '[' *term_seq* ['\|' *term*] ']' . |
| | | |
| *symbol* | ::= | *small_char* {*char*} . |
| *string* | ::= | '"' {*char*} '"' . |
| *real* | ::= | *integer* '.' *digits* ['E' *integer* ] . |
| *integer* | ::= | ['+'\| '-'] *digits* . |
| *digits* | ::= | *digit* {*digit*} . |
| *char* | ::= | *small_char* \| *big_char* \| *digit* \| '_' . |
| *small_char* | ::= | 'a' \| 'b' \| ... \| 'z' \| '+' \| '-' \| '*' \| '/' \| '<' \| '=' \| '>' . |
| *big_char* | ::= | 'A' \| 'B' \| ... \| 'Z' . |
| *digit* | ::= | '0' \| '1' \| ... \| '9' . |

# Chapter 3

# A Direct Semantic Characterization of RELFUN

This is an attempt at a direct semantic formalization of first-order relational-functional languages (the characteristic RELFUN subset) in terms of a generalized model concept. Function-defining conditional equations (or, footed clauses) and active call-by-value expressions (in clause premises) are integrated into first-order theories. Herbrand models are accomodated to relational-functional programs by not only containing ground atoms but also ground molecules, i.e. specific function applications paired with values. Extending SLD-resolution toward innermost conditional narrowing of relational-functional clauses, SLV-resolution is introduced, which, e.g., flattens active expressions. The $T_P$-operator is generalized analogously, e.g. by unnesting ground-clause premises. Soundness and completeness proofs for SLV-resolution naturally extend the corresponding results in logic programming.

## 3.1 Introduction

RELFUN is a logic language primarily extended by call-by-value (eager) functions that may be non-ground, non-deterministic, varying-arity, and higher-order. These functions are defined by extended Horn clauses having a 'foot' premise for value returning. This extension can also be viewed as (directed) conditional equations permitting 'extra' variables in conditions, which may accumulate partial results. It entails the following syntactic changes of PROLOG:

56

**Footed clauses:** Starting with DATALOG, "`:-`"-rules **may be augmented** by an ampersand infix, "**&**", between the normal body premises and the foot premise; facts (empty bodies), by a joined infix, "`:&`".

**Active expressions:** Proceeding to PROLOG, passive structures **are rewritten** using square brackets, "`[...]`", reserving round parentheses, "`(...)`", for RELFUN's active call-by-value expressions (permitted in premises).

As shown by the Fibonacci programs in example 1, RELFUN's function-defining footed clauses (e.g. for `fibfun`) can be developed from PROLOG-like relation-defining Horn clauses (e.g. for `fibrel`) via an intermediate footed-clause form using a generalized relational is-primitive, "`.=`", in a functional, `let`-like manner (e.g. for `fibfis`). When reading such clauses we extend PROLOG's "*... if ...*" for "`... :- ...`" to "*... if ... return ...*" for "`... :- ... & ...`" (or just "*... return ...*" for "`... :& ...`").[1]

**Example 1** *Recursive Fibonacci relations and functions in RELFUN.*

```
fibris(N,F) :- F .= fibfun(N).

fibrel(0,s[0]).
fibrel(s[0],s[0]).
fibrel(s[s[N]],F) :-  fibrel(N,X), fibrel(s[N],Y), plusrel(X,Y,F).

fibfis(0)       :&  s[0].
fibfis(s[0])    :&  s[0].
fibfis(s[s[N]]) :-  X .= fibfis(N), Y .= fibfis(s[N])
                                          & plusfun(X,Y).

fibfun(0)       :&  s[0].
fibfun(s[0])    :&  s[0].
fibfun(s[s[N]]) :&  plusfun(fibfun(N),fibfun(s[N])).


plusrel(0,N,N).
plusrel(s[M],N,P) :-  plusrel(M,s[N],P).

plusfun(0,N)    :&  N.
plusfun(s[M],N) :&  plusfun(M,s[N]).
```

---

[1] Intuitively, the infix "`:&`" corresponds to a (directed, unconditional) "$=$" sign, while the mixfix "`:- ... &`" corresponds to a (directed, conditional) "$\doteq$" sign, where the dots stand for the condition. However, we will not formalize functions using a logic with a distinguished (directed) equality **predicate**, but will 'build in' "`:&`" and "`:- ... &`" even more deeply, as new **connectives**.

Relation definitions in RELFUN employ generalized Horn clauses, namely 'hornish' clauses, which may again call arbitrary functions, either within any argument of a relation call or the right-hand side (rhs) of the ".="-primitive (e.g. in fibris). So the body premises of hornish clauses are relational on the **top-level** (just binding variables, like Horn-clause premises), but may **contain** functional applications (also returning values). Conversely, the head and foot of footed clauses can be regarded as the two sides of an equation, giving these clauses a principal functional flavor, although their body conditions are exactly like the relational top-level premises of hornish clauses. Altogether, RELFUN subsumes hornish and footed clauses as *valued clauses*, which tightly integrate relational and functional characteristics.[2]

The following functional version of J. W. Lloyd's relational slowsort example [Llo87] shows the use of non-ground and non-deterministic subfunction calls for defining a deterministic main function.

**Example 2** *A functional slowsort program in RELFUN.*

```
% Sort filters non-deterministic permutations through sorted:
sort(X) :& sorted(perm(X)).

% Return sorted lists unchanged, fail for unsorted ones:
sorted([]) :& [].
sorted([X]) :& [X].
sorted([X,Y|Z]) :- lesseq(X,Y) & cons(X,sorted([Y|Z])).

% Permute by a non-ground delete call returning U-less lists
% and binding U for a cons call enclosing the perm recursion:
perm([]) :& [].
perm([X|Y]) :& cons(U,perm(delete(U,[X|Y]))).

% Non-deterministically delete X elements from list argument:
delete(X,[X|Y]) :& Y.
delete(X,[Y|Z]) :& cons(Y,delete(X,Z)).

% A less-or-equal relation over s-terms:
lesseq(0,X).
lesseq(s[X],s[Y]) :- lesseq(X,Y).

% cons(h,t) calls h and t by value, [h|t] instantiates h and t:
cons(X,Y) :& [X|Y].
```

---

[2]Still, rather than indiscriminately speaking of 'relational-functional' language constructs, we will didactically distinguish 'relational' and 'functional' constructs on the basis of their principal characteristics.

Since programs for Fibonacci numbers, list sorting, and many other purposes are normally used in a deterministic mode, we think they should be formulated as functions rather than relations, indicating the preferred direction of computation. However, in RELFUN such functions still permit inverse calls (e.g. s[0] .= fibfun(W) non-deterministically binds W to 0 or s[0]) and can make natural internal use of relations (e.g. lesseq) and non-deterministic functions (e.g. perm and delete).

A comprehensive overview of RELFUN and related work as well as pointers to its applications and to its original operational (interpretative), LISP-implemented semantics can be found in chapter 2. Among the tools of the REL-FUN implementation there is a term-rewriting algorithm relationalize for transforming footed and hornish clauses into Horn clauses, thus indirectly characterizing their model-theoretic semantics. However, this semantic indirectness makes our understanding of functions totally dependent on our understanding of relations (inverting the dependency incurred by the LISP-based interpreter), whereas we work towards "equal declarative depth" for both of them.

Here we thus attempt to directly characterize the semantics of 'kernel' REL-FUN, the pure-RELFUN subset exemplifying fixed-arity first-order relational-functional languages, in terms of a generalized model concept: RELFUN models contain both **atoms** (relations) and **directed unconditional equations** (functions). This would permit a common foundation of logic and functional programming, reducing the gap between these declarative paradigms. Through a model-theoretic foundation of relational-functional languages, the semantic characteristics available or lacking in either of these declarative-programming paradigms can be assessed in a way more neutral than via the indirection of mutual implementions of, and cross-translations between these paradigms. For instance, on the basis of our characterization we can study such questions as "How will functional call-by-value expressions enrich (and complicate) the semantics of relational languages?" or "How will the relational meaning of non-ground arguments carry over to the functional meaning of arguments and returned values?" Another important motivation of the present work is to make the many alternative relational-functional integration proposals (see, e.g., [BL86] and [DL86]) comparable on a common ground, revealing their deeper, non-syntactic differences. Finally, we think the model-theoretic treatment can provide us with a long-term yardstick for developing a 'minimal' integration of the essential concepts of relational and functional languages: in the multitude of integration proposals, only "Occam's razor" can help sorting out the **proper integration constructs** from other "nice features".

In fact, with kernel RELFUN we have attempted to operationally explore a tight, minimum integration of the concepts of a relation and a function themselves. Among other things, the classical eager functional expressions (innermost reduction) have been extended to non-deterministic function nestings to accomodate relational non-determinism. Then, the semantic interpretation of functions just uses mappings to **sets** of domain individuals, and expressions are semantically evaluated using **expression assignments**, a natural, set-valued extension of relational term assignments. These semantic extensions are less complicated than the semantics of lazy expressions (outermost reduction) as a relational-functional integration concept, as introduced by other recent proposals (e.g., K-LEAF [GLMP91] and BABEL [MNRA92]): eagerness keeps the semantics strict and simple, whereas laziness accepts the non-strictness overhead to give a meaning to unifications involving non-terminating expressions. While kernel RELFUN's operational integration concepts may be close to a minimum, its current model-theoretic characterization is still quite preliminary and will certainly need further simplification and improvement.

On the other hand, pure-RELFUN extensions of the present treatment could directly incorporate the semantics of varying-arity operations, which can also be reduced to unary ones over lists. Similarly, RELFUN's higher-order operations should not be too difficult to add, as they are restricted to those reducible to first-order operations using an `apply` dummy as introduced for corresponding PROLOG extensions by D. H. D. Warren [War82]. While these two extensions have long existed in the implemented RELFUN system, further extensions such as finite domains and, particularly, finite exclusions (see chapter 4) will first require their own operational test phase before we can think of including them in the formal semantics. Finally, some aspects of our RELFUN extensions of SLD-resolution, Herbrand models, and $T_P$-operators will probably be transferable to other languages.

Our basic semantic treatment draws heavily on chapters 1 and 2 of J. W. Lloyd's book [Llo87], construing a parallel between Horn-clause relations and first-order functions, enabled by suitably generalizing the latter in a non-ground, non-deterministic fashion. This relational-functional parallel in the formal definitions given here derived from considerations in language design such as expressive power, orthogonality, and uniformity of constructs. But it also simplifies transferring foundation theorems of logic programming (as found, e.g., in J. W. Lloyd's book) to eager, non-ground, non-deterministic first-order functional programming and to unified relational-functional programming. It is thus attempted to complement the 'function-translating' characterization of innermost narrowing in [BGM88] by a 'function-modeling' characterization. Since our model notion reflects call-by-value flattening, also our notion of completeness will differ from the general one in [Han94], as illustrated by example 9.

We think that a fundament for functional programming should be 'grounded' on a level as deep as the (Herbrand-)model-theoretic fundament of relational programming. Specifically this means that we will try to establish function definitions as subsets $\{f(a_1, ..., a_n) :\& b, ...\}$ of so-called ground 'molecules' (directed unconditional equations) from the Herbrand 'cross' just like relation definitions are established as subsets $\{r(a_1, ..., a_n), ...\}$ of ground atoms from the Herbrand base. Intuitively, Herbrand cross models employ molecules for the 'pointwise' definition of a (discrete) function, akin to the familiar notion of the 'graph' (or 'extension') of a function as a set of pairs. Avoiding dependencies between the molecules of such a model which correspond to the usual 'functionality' restriction $f(a_1, ..., a_n)$ :& $b \land f(a_1, ..., a_n)$ :& $c \implies b = c$, it will **simplify** this semantics that we permit $b \neq c$ i.e., non-deterministic functions.[3] Unaffected by non-determinism, the **directedness** of functional computation is expressed by the '$f(a_1, ..., a_n)$-to-$b$' order of each molecule $f(a_1, ..., a_n)$ :& $b$ in an Herbrand cross model.

In the following sections the semantics of the first-order-reduced RELFUN kernel is formalized by equivalent *procedural, fixpoint,* and *model-theoretic* means, extending those of logic programming. In particular, the procedural SLD-resolution for Horn-clause programs is extended to *SLV-resolution* for valued-clause programs, e.g. accomodating value returning and operator nesting. Simultaneously, the underlying *Herbrand (base) models*, containing ground atoms (flat relationships), are extended to *Herbrand cross models*, containing ground molecules (flat function applications asymmetrically ":&"-paired with terms). Instead of all ground term equations in the Herbrand base for models of logics with (e.g., symmetry-axiomatized) equality [Fri84], the Herbrand base for cross models thus contains all ground 'innermost' defined-function applications associated with all ground terms, denoting their ultimate computation values (just as the usual Herbrand base contains all ground relation applications, denoting their ultimate truth). For integrated relational-functional programs, such models become united to *Herbrand crossbase models*, containing both atoms and molecules.

On the basis of the unified pure-RELFUN constructs, the impure relational-functional features can also be introduced in a uniform manner. For instance, after proving results corresponding to the "independence of the computation rule" in [Llo87], we could proceed from 'and-parallel' to 'and-sequential' relational-functional premise evaluation, which is the operational semantics actually implemented for RELFUN (just as for PROLOG). Similarly, the resolution/model-theoretic 'or-parallelism' of relational-functional clauses could be weakened toward the operational (but implementation-incomplete!) 'or-sequentialism' of backtracking. Finally, functions **and** relations can be forced to operate (more) deterministically using the same cut, commit, or substitute constructs; however, adapting our model-theoretic approach to such optional determinism specifications may be difficult because of the semantic problems with cut-like notions.

---

[3](Re)specializing RELFUN to a sublanguage with only deterministic functions would cause semantic changes starting off from the interpretation concept. (While our non-deterministic function symbols are assigned mappings to the powerset of the domain, deterministic function symbols could be assigned constructor-like mappings to the domain itself.) Within models the 'deterministic-function' restriction could then be introduced as an axiom, but this would change Herbrand's **sets** to (non-free) **algebras**.

## 3.2 Extending First-Order Theories to First-Order Relational-Functional Theories

We now begin with the formal development of first-order relational-functional programming by 'functionally' extending the "Foundations of Logic Programming" [Llo87], which should also be consulted for references to classical work.

A *first-order relational-functional theory* consists of:

1. An alphabet.

2. A first-order relational-functional language (the well-formed formulas of the theory).

3. A set of axioms (a designated subset of the well-formed formulas).

4. A set of inference rules.

**Definition 1** *The alphabet of a first-order relational-functional theory consists of nine classes of symbols (some notational conventions are given in parentheses, where all letters used may be subscripted):*

1. *Variables (normally denoted by the letters $x$, $y$, and $z$).[4]*

2. *Constants (normally denoted by the letters $a$, $b$, and $c$).*

3. *Constructors[5] (normally denoted by the letters $j$, $k$, and $l$).*

4. *Function symbols (normally denoted by the letters $f$, $g$, and $h$).*

5. *Relation symbols[6] (normally denoted by the letters $p$, $q$, and $r$).*

6. *Functional connectives (two binary infixes denoted by $.=$ and $:\&$ and a ternary mixfix denoted by $:-$ together with $\&$).*

7. *Relational connectives (a unary prefix denoted by $\neg$ and binary infixes denoted by $\wedge$, $\vee$, $:-$, and $\leftrightarrow$).[7]*

8. *Quantifiers (denoted by $\exists$ and $\forall$).*

9. *Punctuation symbols ("[", "]", "(", ")", and ",").*

---

[4] In larger examples we will capitalize variable names and use digit suffixes instead of subscripts, e.g. $x_1$ becoming $X1$, to conform to RELFUN's PROLOG-like naming conventions.

[5] Often called "functors" or even "function symbols" in the literature.

[6] Often called "predicate symbols" in the literature.

[7] Much like in PROLOG's program clauses, ":-" without a consecutive "&" plays the role of "←".

*The union of the classes of function and relation symbols will be referred to as* operation symbols *or, briefly,* operators.

Note that RELFUN's implemented operational semantics does not differentiate subclasses for constructor, function, and relation symbols but contextually distinguishes **uses** of symbols from a united class, even permitting a given symbol to have occurrences in more than one subclass (e.g., the main operator of a body premise will act as a relation but may re-occur in a foot premise, where it will act as a function; also, meta-calls make operators from constructors).

**Definition 2** *A* term *is defined inductively:*

1. *A* variable *is a term.*

2. *A* constant *is a term.*

3. *If $k$ is an $n$-ary constructor and $t_1, \ldots, t_n$ are terms, then $k[t_1, \ldots, t_n]$ is a term, called a* structure.

The above use of square brackets for applying a constructor to arguments clearly sets off 'passive' structures from 'active' operator applications as defined below with the more usual round parentheses. In our semantic treatment of relational-functional languages the bracketing type serves readability but provides no information beyond that already implicit in the symbol classes, 'constructor' vs. 'operator'. In the implemented version of RELFUN, not distinguishing symbol classes, this information is exclusively conveyed by "[...]" vs. "(...)".

In RELFUN *cns* is employed as the binary list constructor (LISP's *cons* or "."), and *nil*, as usual, as the constant denoting the empty list. Externally, a *list term* having the right-recursively nested form $cns[t_1, cns[t_2, cns[\ldots, cns[t_n, t]\ldots]]]$ is written (PROLOG-like) as the linearized varying-arity term $[t_1, t_2, \ldots, t_n]$ for $t = nil$ or, $[t_1, t_2, \ldots, t_n | t]$ for $t$ being a variable. However, we regard the varying-arity form as (passive) applications of a constructor *tup*, understood to precede unprefixed "[...]"-terms.

**Definition 3** *An* expression *is defined inductively:*

1. *A term is an* expression.

2. *If $f$ is an $n$-ary function symbol and $E_1, \ldots, E_n$ are expressions, then $f(E_1, \ldots, E_n)$ is an expression, called an* application; *if all of $E_1, \ldots, E_n$ are terms, $f(E_1, \ldots, E_n)$ is called a* flat application.

Such a notion of expressions is essential in functional programming, but lacks in non-extended logic programming (in [Llo87], "expression" is given a different, peripheral meaning).

**Definition 4** *A* (well-formed) formula *is defined inductively:*

1. *If $r$ is an $n$-ary relation symbol and $E_1, \ldots, E_n$ are expressions, then $r(E_1, \ldots, E_n)$ is a formula, called a* relationship; *if all of $E_1, \ldots, E_n$ are terms, $r(E_1, \ldots, E_n)$ is called a* flat relationship *or, since this is the most basic kind of formula, an* atomic formula *or, simply, an* atom.

2. *If $E$ is an expression and $t$ is a term, then $(t .= E)$ is a formula, called a* setting formula *or, simply, a* setter; *if $E$ is a flat application, $(t .= E)$ is called a* flat setter; *if $E$ is a term, $(t .= E)$ is called a* term setter.

3. *If $e$ is a flat application and $E$ is an expression, then $(e :\& E)$ is a formula; if $E$ is a term, $(e :\& E)$ is called a* molecular formula *or, simply, a* molecule.

4. *If $e$ is a flat application, $E$ is an expression, and $W$ is a formula, then $(e :- W \& E)$ is a formula.* '

5. *If $W_1$ and $W_2$ are formulas, then so are $(\neg W_1)$, $(W_1 \wedge W_2)$, $(W_1 \vee W_2)$, $(W_1 :- W_2)$, and $(W_1 \leftrightarrow W_2)$.*

6. *If $W$ is a formula and $x$ is a variable, then $(\exists x W)$ and $(\forall x W)$ are formulas.*

The restriction of $e$ being a flat application in items *3.* and *4.* reflects the "constructor discipline" [O'D85] of RELFUN's footed clauses. It could be dropped in a more general equational treatment of first-order relational-functional languages. Conversely, instead of letting $W_1$ be an arbitrary formula in $(W_1 :- W_2)$ of item *5.*, it could be immediately restricted to an atomic formula (flat relationship), as required for RELFUN's hornish clauses.

Note that the parentheses employed to build applications and relationships are indispensible parts of the syntax. The parentheses around entire formulas, however, are just used for grouping and will frequently be omitted if no ambiguities arise under the following partial precedence order: "$\neg$", "$\forall$", "$\exists$" precede ".=" precedes "$\wedge$" precedes "$\vee$" precedes "$:\&$", "$:-$ ... &", "$:-$", "$\leftrightarrow$".

There is a close kinship between flat setters and molecules, which will be confirmed in definition 16. Thus, an operation that switches between both formula types will be convenient.

**Definition 5** *The self-inverse setter/molecule swapping operation "$^\otimes$" is defined as an exponentiation operator over sets of molecules, flat setters, and relationships (the $u_i$ must be terms):*[8]

$$r(u_1, \ldots, u_m)^\otimes = r(u_1, \ldots, u_m)$$
$$(t .= g(u_1, \ldots, u_m))^\otimes = g(u_1, \ldots, u_m) :\& t$$

---

[8] If "$^\otimes$" is applicable to a formula $F$, then $(F^\otimes)^\otimes = F$.

$$(g(u_1, \ldots, u_m) : \& \ t)^{\otimes} \ = \ t \ .= g(u_1, \ldots, u_m)$$
$$\{F_1, \ldots, F_n\}^{\otimes} \ = \ \{F_1^{\otimes}, \ldots, F_n^{\otimes}\}$$

**Example 3** $a$, $b$, $c$, $x$, $y$, $k[a, x, b]$, $l[y, y]$, and $k[a, l[y, y], b]$ are terms; $f(y, k[a, l[y, y], b], c, l[y, y])$ is a flat application; $r(b, f(y, k[a, l[y, y], b], c, l[y, y]))$ is a (non-flat) relationship. Furthermore, $f(y, k[a, l[y, y], b], c, l[y, y]) : \& \ k[a, x, b]$ is a molecule; finally, $(f(y, k[a, l[y, y], b], c, l[y, y]) : \& \ k[a, x, b])^{\otimes} = k[a, x, b] .= f(y, k[a, l[y, y], b], c, l[y, y])$ is a flat setter.

**Definition 6** *The* first-order relational-functional language *given by an alphabet consists of the set of all formulas built from the symbols of the alphabet.*

In the following we will focus special kinds of formulas, namely RELFUN's clauses. Unaffected by their Horn-clause extensions (expressions, setters, and foot premises), they are closed formulas by assuming all variables to have a prenex universal quantifier.

**Definition 7** *A (program) clause is a hornish (program) clause or a footed (program) clause. If $w$ is an atomic formula, $e$ is a flat application, $V_1, \ldots, V_n$ are relationships or setters, and $E$ is an expression, then $w \ :\text{-} \ V_1, \ldots, V_n$, abbreviating $w \ :\text{-} \ (V_1 \wedge \ldots \wedge V_n)$, is a* hornish (program) clause *and $e \ :\text{-} \ V_1, \ldots, V_n \ \& \ E$, abbreviating $e \ :\text{-} \ (V_1 \wedge \ldots \wedge V_n) \ \& \ E$, is a* footed (program) clause. *$w$ or $e$ is the* head, *$V_1, \ldots, V_n$ is the* body, *and $E$ is the* foot *of the clause. If $V_1, \ldots, V_n$ are all atoms, the hornish (program) clause $w \ :\text{-} \ V_1, \ldots, V_n$ is also called a* Horn (program) clause. *For $n = 0$, i.e. with an empty body, a hornish (program) clause $w \ :\text{-}$ , abbreviating $w \ :\text{-} \ true$, is written as $w$, while a footed (program) clause $e \ :\text{-} \ \& \ E$, abbreviating $e \ :\text{-} \ true \ \& \ E$, is written as $e \ :\& \ E$.*

**Definition 8** *A ((first-order) relational-functional) program $P$ is a finite set of program clauses $\{c_1, \ldots, c_n\}$. $P$ is usually written (with ".": -terminators) as:*
$c_1 .$
$\ldots$
$c_n .$

A program will play the role of the set of axioms of a first-order relational-functional theory.

**Definition 9** *The* empty (hornish) clause, *denoted $\square$, is the hornish clause of the form $ \ :\text{-}$ , which abbreviates false $ \ :\text{-} \ true$. A* terminal ((t-)footed) clause, *denoted $\triangle(t)$, $t$ a term, is a footed clause of the form $ \ :\& \ t$, which abbreviates $\square \ \& \ t$. The* trivial (hornish) clause, *denoted $\top$, is the hornish clause of the form true $ \ :\text{-} \ true$.*

**Definition 10** *A* relational goal *is a hornish clause of the form*

$$:- V_1, \ldots, V_n$$

*that is, it has an empty head.* A functional goal *is a footed clause of the form*

$$:- V_1, \ldots, V_n \; \& \; E$$

*that is, it has an empty head.*

It should be kept in mind that a relational goal is 'relational' in the usual sense only on the top-level: the $V_i$'s need not be atoms but may be nested relationships or setters. Conversely, a functional goal may of course contain $V_i$'s that are atoms.[9]

## 3.3 Relational-Functional Interpretations and Models

First, we will consider general interpretations of full first-order relational-functional languages. Then, these will be restricted to Herbrand-like interpretations of RELFUN's clause programs. Since the kernel RELFUN formalized here does not contain a negation construct, we will neglect RELFUN's three-valued open-world semantics and its differentiation of the truth values false and unknown (see chapter 2).

**Definition 11** *A* pre-interpretation *$J$ of a first-order relational-functional language $L$ consists of:*

1. *A non-empty set $D$, called the* domain *of the pre-interpretation.*

2. *For each constant in $L$, the assignment of an element in $D$.*

3. *For each n-ary constructor in $L$, the assignment of a mapping from $D^n$ to $D$.*

**Definition 12** *An* interpretation *$I$ of a first-order relational-functional language $L$ consists of a pre-interpretation $J$ with domain $D$ of $L$ together with:*

1. *For each n-ary relation symbol in $L$, the assignment of a mapping from $D^n$ into $\{true, false\}$ (or, equivalently, a relation on $D^n$).*

---

[9]Thus, "relational goal" should perhaps be renamed into "hornish goal", and "functional goal" into "footed goal". However, this would entail new words in the later definitions for "relational"/"functional" derivation, answer, etc.

2. *For each n-ary function symbol in L, the assignment of a mapping from $D^n$ to $2^D$, the powerset of D.*

*We say I is* based on *J.*

**Definition 13** *Let J be a pre-interpretation of a first-order relational-functional language L. A* variable assignment (wrt *J*) *is an assignment to each variable in L of an element in the domain of J.*

**Definition 14** *Let J be a pre-interpretation with domain D of a first-order relational-functional language L and let V be a variable assignment. The* term assignment (wrt *J* and *V*) *of the terms in L is defined as follows:*

1. *Each variable is given its assignment according to V.*

2. *Each constant is given its assignment according to J.*

3. *If $k'$ is the assignment of the n-ary constructor k according to J and $t'_1, \ldots, t'_n$ are the term assignments of $t_1, \ldots, t_n$, then $k'(t'_1, \ldots, t'_n) \in D$ is the term assignment of $k[t_1, \ldots, t_n]$.*

**Definition 15** *Let I be an interpretation with domain D of a first-order relational-functional language L and let V be a variable assignment. The* expression assignment (wrt *I* and *V*) *of the expressions in L is defined as follows:*

1. *If $t'$ is the term assignment of the term t wrt I and V, then the singleton set $\{t'\}$ is the expression assignment of t.*

2. *If $f'$ is the mapping assigned to the n-ary function symbol f by I and $E'_1, \ldots, E'_n$ are the expression assignments of $E_1, \ldots, E_n$, then the union of all $f'(t'_1, \ldots, t'_n) \in 2^D$ for each $t'_1 \in E'_1, \ldots, t'_n \in E'_n$ is the expression assignment of $f(E_1, \ldots, E_n)$.*

**Definition 16** *Let I be an interpretation with domain D of a first-order relational-functional language L and let V be a variable assignment. Then a formula in L can be given a truth value, true or false, (wrt I and V) as follows (we let (a possibly embellished version of) t denote a term, of e, denote a flat application, of E, denote an expression, and of W, denote a formula):*

1. *If the formula has the form $r(E_1, \ldots, E_n)$, then the truth value of the formula is true if there exist $t'_1 \in E'_1, \ldots, t'_n \in E'_n$ such that $r'(t'_1, \ldots, t'_n)$ has truth value true, where $r'$ is the mapping assigned to r by I and $E'_1, \ldots, E'_n$ are the expression assignments of $E_1, \ldots, E_n$ wrt I and V; otherwise, the formula's truth value is false.*

2. *If the formula has the form* $f(t_1, \ldots, t_n)$ :& $E$, *then the truth value of the formula is true if the expression assignment of* $E$ *wrt* $I$ *and* $V$ *is* $E'$ *and* $E' \subseteq f'(t'_1, \ldots, t'_n)$, *where* $f'$ *is the mapping assigned to* $f$ *by* $I$, *and* $t'_1, \ldots, t'_n$ *are the term assignments of* $t_1, \ldots, t_n$ *wrt* $I$ *and* $V$; *otherwise, the formula's truth value is false.*

3. *If the formula has the form* $t$ .= $E$, *then its truth value is true if the expression assignment of* $E$ *wrt* $I$ *and* $V$ *is* $E'$ *and* $t' \in E'$, *where* $t'$ *is the term assignment of* $t$ *wrt* $I$ *and* $V$; *otherwise, its truth value is false.*[10]

4. *If the formula has the form* $e$ :- *false* & $E$, *then its truth value is true. If the formula has the form* $e$ :- *true* & $E$, *then the truth value is that of* $e$ :& $E$.[11]

5. *If the formula has the form* $\neg W$, $W_1 \wedge W_2$, $W_1 \vee W_2$, $W_1$ :- $W_2$, *or* $W_1 \leftrightarrow W_2$, *then the truth value is given by the usual truth tables.*

6. *If the formula has the form* $\forall x W$, *then the truth value of the formula is true if for all* $d \in D$ *the subformula* $W$ *has truth value true wrt* $I$ *and* $V(x/d)$, *where* $V(x/d)$ *is* $V$ *except that* $x$ *is assigned* $d$; *otherwise, the formula's truth value is false.*

7. *If the formula has the form* $\exists x W$, *then its truth value is true if there exists* $d \in D$ *such that* $W$ *has truth value true wrt* $I$ *and* $V(x/d)$; *otherwise, its truth value is false.*

This functionally extended truth concept directly transfers to the classical definitions of, e.g., *model*, *validity*, and *logical consequence*, for which we refer to [Llo87].

**Example 4** *Consider the formula* $\forall x (x$ .= $f(g(x), g(x)))$ *and the following interpretation* $I$. *Let* $D = \{1, 2, \ldots\}$ *be the natural numbers, let* $f$ *be assigned the function that maps two naturals to the singleton set of their product, and let* $g$ *be assigned the function that maps a natural to the set of its divisors. Then* $I$

---

[10]Thus the instance $t$ .= $f(t_1, \ldots, t_n)$ has the same truth value as the instance $f(t_1, \ldots, t_n)$ :& $t$, defined through item 2. The different syntaxes are maintained even in these special cases for marking off the body-goal use of the former from the clause-definition use of the latter. Also, in RELFUN's implemented operational semantics, successful setters return their evaluated rhs, rather than just **true**.

[11]For formalizing RELFUN's "valued conjunctions", definition 3 could introduce a third class of expressions, co-inductively with the formulas of definition 4, making the symbol "&" a binary infix instead of its actual use as part of a ternary mixfix: If $W$ is a formula and $E$ is an expression, then $(W$ & $E)$ is a (conditional) expression. This enables simulating formulas of the form $e$ :- $W$ & $E$ by nestings of the form $e$ :& $(W$ & $E)$. For this, the expression $(true$ & $E)$ can be assigned the value of $E$. However, assigning $false$ to $(false$ & $E)$, blurring the distinction between $(2^D$-valued) expressions and ($\{true, false\}$-valued) formulas, would, e.g., cause $fac(N)$ :& $(zerop(N)$ & $1)$ to return $false$ for $fac(1)$ instead of signalling inapplicability. Therefore, in RELFUN $(false$ & $E)$ is actually assigned the failure-signalling truth value $unknown$, which can be regarded as the empty expression value $\{\} \in 2^D$.

*is a model of the formula because all naturals have at least themselves and 1 as divisors.*

The definitions of groundness and Herbrand universes and bases adapt the corresponding classical notions; the definitions of Herbrand crosses and crossbases extend the notion of Herbrand bases in order to define models of, respectively, functional and relational-functional programs, as motivated in section 3.1.

**Definition 17** *A* ground term, ground atom, *or* ground molecule *is, respectively, a term, atom, or molecule not containing variables.*

**Definition 18** *The* Herbrand universe $U_P$ *of a program P is the set of all ground terms that can be formed out of the constants and constructors appearing in P.*

**Definition 19** *The* Herbrand base $B_P$ *of a program P is the set of all ground atoms that can be formed by using the relation symbols from P with ground terms from the Herbrand universe $U_P$ as arguments.*

**Definition 20** *The* Herbrand cross $C_P$ *of a program P is the set of all ground molecules that can be formed by using the function symbols from P with ground terms from the Herbrand universe $U_P$ as arguments and using ground terms from $U_P$ as foots.*

**Definition 21** *The* Herbrand crossbase $X_P$ *of a program P is the union $B_P \cup C_P$ of its Herbrand base $B_P$ and its Herbrand cross $C_P$.*

**Example 5** *The (deterministic, extra-variables, ".="-less) program $P_1$*

$f(X)$ :- $p(X), q(Y)$ & $g(g(X, Y), Y)$.
$g(a, a)$ :& $k[X]$.
$g(k[X], l[X])$ :& $g(X, X)$.
$p(k[X])$.
$q(l[X])$.

*uses the constructors k and l, and employs the operators f and g (as functions) as well as p and q (as relations).*

*The Herbrand universe $U_{P_1}$ of $P_1$ is*
$\{a, k[a], l[a], k[k[a]], k[l[a]], l[k[a]], l[l[a]], \ldots\}$.

*The Herbrand base $B_{P_1}$ of $P_1$ is*
$\{p(a), q(a), p(k[a]), p(l[a]), q(k[a]), q(l[a]), \ldots\}$.

The *Herbrand cross* $C_{P_1}$ of $P_1$ is
$\{f(a) :\& a, f(a) :\& k[a], f(a) :\& l[a], \ldots,$
$g(a,a) :\& a, g(a,a) :\& k[a], g(a,a) :\& l[a], \ldots,$
$\ldots\}$.

The *Herbrand crossbase* $X_{P_1} = B_{P_1} \cup C_{P_1}$ of $P_1$ is
$\{p(a), q(a), p(k[a]), p(l[a]), q(k[a]), q(l[a]), \ldots,$
$f(a) :\& a, f(a) :\& k[a], f(a) :\& l[a], \ldots,$
$g(a,a) :\& a, g(a,a) :\& k[a], g(a,a) :\& l[a], \ldots,$
$\ldots\}$.

Two generalized model concepts can now be defined, extending the usual Herbrand models for relational programs to models for functional and relational-functional programs.

**Definition 22** *An* Herbrand (base), Herbrand cross, or Herbrand crossbase in-terpretation *is a subset of the Herbrand base, Herbrand cross, or Herbrand cross-base, respectively.*

**Definition 23** *Let $I$ be an Herbrand (base), Herbrand cross, or Herbrand cross-base interpretation and let $P$ be a program. Then $I$ is, respectively, an* Herbrand (base), Herbrand cross, or Herbrand crossbase model *for $P$ if $P$ is true wrt $I$.*

We concentrate the further development on relational-functional Herbrand crossbase models, which, however, constitute disjoint unions of Herbrand cross models and Herbrand (base) models.

The "model intersection" proposition 6.1 of [Llo87] obviously also holds for the crossbase extension.

**Proposition 1 (Model intersection property)** *Let $P$ be a relational-functional program and $\{M_i\}_{i \in I}$ be a non-empty set of Herbrand crossbase mo-dels for $P$. Then $\bigcap_{i \in I} M_i$ is an Herbrand crossbase model for $P$.*

Since every relational-functional program $P$ has $X_P$ as an Herbrand cross-base model, the set of all Herbrand crossbase models for $P$ is non-empty, and proposition 1 permits the following definition.

**Definition 24** *The* least Herbrand crossbase model $M_P$ *for a relational-functional program $P$ is the intersection of all Herbrand crossbase models for $P$.*

**Example 6** *For $u$ assuming all values from $U_{P_1}$, the following Herbrand cross-base interpretation $I$, contained in $X_{P_1}$, is an (the least) Herbrand crossbase* *model of $P_1$ (cf. example 5):*

$\{f(k[a]) :\& k[u], \quad g(a,a) :\& k[u], \quad g(k[a], l[a]) :\& k[u],$
$p(k[u]), \quad q(l[u])\}.$

*Thus, while $P_1$ deterministically returns the non-ground term $k[X]$ for certain arguments of the functions $f$ and $g$ (failing for other ones), the model of $P_1$ contains infinitely non-deterministic molecules that let $f$ and $g$ return the ground terms $k[a], k[k[a]], k[l[a]], \ldots$ for the same argument combinations.*

**Proposition 2** *Let $P$ be a relational-functional program and $I$ an Herbrand crossbase model of $P$ (in particular, the least one). Then there exist a Horn program $\tilde{P}$ and an Herbrand model $\tilde{I}$ of $\tilde{P}$ (in particular, the least one) such that there is a bijection between $I$ and $\tilde{I}$.*

**Example 7** *The relational-functional program $P_1$ of example 5 can be transformed into the following Horn program $\tilde{P}_1$ by flattening the $g$ nesting and introducing result parameters for $f$ and $g$ (note that the $g$-molecule becomes an atom):*

$\tilde{f}(X,R) :\!- p(X), q(Y), \tilde{g}(X,Y,S), \tilde{g}(S,Y,R).$
$\tilde{g}(a,a,k[X]).$
$\tilde{g}(k[X], l[X], R) :\!- \tilde{g}(X,X,R).$
$p(k[X]).$
$q(l[X]).$

*An (the least) Herbrand model $\tilde{I}$ of $\tilde{P}_1$ is (where $u \in U_{\tilde{P}_1} = U_{P_1}$):*

$\{\tilde{f}(k[a], k[u]), \quad \tilde{g}(a, a, k[u]), \quad \tilde{g}(k[a], l[a], k[u]),$
$p(k[u]), \quad q(l[u])\}.$

*The bijection between $I$ and $\tilde{I}$ is obvious: untilded (functional) molecules correspond to tilded (relational) atoms; untilded atoms remain unchanged.*

*While the above bijection, call it $b_{LAST}$, introduces the new parameter in position $n + 1$, there is another bijection, $b_{FIRST}$, introducing it in position 1, as actually done by RELFUN's `relationalize` algorithm (see chapter 2). That is, an Herbrand model such as $\tilde{I}$ alone does not carry the entire information of the original Herbrand crossbase model such as $I$: the type of bijection must be specified along with the Herbrand model, e.g. by $(\tilde{I}, LAST)$, in order to preserve in the relations the computation direction of the original functions (like the 'modes' $\tilde{f}(in, out)$ and $\tilde{g}(in, in, out)$). For instance, while $(b_{LAST})^{-1} \circ b_{LAST}(I) = I$, the composition $(b_{FIRST})^{-1} \circ b_{LAST}$ would transform $I$ to the Herbrand crossbase model*

$\{f(k[u])$ :& $k[a]$, $g(a, k[u])$ :& $a$, $g(l[a], k[u])$ :& $k[a]$,
$p(k[u])$, $q(l[u])\}$

*which is not equivalent to I.*

Let us now proceed to the generalized notions of relational-functional answers and their correctness.

**Definition 25** *Let P be a relational-functional program and $G_r$ and $G_f$ be a relational and a functional goal, respectively. A* relational answer *for $P \cup \{G_r\}$ is a substitution for variables of $G_r$. A functional answer for $P \cup \{G_f\}$ is a term paired with a substitution for variables of $G_f$.*

It should be understood that the substitution does not necessarily contain a binding for every variable in $G_r$ or $G_f$. Since RELFUN's operational semantics considers relations as true-valued functions, a relational answer operationally returns the term **true** along with yielding a substitution.

**Definition 26** *Let P be a relational-functional program, $G_r$ a relational goal* :- $B_1, \ldots, B_k$ *with $\theta$ an answer for $P \cup \{G_r\}$, and $G_f$ a functional goal* :- $B_1, \ldots, B_k$ & $F$ *with $(t, \theta)$ an answer for $P \cup \{G_f\}$. We say that $\theta$ is a* correct (relational) *answer for $P \cup \{G_r\}$ if $\forall((B_1 \wedge \ldots \wedge B_k)\theta)$ is a logical consequence of P. We say that $(t, \theta)$ is a* correct (functional) *answer for $P \cup \{G_f\}$ if $\forall((B_1 \wedge \ldots \wedge B_k \wedge (t .= F))\theta)$ is a logical consequence of P.*

The following lemma shows that functional answers, i.e. "value returning to the top-level", can be simulated by relational answers binding top-level return values to a special variable.

**Lemma 1** *Let P be a relational-functional program, $G_f$ a functional goal* :- $B_1, \ldots, B_k$ & $F$, *and $G_r$ a relational goal* :- $B_1, \ldots, B_k, (x .= F)$ *with $x$ a new variable. Then the following statements are equivalent:*

1. *$(t, \theta)$ is a correct functional answer for $P \cup \{G_f\}$.*

2. *$\theta\{x/t\}$ is a correct relational answer for $P \cup \{G_r\}$.*

**Proof**
$(t, \theta)$ is a correct functional answer for $P \cup \{G_f\}$
*iff*
$\forall((B_1 \wedge \ldots \wedge B_k \wedge (t .= F))\theta)$ is a logical consequence of P
*iff*
$\forall((B_1 \wedge \ldots \wedge B_k \wedge (x .= F))\theta\{x/t\})$ is a logical consequence of P
*iff*
$\theta\{x/t\}$ is a correct relational answer for $P \cup \{G_r\}$.

# 3.4 SLV-Resolution

We now extend SLD-resolution to first-order relational-functional clauses, where the SLD-case will be called *body resolution*. The extended resolution method, similar to innermost conditional narrowing [Fri85], will be called *SLV-resolution* (SL-resolution for "Valued clauses" i.e., RELFUN's definite-clause extension). It provides the set of inference rules of a first-order relational-functional theory; their application conditions specify a partial derivation order. The detailed example 8 at the end of this section will illustrate most SLV-resolution concepts.

**Definition 27** *Let $G_r$ be the relational goal* $:- B_1, \ldots, B_m, \ldots, B_k$; *further let $C$ be the hornish clause $d :- V_1, \ldots, V_v$ or the footed clause $e :- W_1, \ldots, W_w$ & $E$ or the trivial clause $\top$. Then $G_r'$ is (relationally) derived from $G_r$ and $C$ using mgu $\theta$ if one of the following five inference rules applies (we let $t$'s or $u$'s denote terms):*

### Body resolution

1. *$B_m$ is an atom, called the* selected atom, *in $G_r$.*

2. *$C$ is the hornish clause $d :- V_1, \ldots, V_v$ and $\theta$ is the mgu of $B_m$ and $d$.*

3. *$G_r'$ is the relational goal* $:- (B_1, \ldots, B_{m-1}, V_1, \ldots, V_v, B_{m+1}, \ldots, B_k)\theta$.

### ".="-rhs resolution

1. *$B_m$ is a formula of the form $t .= g(u_1, \ldots, u_m)$, called the* selected flat setter, *in $G_r$.*

2. *$C$ is the footed clause $e :- W_1, \ldots, W_w$ & $E$ and $\theta$ is the mgu of $g(u_1, \ldots, u_m)$ and $e$.*

3. *$G_r'$ is the relational goal* $:- (B_1, \ldots, B_{m-1}, W_1, \ldots, W_w, t .= E, B_{m+1}, \ldots, B_k)\theta$.

### Body flattening

1. *$B_m$ in $G_r$ is a formula of the form $r(E_1, \ldots, E_{i-1}, h(E_{i,1}, \ldots, E_{i,n_i}), E_{i+1}, \ldots, E_m)$, called the* selected nested relationship, *and $h(E_{i,1}, \ldots, E_{i,n_i})$ is an* embedded application, *called the* selected (relationship-)embedded application.

2. *$C$ is the trivial clause $\top$ and $\theta$ is the identity substitution (hence, trivially, an mgu).*

3. *$x$ is a new variable.*

4. *$G_r'$ is the relational goal* $:- B_1, \ldots, B_{m-1}, x .= h(E_{i,1}, \ldots, E_{i,n_i}), r(E_1, \ldots, E_{i-1}, x, E_{i+1}, \ldots, E_m), B_{m+1}, \ldots, B_k$.

**".="-rhs flattening**

1. $B_m$ in $G_r$ is a formula of the form $t \;.=\; g(E_1, \ldots, E_{i-1}, h(E_{i,1}, \ldots, E_{i,n_i}), E_{i+1}, \ldots, E_m)$, called the selected nested setter, and $h(E_{i,1}, \ldots, E_{i,n_i})$ is an embedded application, called the selected (".=")-embedded application.

2. $C$ is the trivial clause $\top$ and $\theta$ is the identity substitution (hence, trivially, an mgu).

3. $x$ is a new variable.

4. $G'_r$ is the relational goal $:- B_1, \ldots, B_{m-1}, x \;.=\; h(E_{i,1}, \ldots, E_{i,n_i})$, $t \;.=\; g(E_1, \ldots, E_{i-1}, x, E_{i+1}, \ldots, E_m), B_{m+1}, \ldots, B_k$.

**Term unification**

1. $B_m$ is a formula of the form $t_1 \;.=\; t_2$, called the selected term setter, in $G_r$.

2. $C$ is the trivial clause $\top$ and $\theta$ is the mgu of $t_1$ and $t_2$.

3. $G'_r$ is the relational goal $:- (B_1, \ldots, B_{m-1}, B_{m+1}, \ldots, B_k)\theta$.

**Definition 28** *Let $G_f$ be the functional goal $:- B_1, \ldots, B_k \;\&\; F$; further let $C$ be the hornish clause $d :- V_1, \ldots, V_v$ or the footed clause $e :- W_1, \ldots, W_w \;\&\; E$ or the trivial clause $\top$. Then $G'_f$ is (functionally) derived from $G_f$ and $C$ using mgu $\theta$ if one of the following three inference rules applies (we let $u$'s denote terms):*

**Relational subderivation (using one of the five rules of definition 27)**

1. $G_r$ is $:- B_1, \ldots, B_k$, called the selected relational subgoal *of* $G_f$.

2. $G'_r$ is relationally derived from $G_r$ and $C$ using mgu $\theta$.

3. $G'_f$ is the functional goal $:- G'_r \;\&\; F\theta$.

**Foot resolution**

1. $F$ is a formula of the form $g(u_1, \ldots, u_m)$, called the selected flat application, in $G_f$.

2. $C$ is the footed clause $e :- W_1, \ldots, W_w \;\&\; E$ and $\theta$ is the mgu of $g(u_1, \ldots, u_m)$ and $e$.

3. $G'_f$ is the functional goal $:- (B_1, \ldots, B_k, W_1, \ldots, W_w \;\&\; E)\theta$.

**Foot flattening**

1. $F$ in $G_f$ is a formula of the form $g(E_1, \ldots, E_{i-1}, h(E_{i,1}, \ldots, E_{i,n_i}), E_{i+1}, \ldots, E_m)$, called the selected nested application, and $h(E_{i,1}, \ldots, E_{i,n_i})$ is an embedded application, called the selected (application-)embedded application.

2. $C$ is the trivial clause $\top$ and $\theta$ is the identity substitution (hence, trivially, an mgu).

3. $x$ is a new variable.

4. $G'_f$ is the functional goal $\ :\text{-}\ B_1, \ldots, B_k, x\ .= h(E_{i,1}, \ldots, E_{i,n_i})$ & $g(E_1, \ldots, E_{i-1}, x, E_{i+1}, \ldots, E_m)$.

Although we first presented relational goals (in definition 27) and then extended them to functional goals (in definition 28), the inference rules would not have to distinguish body and foot premises for their "selection function" (or, item *1.* of each rule), and they do not in the actual implementation: (relational) body resolution and (functional) foot resolution, as well as body and foot flattening, could be treated together. Similarly, inference rules operating in the top-level of premises and in ".="-rhs's have a common realization: (relational) body resolution and (functional) ".="-rhs resolution, as well as body flattening and ".="-rhs flattening, could be identified. However, our more discriminative presentation will clarify the case analysis of the soundness proof.

**Definition 29** *Let $P$ be a relational-functional program and $G$ be a (relational or functional) goal. A (relational resp. functional) SLV-derivation of $P \cup \{G\}$ consists of a finite or infinite sequence $G_0 = G, G_1, G_2, \ldots$ of (relational resp. functional) goals, a sequence $C_1, C_2, \ldots$ of variants of program clauses of $P \cup \{\top\}$, $\top$ the trivial clause, and a sequence $\theta_1, \theta_2, \ldots$ of mgu's such that each $G_{i+1}$ is derived from $G_i$ and $C_{i+1}$ using $\theta_{i+1}$.*

**Definition 30** *A (relational) SLV-refutation of $P \cup \{G_r\}$, $G_r$ a relational goal, is a finite SLV-derivation of $P \cup \{G_r\}$ that has the empty hornish clause $\square$ as the last goal in the derivation. A (functional) SLV-refutation of $P \cup \{G_f\}$, $G_f$ a functional goal, is a finite SLV-derivation of $P \cup \{G_f\}$ that has the terminal footed clause $\triangle(t)$ as the last goal in the derivation. If $G_n = \square$ or $G_n = \triangle(t)$, we say the refutation has length n.*

**Definition 31** *An unrestricted (relational or functional) SLV-refutation is a (relational or functional) SLV-refutation, except that the substitutions $\theta_i$ are not required to be most general unifiers. They are only required to be unifiers.*

**Definition 32** *Let $P$ be a relational-functional program. The relational success set of $P$ is the set of all ground atoms $a \in B_P$ such that $P \cup \{\ :\text{-}\ a\}$ has a relational SLV-refutation. The functional success set of $P$ is the set of all ground molecules $(e\ :\&\ t) \in C_P$ such that $P \cup \{\ :\&\ e\}$ has a functional SLV-refutation with last goal $\triangle(t)$. The success set of $P$ is the union of the relational and functional success sets of $P$.*

**Proposition 3** *Let $P$ be a relational-functional program. The functional success set of $P$ is the set of all ground molecules $(e \;:\& \; t) \in C_P$ such that $P \cup \{ \; :- (t \;.= e)\}$ has a relational SLV-refutation.*

**Proof**
*The ground flat setter $(t \;.= e) = (e \;:\& \; t)^{\otimes}$ leads to a relational SLV-refutation iff $e$, also being the corresponding molecule's ground flat application, leads to a functional SLV-refutation with last goal $\triangle(t)$.*

**Definition 33** *Let $P$ be a relational-functional program; further, let $G_r$ be a relational goal. Suppose there is an SLV-refutation of $P \cup \{G_r\}$ and let $\theta_1, \ldots, \theta_n$ be its sequence of mgu's. A computed (relational) answer for $P \cup \{G_r\}$ is the substitution $\theta$ obtained by restricting the composition $\theta_1 \ldots \theta_n$ to the variables of $G_r$.*

**Definition 34** *Let $P$ be a relational-functional program; further, let $G_f$ be a functional goal. Suppose there is an SLV-refutation of $P \cup \{G_f\}$ and let $\theta_1, \ldots, \theta_n$ be its sequence of mgu's and let $\triangle(t)$ be its last goal. A computed (functional) answer for $P \cup \{G_f\}$ is the pair $(t\theta_1 \ldots \theta_n, \theta)$, with the term $t$ extracted from $\triangle(t)$ and the substitution $\theta$ obtained by restricting the composition $\theta_1 \ldots \theta_n$ to the variables of $G_f$.*

**Lemma 2** *Let $P$ be a relational-functional program, $G_f$ a functional goal $:- B_1, \ldots, B_k \;\& \; F$, and $G_r$ a relational goal $:- B_1, \ldots, B_k, (x \;.= F)$ with $x$ a new variable. Then the following statements are equivalent:*

1. *$(t, \theta)$ is a computed functional answer for $P \cup \{G_f\}$.*

2. *$\theta\{x/t\}$ is a computed relational answer for $P \cup \{G_r\}$.*

**Proof**
*$(t, \theta)$ is a computed functional answer for $P \cup \{G_f\}$*
*iff*
*there is an SLV-refutation of $P \cup \{G_f\}$ with a sequence of mgu's $\theta_1, \ldots, \theta_n$ and last goal $\triangle(u)$ such that $t$ is $u\theta_1 \ldots \theta_n$ and $\theta$ restricts the composition $\theta_1 \ldots \theta_n$ to the variables of $G_f$*
*iff*
*there is an SLV-refutation of $P \cup \{G_r\}$ with a sequence of mgu's $\theta_1, \ldots, \theta_n, \{x/t\}$ such that $\theta\{x/t\}$ restricts the composition $\theta_1 \ldots \theta_n\{x/t\}$ to the variables of $G_r$*
*iff*
*$\theta\{x/t\}$ is a computed relational answer for $P \cup \{G_r\}$.*

**Example 8** *The (non-deterministic, no-extra-variables, ".="-using) program* $P_2$

$f(X) :- p(g(a), g(X))$ & $h(g(X))$.
$g(a)$ :& $c$.
$g(a)$ :& $h(c)$.
$h(X)$ :& $b$.
$p(X, c) :- X$ .= $h(a), q(h(X))$.
$q(b)$.

*uses no constructors, hence belongs to the DATALOG-extending DATA-FUN subset of RELFUN; it has the finite Herbrand universe $\{a, b, c\}$, hence a finite Herbrand crossbase.*

*A functional SLV-refutation of $P_2 \cup \{$ :& $f(Y)\}$ is:*

$G_0 = G =$ :& $f(Y)$
*Foot resolution of $f(Y)$ with $C_1 = f(X1) :- p(g(a), g(X1))$ & $h(g(X1))$,*
$$\theta_1 = \{Y/X1\}:$$
$G_1 =$ :- $p(g(a), g(X1))$ & $h(g(X1))$
*Body flattening of $p(g(a), \ldots)$ with $C_2 = \top$, $\theta_2 = \{\}$:*
$G_2 =$ :- $Z1$ .= $g(a), p(Z1, g(X1))$ & $h(g(X1))$
*".="-rhs resolution of $Z1$ .= $g(a)$ with $C_3 = g(a)$ :& $h(c)$, $\theta_3 = \{\}$:*
$G_3 =$ :- $Z1$ .= $h(c), p(Z1, g(X1))$ & $h(g(X1))$
*".="-rhs resolution of $Z1$ .= $h(c)$ with $C_4 = h(X2)$ :& $b$, $\theta_4 = \{X2/c\}$:*
$G_4 =$ :- $Z1$ .= $b, p(Z1, g(X1))$ & $h(g(X1))$
*Term unification of $Z1$ .= $b$ with $C_5 = \top$, $\theta_5 = \{Z1/b\}$:*
$G_5 =$ :- $p(b, g(X1))$ & $h(g(X1))$
*Body flattening of $p(\ldots, g(X1))$ with $C_6 = \top$, $\theta_6 = \{\}$:*
$G_6 =$ :- $Z2$ .= $g(X1), p(b, Z2)$ & $h(g(X1))$
*".="-rhs resolution of $Z2$ .= $g(X1)$ with $C_7 = g(a)$ :& $c$, $\theta_7 = \{X1/a\}$:*
$G_7 =$ :- $Z2$ .= $c, p(b, Z2)$ & $h(g(X1))$
*Term unification of $Z2$ .= $c$ with $C_8 = \top$, $\theta_8 = \{Z2/c\}$:*
$G_8 =$ :- $p(b, c)$ & $h(g(X1))$
*Body resolution of $p(b, c)$ with $C_9 = p(X3, c) :- X3$ .= $h(a), q(h(X3))$,*
$$\theta_9 = \{X3/b\}:$$
$G_9 =$ :- $b$ .= $h(a), q(h(b))$ & $h(g(X1))$
*".="-rhs resolution of $b$ .= $h(a)$ with $C_{10} = h(X4)$ :& $b$, $\theta_{10} = \{X4/a\}$:*
$G_{10} =$ :- $b$ .= $b, q(h(b))$ & $h(g(X1))$
*Term unification of $b$ .= $b$ with $C_{11} = \top$, $\theta_{11} = \{\}$:*
$G_{11} =$ :- $q(h(b))$ & $h(g(X1))$
*Body flattening of $q(h(b))$ with $C_{12} = \top$, $\theta_{12} = \{\}$:*
$G_{12} =$ :- $Z3$ .= $h(b), q(Z3)$ & $h(g(X1))$
*".="-rhs resolution of $Z3$ .= $h(b)$ with $C_{13} = h(X5)$ :& $b$, $\theta_{13} = \{X5/b\}$:*
$G_{13} =$ :- $Z3$ .= $b, q(Z3)$ & $h(g(X1))$

*Term unification of $Z3$ .= $b$ with $C_{14} = \top$, $\theta_{14} = \{Z3/b\}$:*
$G_{14} = $ :- $q(b)$ & $h(g(X1))$
*Body resolution of $q(b)$ with $C_{15} = q(b)$, $\theta_{15} = \{\}$:*
$G_{15} = $ :& $h(g(a))^{12}$
*Foot flattening of $h(g(a))$ with $C_{16} = \top$, $\theta_{16} = \{\}$:*
$G_{16} = $ :- $Z4$ .= $g(a)$ & $h(Z4)$
*".="-rhs resolution of $Z4$ .= $g(a)$ with $C_{17} = g(a)$ :& $c$, $\theta_{17} = \{\}$:*
$G_{17} = $ :- $Z4$ .= $c$ & $h(Z4)$
*Term unification of $Z4$ .= $c$ with $C_{18} = \top$, $\theta_{18} = \{Z4/c\}$:*
$G_{18} = $ :& $h(c)$
*Foot resolution of $h(c)$ with $C_{19} = h(X6)$ :& $b$, $\theta_{19} = \{X6/b\}$:*
$G_{19} = $ :& $b$

*This length-19 refutation happens to use RELFUN's implemented PROLOG-like 'leftmost' computation rule (however, RELFUN implements flattening in a condensed 'and-parallel' fashion). Operationally speaking, "$f(Y)$ returns $b$ and binds $Y$ to $a$": The refutation has last goal $G_{19} = \triangle(b)$, and $\theta_1 \ldots \theta_{19}$ restricted to $Y$ is $\{Y/a\}$; hence the computed functional answer is $(b, \{Y/a\})$.*

*The equivalent computed relational answer for $P_2 \cup \{$ :- $Z$ .= $f(Y)\}$ is $\{Y/a, Z/b\}$. Here, the refutation uses ".="-rhs resolutions and performs an ".="-rhs flattening instead of the corresponding rules operating on the foot, and it needs a final term unification. Functional computation is somewhat hidden in the auxiliary setter's rhs. However, the kernel subderivations of the functional and relational refutations are essentially the same.*

*The success set of $P_2$ is (functional and relational partitions displayed in separate lines):[13]*

$\{f(a)$ :& $b$, $g(a)$ :& $b$, $g(a)$ :& $c$, $h(a)$ :& $b$, $h(b)$ :& $b$, $h(c)$ :& $b$,
$q(b)$, $p(b, c)\}$

**Example 9** *Employing the programs $Q_f$ and $Q_r$, defined in the table below, $Q_f \cup \{$ :& $omegaf()\}$ has no functional SLV-refutation, just as the equivalent $Q_r \cup \{$ :- $omegar(U)\}$ has no relational SLD-refutation. The procedural call-by-value non-termination of such omegaf and omegar goals (independent of a leftmost or rightmost computation rule) is reflected in the models of $Q_f$ and $Q_r$ below by the non-existing molecule omegaf() :& $b$ and atom omegar(b), respectively, whose bottom-up construction would presuppose a psif molecule and a psir atom. (For the call-by-name termination of the functional $Q_f \cup \{$ :& $omegaf()\}$ with $b$ there is no obvious relational analogue.)*

---

[12]The binding $\theta_7 = \{X1/a\}$ from the relational subderivation $G_2, \ldots, G_{15}$ is applied here.
[13]In higher-order RELFUN, this can be obtained from the computed answers of an operator-variable, varying-arity goal (see chapter 2) such as :& $Op(|Args)$.

| Least Herbrand model (of $Q_r$): | Least Herbrand cross model (of $Q_f$): |
|---|---|
| $\{chir(a,b),$ $\quad chir(b,b)\}$ | $\{chif(a) \text{ :\& } b,$ $\quad chif(b) \text{ :\& } b\}$ |
| Relational program ($Q_r$): `chir(X,b).` `psir(a,Y) :- psir(a,Y).` `omegar(S) :- psir(a,I), chir(I,S).` | Functional program ($Q_f$): `chif(X) :& b.` `psif(a) :& psif(a).` `omegaf() :& chif(psif(a)).` |

# 3.5 Soundness of SLV-Resolution

While the following result addresses relational goals, only the first of the five SLV-resolution rules to be considered corresponds to the classical case of logic programming as proved by K. L. Clark.

**Theorem 1 (Soundness of relational SLV-resolution)** *Let $P$ be a relational-functional program and $G_r$ a relational goal. Then every computed answer for $P \cup \{G_r\}$ is a correct answer for $P \cup \{G_r\}$.*

**Proof**
*Let $G_r$ be the relational goal* `:- `$B_1, \ldots, B_k$ *and* $\theta_1, \ldots, \theta_n$ *be the sequence of mgu's used in an SLV-refutation of* $P \cup \{G_r\}$. *We have to show that* $\forall((B_1 \wedge \ldots \wedge B_k)\theta_1 \ldots \theta_n)$ *is a logical consequence of* $P$. *The result is proved by induction on the length of the refutation.*

*Suppose first that $n = 1$. This means that $G_r$ is a goal of the form* `:- `$B_1$, *to which either of two of the five SLV-resolution rules applies:*

**Body resolution** $B_1$ *is an atom, the program has a unit clause of the form* $d$ `:- `, *and* $B_1\theta_1 = d\theta_1$. *Since* $B_1\theta_1$ `:-` *is an instance of a unit clause of* $P$, *it follows that* $\forall(B_1\theta_1)$ *is a logical consequence of* $P$.

**".="-rhs resolution** *Cannot derive* $\square$ *in one step.*

**Body flattening** *Cannot derive* $\square$ *in one step.*

**".="-rhs flattening** *Cannot derive* $\square$ *in one step.*

**Term unification** $B_1$ *is a formula of the form* $t_1 \text{ .= } t_2$ *and* $\theta_1$ *is the mgu of* $t_1$ *and* $t_2$. *Since* $t_1\theta_1 = t_2\theta_1$, *it follows that* $\forall(B_1\theta_1)$ *is valid, hence, trivially, is a logical consequence of* $P$.

*Next suppose that the result holds for computed answers that come from SLV-refutations of length $n - 1$. Suppose $\theta_1, \ldots, \theta_n$ is the sequence of mgu's used in a refutation of $P \cup \{G_r\}$ of length $n$. One of the five SLV-resolution rules applies:*

**Body resolution** *Let $B_m$ be the selected atom of $G_r$ and the hornish clause $d :- V_1, \ldots, V_v$ ($v \geq 0$) be the first input clause. By the induction hypothesis, $\forall((B_1 \wedge \ldots \wedge B_{m-1} \wedge V_1 \wedge \ldots \wedge V_v \wedge B_{m+1} \wedge \ldots \wedge B_k)\theta_1 \ldots \theta_n)$ is a logical consequence of $P$. Thus, if $v > 0$, $\forall((V_1 \wedge \ldots \wedge V_v)\theta_1 \ldots \theta_n)$ is a logical consequence of $P$. In this case, as well as for $v = 0$, $\forall(B_m\theta_1 \ldots \theta_n)$, which is the same as $\forall(d\theta_1 \ldots \theta_n)$, is a logical consequence of $P$. Hence $\forall((B_1 \wedge \ldots \wedge B_k)\theta_1 \ldots \theta_n)$ is a logical consequence of $P$.*

**".="-rhs resolution** *Let $B_m$ be the selected flat setter $t .= g(u_1, \ldots, u_m)$ of $G_r$ and the footed clause $e :- W_1, \ldots, W_w$ & $E$ ($w \geq 0$) be the first input clause. By the induction hypothesis, $\forall((B_1 \wedge \ldots \wedge B_{m-1} \wedge W_1 \wedge \ldots \wedge W_w \wedge t .= E \wedge B_{m+1} \wedge \ldots \wedge B_k)\theta_1 \ldots \theta_n)$ is a logical consequence of $P$. Thus, for $w \geq 0$, $\forall((W_1 \wedge \ldots \wedge W_w \wedge t .= E)\theta_1 \ldots \theta_n)$ is a logical consequence of $P$. Consequently, $\forall(B_m\theta_1 \ldots \theta_n)$, which is the same as $\forall((t .= e)\theta_1 \ldots \theta_n)$, is a logical consequence of $P$. Hence $\forall((B_1 \wedge \ldots \wedge B_k)\theta_1 \ldots \theta_n)$ is a logical consequence of $P$.*

**Body flattening** *Let $B_m$ be the selected nested relationship $r(E_1, \ldots, E_{i-1}, h(E_{i,1}, \ldots, E_{i,n_i}), E_{i+1}, \ldots, E_m)$ with the selected embedded application $h(E_{i,1}, \ldots, E_{i,n_i})$ of $G_r$. By the induction hypothesis, $\forall((B_1 \wedge \ldots \wedge B_{m-1} \wedge (x .= h(E_{i,1}, \ldots, E_{i,n_i})) \wedge r(E_1, \ldots, E_{i-1}, x, E_{i+1}, \ldots, E_m) \wedge B_{m+1} \wedge \ldots \wedge B_k)\theta_1 \ldots \theta_n)$, $x$ the new variable chosen by the SLV-refutation, is a logical consequence of $P$. Thus, $\forall((x .= h(E_{i,1}, \ldots, E_{i,n_i}))\theta_1 \ldots \theta_n)$ and $\forall(r(E_1, \ldots, E_{i-1}, x, E_{i+1}, \ldots, E_m)\theta_1 \ldots \theta_n)$ are logical consequences of $P$. Consequently, $\forall(B_m\theta_1 \ldots \theta_n)$ is a logical consequence of $P$. Hence $\forall((B_1 \wedge \ldots \wedge B_k)\theta_1 \ldots \theta_n)$ is a logical consequence of $P$.*

**".="-rhs flattening** *Let $B_m$ be the selected nested setter $t .= g(E_1, \ldots, E_{i-1}, h(E_{i,1}, \ldots, E_{i,n_i}), E_{i+1}, \ldots, E_m)$ with the selected embedded application $h(E_{i,1}, \ldots, E_{i,n_i})$ of $G_r$. By the induction hypothesis, $\forall((B_1 \wedge \ldots \wedge B_{m-1} \wedge (x .= h(E_{i,1}, \ldots, E_{i,n_i})) \wedge (t .= g(E_1, \ldots, E_{i-1}, x, E_{i+1}, \ldots, E_m)) \wedge B_{m+1} \wedge \ldots \wedge B_k)\theta_1 \ldots \theta_n)$, $x$ the new variable chosen by the SLV-refutation, is a logical consequence of $P$. Thus, $\forall((x .= h(E_{i,1}, \ldots, E_{i,n_i}))\theta_1 \ldots \theta_n)$ and $\forall((t .= g(E_1, \ldots, E_{i-1}, x, E_{i+1}, \ldots, E_m))\theta_1 \ldots \theta_n)$ are logical consequences of $P$. Consequently, $\forall(B_m\theta_1 \ldots \theta_n)$ is a logical consequence of $P$. Hence $\forall((B_1 \wedge \ldots \wedge B_k)\theta_1 \ldots \theta_n)$ is a logical consequence of $P$.*

**Term unification** *Let $B_m$ be the selected term setter $t_1 .= t_2$ of $G_r$. By the induction hypothesis, $\forall((B_1 \wedge \ldots \wedge B_{m-1} \wedge B_{m+1} \wedge \ldots \wedge B_k)\theta_1 \ldots \theta_n)$ is a logical consequence of $P$. Since $t_1\theta_1 \ldots \theta_n = t_2\theta_1 \ldots \theta_n$, it follows that $\forall(B_m\theta_1 \ldots \theta_n)$ is valid, hence, trivially, is a logical consequence of $P$. Hence $\forall((B_1 \wedge \ldots \wedge B_k)\theta_1 \ldots \theta_n)$ is a logical consequence of $P$.*

The result for relational goals naturally carries over to functional goals.

**Corollary 1 (Soundness of functional SLV-resolution)** *Let $P$ be a relational-functional program and $G_f$ a functional goal. Then every computed answer for $P \cup \{G_f\}$ is a correct answer for $P \cup \{G_f\}$.*

**Proof**
*By lemmas 2 and 1 there is an equivalent relational goal with computed and correct answers for which the soundness result of theorem 1 holds.*

**Corollary 2** *The success set of a relational-functional program is contained in its least Herbrand crossbase model.*

**Proof**
*Let the program be $P$ and suppose $F \in X_P$ is in the success set of $P$. By proposition 3, the success set of $P$ is the set of all $F \in X_P$ such that $P \cup \{\ :\text{-}\ F^{\otimes}\}$ has a relational refutation. By theorem 1, $F^{\otimes}$, hence $F$, is a logical consequence of $P$. Thus, $F$ is true wrt all Herbrand crossbase models of $P$, hence is in $P$'s least Herbrand crossbase model.*

# 3.6 Least Herbrand Crossbase Models as Fixpoints

We now define $T_P$-like immediate-consequence operators on Herbrand crossbase interpretations. For this we employ *unnesting* of clause premises, a fixpoint-semantics, ground-formula analogue to flattening in SLV-resolution. Instead of introducing new variables, unnesting chooses any ground terms from the Herbrand universe, as "returned values", to link the subformulas generated from the original formula.

**Definition 35** *A set of unnested setters $unnestis_P(t\ .=\ E)$ of a ground setter $t\ .=\ E$ for a program $P$ is defined recursively as the non-deterministic mapping*

$$unnestis_P(t\ .=\ g(u_1, \ldots, u_m)) =$$
$$\{t\ .=\ g(u_1, \ldots, u_m)\}\ if\ \{u_1, \ldots, u_m\} \subseteq U_P$$
$$unnestis_P(t\ .=\ g(E_1, \ldots, E_{i-1}, h(E_{i,1}, \ldots, E_{i,n_i}), E_{i+1}, \ldots, E_m)) =$$
$$unnestis_P(u\ .=\ h(E_{i,1}, \ldots, E_{i,n_i}))\ \cup$$
$$unnestis_P(t\ .=\ g(E_1, \ldots, E_{i-1}, u, E_{i+1}, \ldots, E_m))$$
$$for\ some\ u \in U_P$$

**Definition 36** *A set of* unnested formulas $unnest_P(V)$ *of a ground relationship or setter $V$ for a program $P$ is defined as the non-deterministic mapping*

$$unnest_P(r(u_1, \ldots, u_m)) =$$
$$\{r(u_1, \ldots, u_m)\} \; if \; \{u_1, \ldots, u_m\} \subseteq U_P$$
$$unnest_P(r(E_1, \ldots, E_{i-1}, h(E_{i,1}, \ldots, E_{i,n_i}), E_{i+1}, \ldots, E_m)) =$$
$$unnestis_P(u \; .= \; h(E_{i,1}, \ldots, E_{i,n_i})) \; \cup$$
$$unnest_P(r(E_1, \ldots, E_{i-1}, u, E_{i+1}, \ldots, E_m))$$
$$for \; some \; u \in U_P$$
$$unnest_P(t \; .= \; t) =$$
$$\{\} \; if \; t \in U_P$$
$$unnest_P(t \; .= \; g(E_1, \ldots, E_m)) =$$
$$unnestis_P(t \; .= \; g(E_1, \ldots, E_m))$$

A first auxiliary immediate-consequence operator, $TB_P$, generates atoms from atoms and molecules.

**Definition 37** *Let $P$ be a relational-functional program. The mapping $TB_P$ : $2^{X_P} \to 2^{B_P}$ is defined as follows. Let $I \in 2^{X_P}$ be an Herbrand crossbase interpretation. Then:*

$$TB_P(I) = \{w \in B_P \mid \; w \; :\text{-} \; V_1, \ldots, V_n \text{ is a ground instance of a clause in } P,$$
$$unnest_P(V_k)^{\otimes} \subseteq I \text{ for } 1 \leq k \leq n\}$$

If each $V_k$ has the Horn-premise form $r(u_1, \ldots, u_n)$ of an atom, $unnest_P(V_k)^{\otimes}$ just denotes the unit set $\{V_k\}$, hence $TB_P$ becomes the $T_P$ operator of M. H. van Emden and R. Kowalski.

**Proposition 4** *Let $P$ be a relational-functional program containing Horn clauses only and $I \in 2^{B_P}$ be an Herbrand interpretation. Then the mapping $TB_P$ restricted to $2^{B_P} \subseteq 2^{X_P}$ specializes to the mapping $T_P : 2^{B_P} \to 2^{B_P}$ defined as:*

$$T_P(I) = \{w \in B_P \mid \; w \; :\text{-} \; V_1, \ldots, V_n \text{ is a ground instance of a clause in } P,$$
$$V_k \in I \text{ for } 1 \leq k \leq n\}$$

Note how the intuitive understanding of $T_P$ is extended by $TB_P$: as $T_P(I)$ 'guesses' a ground clause of $P$ and then checks whether its premise atoms are members of $I$, $TB_P(I)$ 'guesses' a ground clause of $P$, then 'guesses' an unnesting (zero/one atoms and one/zero or more setters) from each of its premises, and then checks whether the "$\otimes$"-corresponding atoms and molecules constitute subsets of $I$.

A second auxiliary immediate-consequence operator, $TC_P$, generates molecules from atoms and molecules.

**Definition 38** *Let $P$ be a relational-functional program. The mapping $TC_P$ : $2^{X_P} \to 2^{C_P}$ is defined as follows. Let $I \in 2^{X_P}$ be an Herbrand crossbase interpretation. Then:*

$$TC_P(I) = \{e :\& t \in C_P \mid \quad e :- V_1, \ldots, V_n \,\&\, E \text{ is a ground instance}$$
$$\text{of a clause in } P,$$
$$unnest_P(V_k)^{\otimes} \subseteq I \text{ for } 1 \leq k \leq n,$$
$$unnest_P(t \,.= E)^{\otimes} \subseteq I\}$$

**Example 10** *The program $P_2$ (cf. example 8) with $U_{P_2} = \{a, b, c\}$ contains the footed clause $f(X) :- p(g(a), g(X)) \,\&\, h(g(X))$. Suppose a $TC_{P_2}$ application selects the ground instance $f(a) :- p(g(a), g(a)) \,\&\, h(g(a))$, i.e. $V_1 = p(g(a), g(a))$ and $E = h(g(a))$. Then $unnest_{P_2}(V_1)$ can select $\{p(b, c), \ b \,.= g(a), \ c \,.= g(a)\}$, so that $unnest_{P_2}(V_1)^{\otimes} = \{p(b, c), \quad g(a) :\& b, \quad g(a) :\& c\}$. Further suppose $TC_{P_2}$'s set formation selects $t = b$ and $unnest_{P_2}(t \,.= E)$ selects $\{b \,.= h(c), \ c \,.= g(a)\}$, so that $unnest_{P_2}(t \,.= E)^{\otimes} = \{h(c) :\& b, \ g(a) :\& c\}$. Now, if some interpretation $I$ has $\{p(b, c), \ g(a) :\& b, \ g(a) :\& c, \ h(c) :\& b\}$ as a subset, $TC_{P_2}(I)$ will contain the element $f(a) :\& b$.*

Since the sets produced by unnesting are always finite, the atoms and setters resulting from $unnest_P(V_k)$ and $unnest_P(t \,.= E)$ can be regarded as premises of a 'virtual' ground clause $e :- unnest_P(V_1)^{\epsilon}, \ldots, unnest_P(V_n)^{\epsilon}, unnest_P(t \,.= E)^{\epsilon} \,\&\, t.$ ("$\{\ldots\}^{\epsilon}$" denotes the sequence of *elements* of "$\{\ldots\}$".) The corresponding non-ground clause can be obtained by transforming the original program $P$ via static flattening and denotative normalization (see chapter 5). Therefore, each application of $TC_P$ can be regarded as a condensed form of the application of a less powerful operator indexed by the more lengthy transformed program ($T_P$'s extension would be confined to clauses with atomic and flat-setter bodies and term foots).

**Example 11** *A virtual ground clause of $f(a) :- p(g(a), g(a)) \,\&\, h(g(a))$ from example 10 is $f(a) :- b \,.= g(a), c \,.= g(a), p(b, c), c \,.= g(a), b \,.= h(c) \,\&\, b$. Its nonground abstraction $f(X) :- Y1 \,.= g(a), Y2 \,.= g(X), p(Y1, Y2), Y3 \,.= g(X), Y4 \,.= h(Y3) \,\&\, Y4$ is the flattened, denotative normalization of $f(X) :- p(g(a), g(X)) \,\&\, h(g(X))$, the original non-ground clause.*

The main immediate-consequence operator, $TX_P$, just unites the two auxiliary ones.

**Definition 39** *Let $P$ be a relational-functional program. The mapping $TX_P$ : $2^{X_P} \to 2^{X_P}$ is defined as follows. Let $I \in 2^{X_P}$ be an Herbrand crossbase interpretation. Then:*

$$TX_P(I) = TB_P(I) \cup TC_P(I)$$

**Example 12** *Let $P_1$ be the relational-functional program of example 5 and $I$ the interpretation $\{g(k[a],l[a]) \quad :\& \quad k[a], \; p(k[a]), \; q(l[a])\} \in 2^{X_{P_1}}$. Since $unnest_{P_1}(k[a] \;.= g(g(k[a],l[a]),l[a]))^{\otimes}$ can select $\{g(k[a],l[a]) \quad :\& \quad k[a]\}$, we obtain $TX_{P_1}(I) = \{f(k[a]) \quad :\& \quad k[a], \; g(a,a) \quad :\& \quad k[u], \; p(k[u]), \; q(l[u])\}$ for $u \in U_{P_1}$.*

Clearly, $TX_P$ is monotonic on the complete lattice $2^{X_P}$ under the partial order "$\subseteq$". Like $T_P$ in [Llo87], it can be shown to be continuous.

**Proposition 5** *Let $P$ be a relational-functional program. Then the mapping $TX_P$ is continuous.*

**Proof**
Let $S$ be a directed subset of $2^{X_P}$, $V_k$ be a ground relationship or setter, for $1 \leq k \leq n$, and $t \;.= E$ be a ground setter. Each $unnest_P(V_k)^{\otimes}$ being a finite set, we can first note that $\bigcup_{k=1}^{n} unnest_P(V_k)^{\otimes} \subseteq lub(S)$ iff $\bigcup_{k=1}^{n} unnest_P(V_k)^{\otimes} \subseteq I$ for some $I \in S$; furthermore, $unnest_P(t \;.= E)^{\otimes}$ being a finite set, $\bigcup_{k=1}^{n} unnest_P(V_k)^{\otimes} \cup unnest_P(t \;.= E)^{\otimes} \subseteq lub(S)$ iff $\bigcup_{k=1}^{n} unnest_P(V_k)^{\otimes} \cup unnest_P(t \;.= E)^{\otimes} \subseteq I$ for some $I \in S$. In order to show that $TX_P$ is continuous we have to show $TX_P(lub(S)) = lub(TX_P(S))$ for each directed subset $S$. Since $TX_P$ denotes the disjoint union of $TB_P$'s and $TC_P$'s values we show the equality of both subsets individually:

$w \in TB_P(lub(S))$
*iff*
$w :- V_1, \ldots, V_n$ *is a ground instance of a clause in $P$ and* $\bigcup_{k=1}^{n} unnest_P(V_k)^{\otimes} \subseteq lub(S)$
*iff*
$w :- V_1, \ldots, V_n$ *is a ground instance of a clause in $P$ and* $\bigcup_{k=1}^{n} unnest_P(V_k)^{\otimes} \subseteq I$ *for some $I \in S$*
*iff*
$w \in TB_P(I)$ *for some $I \in S$*
*iff*
$w \in lub(TB_P(S))$

$e :\& t \in TC_P(lub(S))$
*iff*
$e :- V_1, \ldots, V_n \; \& \; E$ *is a ground instance of a clause in $P$ and* $\bigcup_{k=1}^{n} unnest_P(V_k)^{\otimes} \cup unnest_P(t \;.= E)^{\otimes} \subseteq lub(S)$
*iff*
$e :- V_1, \ldots, V_n \; \& \; E$ *is a ground instance of a clause in $P$ and* $\bigcup_{k=1}^{n} unnest_P(V_k)^{\otimes} \cup unnest_P(t \;.= E)^{\otimes} \subseteq I$ *for some $I \in S$*
*iff*
$e :\& t \in TC_P(I)$ *for some $I \in S$*
*iff*
$e :\& t \in lub(TC_P(S))$

Herbrand crossbase models can be characterized in terms of $TX_P$.

**Proposition 6** *Let $P$ be a relational-functional program and $I$ be an Herbrand crossbase interpretation of $P$. Then $I$ is a crossbase model for $P$ iff $TX_P(I) \subseteq I$.*

**Proof**
*$I$ is a crossbase model for $P$*
*iff*
*for each ground instance $w$ :- $V_1, \ldots, V_n$ or $e$ :- $V_1, \ldots, V_n$ & $E$ of each clause in $P$ we have, respectively, $\bigcup_{k=1}^{n} unnest_P(V_k)^{\otimes} \subseteq I$ implies $w \in I$ or $\bigcup_{k=1}^{n} unnest_P(V_k)^{\otimes} \cup unnest_P(t \mathrel{.=} E)^{\otimes} \subseteq I$ implies $e$ :& $t \in I$*
*iff*
*$TX_P(I) \subseteq I$*

Using these propositions and general fixpoint results, we can extend the fixpoint characterization of the least Herbrand model of logic programs by M. H. van Emden and R. Kowalski to a characterization of the least Herbrand crossbase model of relational-functional programs (for the "$\uparrow$"-notation see [Llo87]).

**Theorem 2 (Fixpoint characterization of least Herbrand crossbase model)**
*Let $P$ be a relational-functional program. Then $M_P = lfp(TX_P) = TX_P \uparrow \omega$.*

**Proof**

$$
\begin{aligned}
M_P &= glb\{I \mid I \text{ is an Herbrand crossbase model for } P\} \\
&= glb\{I \mid TX_P(I) \subseteq I\}, \text{ by proposition 6} \\
&= lfp(TX_P), \text{ by proposition 5.1 in } [Llo87] \\
&= TX_P \uparrow \omega, \text{ by proposition 5.4 in } [Llo87] \text{ and proposition 5}
\end{aligned}
$$

**Example 13** *The 8-element least Herbrand crossbase model of the program $P_2$ of example 8 (in section 3.4) can be computed bottom-up by the following $TX_{P_2}$ iterations (details of the last step were shown in example 10):*

$TX_{P_2} \uparrow 0 =$
$\{\}$

$TX_{P_2} \uparrow 1 = TX_{P_2} \uparrow 0 \cup$
$\{g(a) \mathrel{:\&} c, \; h(a) \mathrel{:\&} b, \; h(b) \mathrel{:\&} b, \; h(c) \mathrel{:\&} b,$
$q(b)\}$

$TX_{P_2} \uparrow 2 = TX_{P_2} \uparrow 1 \cup$
$\{g(a) \mathrel{:\&} b,$
$p(b,c)\}$

$M_{P_2} = lfp(TX_{P_2}) = TX_{P_2} \uparrow \omega = TX_{P_2} \uparrow 3 = TX_{P_2} \uparrow 2 \cup$
$\{f(a) \mathrel{:\&} b\}$

*This is equal to the success set of $P_2$ given in example 8.*

# 3.7 Completeness of SLV-Resolution

Like for soundness, we will again use proposition 3 as well as lemmas 1 and 2; hence the following mgu and lifting lemmas will only be needed for relational goals. The symbol "$\overset{G}{=}$" will denote equality between substitutions after restriction of the rhs substitution to the variables of the goal $G$.

**Lemma 3 (Mgu lemma)** *Let $P$ be a relational-functional program and $G_r$ a relational goal. Suppose that $P \cup \{G_r\}$ has an unrestricted SLV-refutation. Then $P \cup \{G_r\}$ has an SLV-refutation of the same length such that, if $\theta_1, \ldots, \theta_n$ are the unifiers from the unrestricted SLV-refutation and $\theta'_1, \ldots, \theta'_n$ are the mgu's from the SLV-refutation, then there exists a substitution $\gamma$ such that $\theta_1 \ldots \theta_n \overset{G_r}{=} \theta'_1 \ldots \theta'_n \gamma$.*

**Proof**
*The induction proof is as for lemma 8.1 in [Llo87] except that unifiers and mgu's need not derive from (body) resolution but can derive from the other rules of SLV-resolution (flattening in unrestricted SLV-refutations, like in SLV-refutations, produces identity substitutions).*

**Lemma 4 (Lifting lemma)** *Let $P$ be a relational-functional program, $G_r$ a relational goal, and $\theta$ a substitution. Suppose there exists an SLV-refutation of $P \cup \{G_r \theta\}$. Then there exists an SLV-refutation of $P \cup \{G_r\}$ of the same length such that, if $\theta_1, \ldots, \theta_n$ are the mgu's from the SLV-refutation of $P \cup \{G_r \theta\}$ and $\theta'_1, \ldots, \theta'_n$ are the mgu's from the SLV-refutation of $P \cup \{G_r\}$, then there exists a substitution $\gamma$ such that $\theta \theta_1 \ldots \theta_n \overset{G_r}{=} \theta'_1 \ldots \theta'_n \gamma$.*

**Proof**
*The proof is as for lemma 8.2 in [Llo87] with the qualification already noted for lemma 3, which is crucially applied here.*

The converse of corollary 2 extends the logic-programming completeness result of K. R. Apt and M. H. van Emden to relational-functional programming.

**Theorem 3** *The success set of a relational-functional program is equal to its least Herbrand crossbase model.*

**Proof**
*Let the program be $P$. By corrollary 2 it suffices to show that the least Herbrand crossbase model of $P$ is contained in the success set of $P$. Let $F$ denote the ground atom $d$ or molecule $f : \& t$. By proposition 3 we need only consider the relational goals denoted by $F^\otimes$. Suppose $F$ is in the least Herbrand crossbase model of $P$. By theorem 2, $F \in TX_P \uparrow n$ for some $n \in \omega$. We prove by induction on $n$ that $F \in TX_P \uparrow n$ implies that $P \cup \{ :\text{-} F^\otimes \}$ has a refutation (i.e., $d \in TX_P \uparrow n$*

*implies that $P \cup \{ :- d\}$ has a refutation and $f :\& t \in TX_P \uparrow n$ implies that $P \cup \{ :- t .= f\}$ has a refutation). Hence $F$ will be in the success set.*

*Suppose first that $n = 1$. Then $F \in TX_P \uparrow 1$ means that $F$ is a ground instance of an atom or molecule from $P$. Clearly, $P \cup \{ :- d\}$ and $P \cup \{ :- t .= f\}$ have a refutation (a body resolution and an ".="-rhs resolution followed by a term unification, respectively).*

*Now suppose that the result holds for $n - 1$. We distinguish the two cases for $F$. First, let $d \in TX_P \uparrow n$. By the definition of $TX_P$ there exists a ground instance of a clause $w :- V_1, \ldots, V_m$ and an unnesting of its premises such that $d = w\theta$ and $\bigcup_{k=1}^{m} unnest_P(V_k\theta)^{\otimes} \subseteq TX_P \uparrow (n - 1)$ for some unifier $\theta$. By the induction hypothesis, for each formula $A$ in the selected $unnest_P(V_k\theta)$, for $1 \leq k \leq m$, $P \cup \{ :- A\}$ has a refutation. Hence, $P \cup \{ :- V_k\theta\}$ has a refutation, mimicking unnesting by flattening. Because each $V_k\theta$ is ground and flattening only introduces new variables, these refutations can be combined into a refutation of $P \cup \{ :- (V_1, \ldots, V_m)\theta\}$. Thus $P \cup \{ :- d\}$ has an unrestricted refutation and we can apply the mgu lemma to obtain a refutation of $P \cup \{ :- d\}$.*

*Second, let $f :\& t \in TX_P \uparrow n$. By the definition of $TX_P$ there exists a ground instance of a clause $e :- V_1, \ldots, V_m \& E$ and an unnesting of its premises such that $f = e\theta$ and $\bigcup_{k=1}^{m} unnest_P(V_k\theta)^{\otimes} \cup unnest_P(t .= E\theta)^{\otimes} \subseteq TX_P \uparrow (n-1)$ for some unifier $\theta$. By the induction hypothesis, for each formula $A$ in the selected $unnest_P(V_k\theta)$, for $1 \leq k \leq m$, and $unnest_P(t .= E\theta)$, $P \cup \{ :- A\}$ has a refutation. Hence, $P \cup \{ :- V_k\theta\}$ and $P \cup \{ :- t .= E\theta\}$ have a refutation, mimicking unnesting by flattening. Because each $V_k\theta$ and $t .= E\theta$ are ground and flattening only introduces new variables, these refutations can be combined into a refutation of $P \cup \{ :- (V_1, \ldots, V_m, t .= E)\theta\}$. Thus $P \cup \{ :- t .= f\}$ has an unrestricted refutation and we can apply the mgu lemma to obtain a refutation of $P \cup \{ :- t .= f\}$.*

For proving that every correct (relational or functional) answer is an instance of a computed (relational or functional) answer we first transfer lemma 8.5 from [Llo87].

**Lemma 5** *Let $P$ be a relational-functional program and $F$ a relationship or setter. Suppose that $\forall(F)$ is a logical consequence of $P$. Then there exists an SLV-refutation of $P \cup \{ :- F\}$ with the identity substitution as the computed answer.*

**Proof**

*Suppose $F$ has variables $x_1, \ldots, x_n$, anywhere in the relationship or on both sides of the setter. Let $a_1, \ldots, a_n$ be distinct constants not appearing in $P$ or $F$ and let $\theta$ be the substitution $\{x_1/a_1, \ldots, x_n/a_n\}$. Then it is clear that $F\theta$ is a logical consequence of $P$. Also, $F\theta$ being ground, each formula $A$ in some $unnest_P(F\theta)$ is a logical consequence of $P$. Since each $A$ is ground, theorem 3 shows that $P \cup \{ :- A\}$ has a refutation. Thus, $P \cup \{ :- F\theta\}$ has a refutation, mimicking unnesting by flattening. Since flattening only introduces new variables and the $a_i$ do not appear in $P$ or $F$, by replacing $a_i$ by $x_i$, for $1 \leq i \leq n$, in this* *refutation, we obtain a refutation of $P \cup \{ :\text{-} F\}$ with the identity substitution as the computed answer.*

Now, K. L. Clark's completeness result can be extended from logic to relational-functional programming. For relational goals we can adapt the formulation for definite goals in [Llo87].

**Theorem 4 (Completeness of relational SLV-resolution)** *Let $P$ be a relational-functional program and $G_r$ a relational goal. For every correct answer $\theta$ for $P \cup \{G_r\}$ there exists a computed answer $\sigma$ for $P \cup \{G_r\}$ and a substitution $\gamma$ such that $\theta \stackrel{G_r}{=} \sigma\gamma$.*

**Proof**
*Let the relational goal $G_r$ be $:\text{-} B_1, \ldots, B_k$. Since $\theta$ is correct, $\forall((B_1 \wedge \ldots \wedge B_k)\theta)$ is a logical consequence of $P$. By lemma 5 there exists a refutation of $P \cup \{ :\text{-} B_i\theta\}$ such that the computed answer is the identity, for $1 \le i \le k$. We can combine these refutations into a refutation of $P \cup \{ :\text{-} G_r\theta\}$ such that the computed answer is the identity.*
*Suppose the sequence of mgu's of the refutation of $P \cup \{ :\text{-} G_r\theta\}$ is $\theta_1, \ldots, \theta_n$. Then $G_r\theta\theta_1 \ldots \theta_n = G_r\theta$. By the lifting lemma there exists a refutation of $P \cup \{ :\text{-} G_r\}$ with mgu's $\theta'_1, \ldots, \theta'_n$ such that $\theta\theta_1 \ldots \theta_n \stackrel{G_r}{=} \theta'_1 \ldots \theta'_n\gamma'$, for some substitution $\gamma'$. Let $\sigma$ be $\theta'_1 \ldots \theta'_n$ restricted to the variables in $G_r$. Then $\theta \stackrel{G_r}{=} \sigma\gamma$, where $\gamma$ is an appropriate restriction of $\gamma'$.*

Again, the result for relational goals naturally carries over to functional goals.

**Corollary 3 (Completeness of functional SLV-resolution)** *Let $P$ be a relational-functional program and $G_f$ a functional goal. For every correct answer $(t, \theta)$ for $P \cup \{G_f\}$ there exists a computed answer $(s, \sigma)$ for $P \cup \{G_f\}$ and a substitution $\gamma$ such that $\theta \stackrel{G_f}{=} \sigma\gamma$ and $t = s\gamma$.*

**Proof**
*By lemmas 1 and 2 there is an equivalent relational goal with correct and computed answers for which the completeness result of theorem 4 holds.*

## 3.8  Conclusions

Kernel RELFUN reciprocally extends Horn relations and eager functions just enough to yield a unified operator concept. Other, not integration-relevant but uniformity-preserving extensions such as finite domains are relegated to outer RELFUN shells.

Both relational essentials, non-ground, non-deterministic operators (R1, R2), and one of the functional essentials, application values (F1), of chapter 1 are semantically incorporated into the kernel. The other functional essential, higher-order operators (F2), is incorporated only syntactically. While this considerably simplified the model theory, there remains the challenge of adapting Henkin models [Llo94], Hoare powerdomains [GMHGRA97], or some other higher-order semantics for the first-order relational-functional essentials (R1, R2, F1): Except from the (presumably, rare) cases where its full expressive power is needed, this adaptation should preserve the simplicity of our current higher-order notation (F2), compatible with Herbrand models.

We could not go here into the topic of eagerness vs. laziness [HLW92], which we feel is still an open issue for declarative integrations. But our RELFUN experience suggests that the simpler eager evaluation strategy may be superior in practice. Presumed advantages of laziness may turn out to be reproducible eagerly, as in the proposal to replace lazy streams by free length-counting logic variables [Der95]. This issue should be further studied by systematically comparing eager and lazy versions of declarative programs.

Another open discussion is deterministic vs. non-deterministic functions. However, here we opted for allowing the more general non-deterministic case even in the RELFUN kernel: thus assimilating functions to (per se non-deterministic) relations, our tight relational-functional integration is actually simplified.

Future work should profit from detailed comparisons with the rewriting logic of [GMHGRA97], since, like RELFUN, it uses non-deterministic functions and, unlike RELFUN, lazy narrowing, as well as into the standardization proposal Curry [Han97], since, unlike RELFUN, it uses deterministic functions and needed narrowing.

# Chapter 4

# Finite Domains and Exclusions as First-Class Citizens

Languages based on logical variables can regard finite domains, finite exclusions, and, generally, types as values. Like a variable can be bound to a non-ground structure which can be later specialized through in-place assignment of some inner variables, it can also be bound to, say, a domain structure which can be specialized later through 'in-place deletion' of some of its elements (e.g. by intersection with other domain structures). While finite domains prescribe the elements of a disjunctive structure, the complementary finite exclusions forbid the elements of a conjunctive structure. Domains and exclusions can be values of variables or occur inside clauses as/in terms or within an occurrence-binding construct (useful to name arbitrary terms). In a relational-functional language (e.g., RELFUN) they can also be returned as values of functions. Altogether, domains and exclusions become first-class citizens. Because they are completely handled by an extended unification routine, they do not require delay techniques needed in (more expressive) constraint systems. Still, their backtracking-superseding 'closed' representation leads to smaller proof trees (efficiency), and abstracted, intensional answers (readability). Anti-unification (for generalization) exchanges the roles of domains and exclusions. The operational semantics of domains, exclusions, and occurrence bindings is specified by a RELFUN meta-unify function (and implemented in pure LISP).

## 4.1  Introduction

Characteristic for logic programming (LP) is its uniform variable concept: the single construct of logical variables is usable in different *modes* (input, output, or mixed). However, mainly for efficiency (control) reasons, *committed-choice languages* have compromised this uniformity: they distinguish modes at the user level (e.g., 'read-only' annotations). Similarly, *finite domains*, which turned out to be most useful in constraint systems [Van89], can entail a compromised variable concept: they introduce 'domain' variables separately from logical variables, limiting which variables may be unified with which kind of term (e.g., domain variables must not be bound to logical variables).

The latter problem leads us to the issue of extending LP languages by a clean construct for finite domains (generally, types), deeply integrated with existing LP constructs. In other words, we come to this basic question: Is there a method of optional, predeclaration-free, variable domain restriction (generally, variable typing) fully in the spirit of logical variables? This can be answered affirmatively by applying the following principle: Instead of introducing a new kind of variable with an associated domain (type) **and** a possible value, regard the domain (type) **as** an initial value. A domain value can then be successively *constrained* or *specialized* (e.g. by intersecting it with other domain terms) until it ultimately fails or becomes an ordinary value. (The empty domain is identified with failure, the singleton domain with its single element.)

The 'type-as-value' principle will also be applied to a new type-like construct, namely *finite exclusions*, complementary to finite domains.[1] An exclusion term specifies the values that **cannot** be assigned to a variable. It becomes specialized on unification with other exclusions (here performing union!), fails when unified with one of its argument values, and transmutes to an ordinary value unequal to any of its arguments. (The empty exclusion is identified with success.)

On domain-exclusion unification the exclusion values are set-theoretically subtracted from the domain values. Thus, while a domain corresponds to a *disjunction of solved equalities*, an exclusion corresponds to a *conjunction of solved disequalities*, where 'solved' stands for single-variable constraints. General disequality constraints were introduced to LP by PROLOG II/III [Col87]. By considering only the special case of solved (dis)equalities we can regard constraints as typed logical variables: all their value specializations can be handled as part of the unification routine of LP languages, without need for the goal-delaying mechanisms on which constraint languages are often based.

After having established finite domains and exclusions as values of variables, we will show that they may also be used 'anonymously' anywhere a term can occur (e.g. as top-level arguments of clauses). The final step then is to allow domain and exclusion terms also as values returned by functions of functional LP extensions such as RELFUN (see chapter 2). Altogether, domains and exclu-

---

[1] We will not expand much on further type-like constructs as values, but should note here that certain unary predicates $p$ (e.g. woman) could be marked (with a "$"-prefix) as user-defined sorts $\$p$ (here $woman) that may be assigned to variables, where unification applies $p$ to an ordinary value (e.g. mary) or looks up $\$p$'s *glb* (e.g. $mother) with another marked predicate (e.g. $parent) in a finite sort lattice. For a realistic application of RELFUN sorts see our ontology of Mathematics International at http://www.mathematik.uni-kl.de/~ontology/.

sions become first-class citizens of cleanly extended relational, functional, and relational-functional languages.

## 4.2 Domain Terms

As the predefined term for finite domains we will use variable-length dom structures. They are built from an arbitrary finite number, $n$, of unordered, repetition-free[2] constants, $c_i$:[3]

$$\text{dom}[c_1, \ldots, c_n]$$

In general, dom structures can be used like ordinary terms.

The empty and singleton domains reduce as follows (unknown indicates failure):

$$\text{dom}[] \quad \longrightarrow \quad \text{unknown}$$
$$\text{dom}[c] \quad \longrightarrow \quad c$$

In our RELFUN implementation, the behavior of dom structures is handled by an extension of the unification routine (cf. appendix 4.10). This behavior will be described by employing RELFUN's generalized is-primitive ".=" for unification:

$$term \ .= \ expression$$

unifies *term* (e.g. a variable) with the value of *expression* (e.g. another term).

For instance, the (left-to-right-ordered) conjunction

```
X .= dom[1,2,3], X .= dom[2,3,4,5]
```

initializes X with the three-element domain containing the integers 1, 2, and 3, and then intersects it with the four-element domain containing 2, 3, 4, and 5, thus specializing the X value to the two-element domain dom[2,3]. Similarly, the conjunction

```
X .= dom[1,2,3], X .= dom[2,3,4,5], X .= dom[1,3,5]
```

---

[2]In accordance with RELFUN's call-by-value semantics, we also permit active dom (and exc) *calls*, using round parentheses, which remove repetitions before constructing passive dom (and exc) *structures*, using square brackets.

[3]Unlike many finite-domain systems, we introduce no special treatment for integer domains here. Conversely, generalizing domain elements beyond arbitrary constants would entail complications in using finite domains: even ground structures as in dom[f[a],f[b]] would suggest that unification with f[X] be successful, non-deterministically binding X to a or b, where in fact the advantage of finite domains is their deterministic behavior, as in dom[a,b] unified with X, just binding X to the entire domain term. Rules for reducing a unification like f[X] .= dom[f[a],f[b]] to the deterministic X .= dom[a,b], perhaps via f[X] .= f[dom[a,b]], would be a challenge for non-constant-element extensions of finite domains.

specializes X to a singleton domain, i.e. is equivalent to

```
X .= 3
```

However,

```
X .= dom[1,2,3], X .= dom[2,3,4,5], X .= dom[1,3,5],
                                    X .= dom[1,2,4,8]
```

fails since X now degenerates to the empty domain.

Note that all orders of successive domain constraining are (result-)equivalent, including the usual left-to-right order of PROLOG's implementation of SLD resolution, which we could thus keep for our domain implementation: information about the current domain specialization can always immediately be stored as variable values, and goals need never be delayed.

There is an analogy between our finite-domain structures and the well-known non-ground structures of LP: binding a variable to a finite-domain structure corresponds to binding a variable to a non-ground structure. In both cases, when unified with another such variable, its value may become specialized:

1. Some elements of the domain structure may become deleted. (The domain structure can thus transmute to a single element.)

2. Some inner variables of the non-ground structure may become bound. (The non-ground structure can thus become a ground structure.)

This extension thus preserves the 'specializing-assignment' property of logic programming (a given value can be subsequently specialized, while arbitrary reassignment of a variable leads to failure).[4]

Two conjunctions exhibit the analogy:

```
X .= dom[1,2,3], Y .= dom[2,3,4,5], X .= Y
```

deletes 1 from X, 4 and 5 from Y, assigning dom[2,3] to X and Y.

```
X .= f[A,B,3,4,5], Y .= f[1,B,3,D,E], X .= Y
```

---

[4]Of course, assigning type-like (e.g. domain or non-ground) structures to variables as initial 'non-terminal' values and specializing them to 'terminal' values after successful (unifying) type checks is only possible for specializing-assignment (LP) languages: in reassignment (imperative) languages, a variable **has** to preserve its original type 'value' – in a separate 'slot' – when assigning a terminal value to it because the type will be needed unchanged on reassigning further terminal values. This prevention of the type-as-value principle, and consequently of type 'first-classness', can be construed as one more disadvantage of imperative languages.

binds A to 1, D and E to 4 and 5, respectively, assigning f[1,B,3,4,5] to X and Y.

Note that the final (right-most) result of domain specializations need not be a single value such as 3 but can still be a domain value such as dom[2,3], because such an 'intensional answer' is perfectly legitmate in our language; lack of further specialization possibilities does not lead to 'floundering' goals.

We can carry the analogy one step further. Instead of being assigned to a variable, a non-ground structure can occur directly everywhere a term can occur in a formula (e.g., within another structure). Such 'anonymous use' can also be permitted for finite-domain structures. An anonymous non-ground structure or domain structure has the same advantages as an anonymous variable: by eliminating variable names, 'single-occurrence' and 'back-substitutable' variables (non-ground structures, domain structures) can be immediately identified as such, programs become more concise, and no spurious bindings will be created.

For instance, since the variables X and Y are only used as intermediate stores, the above conjunctions via back-substitution become single expressions:

dom[1,2,3] .= dom[2,3,4,5]

succeeds, bindingless, with the intersection domain dom[2,3].

f[A,B,3,4,5] .= f[1,B,3,D,E]

succeeds, not creating spurious bindings (just A = 1, D = 4, and E = 5), with the most general common non-ground structure f[1,B,3,4,5].

## 4.3 Exclusion Terms

While finite domains *prescribe some constant of a disjunction*, finite exclusions *forbid every constant of a conjunction*. Thus the constants in an exclusion structure are implicitly 'negative'. If a variable is constrained by an exclusion and a domain assignment (in any order), both possibly singleton, the constants of the exclusion delete equal constants of the domain (set difference). If a variable is constrained by two exclusion assignments, their constants are taken together (set union), which **specializes** the original values.

Our predefined term for finite exclusions will be variable-length exc structures. They are again built from an arbitrary finite number, $n$, of unordered, repetition-free constants, $c_i$:

$$exc[c_1,\ldots,c_n]$$

In general, also exc structures can be used like ordinary terms.

The empty exclusion reduces as follows (the anonymous variable, "_", indicates success):

$$\texttt{exc[]} \quad \longrightarrow \quad \_$$

A singleton exclusion cannot be reduced context-freely since its element represents a single 'negative' constant, which has to await a unification partner.

In RELFUN, exc structures are again handled by an extension of the unification routine (cf. appendix 4.10).

For instance, these conjunctions show three principal unifications of exc structures:

```
X .= exc[1,2,3], Y .= dom[2,3,4,5], X .= Y
X .= dom[1,2,3], Y .= exc[2,3,4,5], X .= Y
X .= exc[1,2,3], Y .= exc[2,3,4,5], X .= Y
```

The first binds X to an exclusion of 1, 2, and 3, Y to dom[2,3,4,5], and then subtracts the former from the latter, specializing both X and Y to dom[4,5]. The second symmetrically 'excludes' 2 through 5 from dom[1,2,3], ultimately binding X and Y to dom[1] or 1. The third leads to X and Y being bound to the united exclusion exc[1,2,3,4,5].

Note that an exclusion can result from unification only if both respective unification partners are exc structures. If one partner is a dom structure or a constant, either of these kinds of terms also appears in successful results; exc structures "subtract and disappear". Thus, the first result, dom[4,5], is a – sufficiently specialized – finite domain ("Only constants 4 or 5 are allowed"), while, say, exc[1,2,3,6,...] would not be a – sufficiently specialized – finite exclusion ("All constants but 1 and 2 and 3 and 6 and ... are allowed").

Like for domains, we can choose any order of exclusion constraining, and thus keep the left-to-right order: the negative information of exclusions is also stored as part of the variable substitution, not with goals, which, again, need never be delayed. Also, if only exclusions are involved, the right-most result of exclusion specializations still is a 'negative answer' such as exc[1,2,3,4,5]; if all intermediate values are identical singleton exclusions, a 'negative singleton answer' such as exc[3] arises.

Exclusions can also be used anonymously, with the same advantages as mentioned for anonymous domains (see end of section 4.2). For instance, shortening the above conjunctions, the expressions

```
exc[1,2,3] .= dom[2,3,4,5]
dom[1,2,3] .= exc[2,3,4,5]
exc[1,2,3] .= exc[2,3,4,5]
```

succeed bindingless with, respectively, the difference domain dom[4,5], the difference constant 1, and the united exclusion exc[1,2,3,4,5].

Summarizing the domain and exclusion constructs, a 'domain assignment'

$$X = \text{dom}[c_1, \ldots, c_n]$$

corresponds to the disjunction of $X$-solved equalities

$$X = c_1 \vee \ldots \vee X = c_n \qquad (4.1)$$

with "=" being used like RELFUN's ".=", while an 'exclusion assignment'

$$X = \text{exc}[c_1, \ldots, c_n]$$

corresponds to the conjunction of $X$-solved disequalities (where $(2) = \neg(1)$ shows that exclusions are negated domains)

$$X \neq c_1 \wedge \ldots \wedge X \neq c_n \qquad (4.2)$$

with "$\neq$" having no direct analogue in RELFUN. However, since in such conjunctions (in RELFUN written with "," instead of "$\wedge$") exclusion values become united, the equivalent $n$-ary exclusion assignment

$$X \,.= \text{exc}[c_1, \ldots, c_n]$$

naturally corresponds to the following conjunction of $n$ unary ones:

$$X \,.= \text{exc}[c_1], \ \ldots, \ X \,.= \text{exc}[c_n]$$

Thus, finite exclusions express negative information as base constraints or **values** ('object-centered') that can be simply passed around and unified like positive information, while LP extensions via a "$\neq$" **connective** (symmetric) suggest two-variable generator constraints like $X \neq Y$, normally entailing another layer of complexity such as the need to delay a disequality until a variable becomes bound. (A possible non-ground extension of exclusions for representing two-variable constraints will be discussed in section 4.9.)

## 4.4 Occurrence Bindings

Let us further introduce a generally useful construct for binding a variable to some (initial) value(s) at one or more of its occurrences in arbitrary formulas. If this is a type-like value, e.g. a non-ground structure or a domain or an exclusion, it can become specialized by subsequent unification.

Occurrence bindings are written as binary bnd structures built from a variable, $v$, and a term, $t$:[5]

$$\text{bnd}[v, t]$$

---

[5]One could also use an infix notation like $v:t$ for increased conciseness. If $t$ was the sort-marked predicate $\$p$, bnd$[v, \$p]$ would then shorten to $v:\$p$. The current implementation still has restrictions wrt the $t$'s allowed in bnds. Section 4.5.2 will detail on the elimination of occurrence bindings.

In general, bnd structures can be used as terms.

Taking a non-ground-structure example,

```
bnd[X,f[A,B,3,4,5]] .= f[1,B,3,D,E]
```

binds X to f[A,B,3,4,5], which is then unified with f[1,B,3,D,E], binding A to 1, D and E to 4 and 5, respectively, thus specializing the X value to f[1,B,3,4,5].

An analogous finite-domain example,

```
bnd[X,dom[1,2,3]] .= dom[2,3,4,5]
```

binds X to dom[1,2,3], which is then unified with dom[2,3,4,5], thus specializing the X value to dom[2,3].

A complementary finite-exclusion example,

```
bnd[X,exc[1,2,3]] .= dom[2,3,4,5]
```

binds X to exc[1,2,3], which is then unified with dom[2,3,4,5], thus specializing the X value to dom[4,5].

If the unification partner of an occurrence binding is directly given, here as the ".="-rhs (right-hand side), the bnd structure can always be equivalently replaced by an initializing ('pre-typing') ".="-call:

```
X .= f[A,B,3,4,5], X .= f[1,B,3,D,E]
X .= dom[1,2,3],   X .= dom[2,3,4,5]
X .= exc[1,2,3],   X .= dom[2,3,4,5]
```

For bnds in clause heads, however, the unification partner is not directly given, as will be illustrated by the relational examples in section 4.5.2.

The binding construct, pairing a variable with a value, can again be assigned to a variable. Actually, in our implementation it is generated from dom/exc-bound variables at the end of reference chains to keep track of domain/exclusion specializations (while non-ground structures can be specialized via direct in-place assignments).

# 4.5 Domains/Exclusions in Relation Definitions

## 4.5.1 Facts and dom/exc Reductions

Starting with domains, the fact with a single-occurrence variable X,

```
likes(john,bnd[X,dom[ann,mary,susan]]).
```

is equivalent to the fact using the domain anonymously (regard "X" as "_"):

```
likes(john,dom[ann,mary,susan]).
```

Both can be equivalently queried by ("%" precedes comments)

```
likes(john,mary)  % success
likes(john,peggy) % failure
likes(john,Whom)  % success: Whom = dom[ann,mary,susan]
likes(john,dom[mary,peggy,susan])  % success
likes(john,bnd[Whom,dom[mary,peggy,susan]])
                  % success: Whom = dom[mary,susan]
likes(john,exc[mary,peggy])  % success
likes(john,bnd[Whom,exc[mary,peggy]])
                  % success: Whom = dom[ann,susan]
```

We can reduce the dom fact, obtaining the three 'multiplied out' facts

```
likes(john,ann).
likes(john,mary).
likes(john,susan).
```

Note that the queries would be answered equivalently. However, 'intensional' answers (delivering one closed dom structure) would become 'extensional' answers (enumerating several constants); so the bnd/dom query, instead of binding Whom to dom[mary,susan], would first bind Whom to mary, and then, via backtracking, to susan.

If we let $cls_{i_1,\dots,i_k}(x)$ denote a clause with term $x$ at some position $i_1,\dots,i_k$ ($i_1 = 0$ being the head, $i_1 = 1$ the first premise, ...,[6] $i_2 = 0$ being $i_1$'s operator/constructor, $i_2 = 1$ its first argument, ..., etc.) and $cls_\sim(x)$ a clause not having the term $x$ at any position, then a general *multout* algorithm can be defined recursively via an equation schema (treating queries as answer-head rules):

---

[6]Since the last premise may constitute the value of a functional clause, the *multout* algorithm below will also work for function definitions.

$$multout(cls_\sim(\text{dom}[c_1,\ldots,c_n])) \;\;=\;\; cls_\sim(\text{dom}[c_1,\ldots,c_n])$$

$$multout(cls_{i_1,\ldots,i_k}(\text{dom}[c_1,\ldots,c_n])) \;\;=\;\; \begin{cases} multout(cls_{i_1,\ldots,i_k}(c_1)) \\ \ldots \\ multout(cls_{i_1,\ldots,i_k}(c_n)) \end{cases}$$

For example, $multout(\texttt{likes(john,dom[ann,mary,susan]}))$ matches the second equation via the instantiation $multout(cls_{0,2}(\text{dom[ann,mary,susan]}))$, whose rhs's through the first equation lead to the three domless facts shown above.

Continuing with exclusions, the fact with a single-occurrence variable X,

```
likes(john,bnd[X,exc[mary,claire,linda]]).
```

is equivalent to the fact using the exclusion anonymously (since "X" is "_"):

```
likes(john,exc[mary,claire,linda]).
```

Both can be interchangeably queried by

```
likes(john,mary) % failure
likes(john,peggy) % success
likes(john,Whom) % success: Whom = exc[mary,claire,linda]
likes(john,dom[mary,peggy,susan])  % success
likes(john,bnd[Whom,dom[mary,peggy,susan]])
                % success: Whom = dom[peggy,susan]
likes(john,exc[mary,peggy]) % success
likes(john,bnd[Whom,exc[mary,peggy]])
                % success: Whom = exc[peggy,mary,claire,linda]
```

If we have a 'closed universe' of a finite number, say 8, of individuals, e.g. $\{ann, claire, john, linda, mary, peggy, susan, tina\}$, we could reduce the exc fact, obtaining the five 'complemented out' facts

```
likes(john,ann).
likes(john,john).
likes(john,peggy).
likes(john,susan).
likes(john,tina).
```

where the bnd/dom query would now first bind Whom to peggy, then, via backtracking, to susan. (These facts are also the multiplied out form of a dom fact.)

If the 'non-Horn' extension of a (classic, strong) negation construct is available for facts, e.g. via false-valued functions in RELFUN, one could also approximate the exc fact in an 'open universe', with infinite complements, by

```
likes(john,dom[mary,claire,linda]) !& false.
likes(john,X).
```

Queries as shown above could now bind a second argument Whom to the dom by (successfully!) returning false, but would, e.g., also return a bindingless false for mary (rather than yielding unknown due to unification failure). The impurity of the cut-protected 'catch-all' fact seems to favor our proposal to express such special cases of negation by the special-purpose construct exc directly in clause heads, permitting non-Horn clauses as "Horn clauses + exclusions".

## 4.5.2   Clauses and bnd-to-".=" Reductions

A typed version of a well-known PROLOG program contains a rule with a non-single-occurrence variable X, whose head occurrence is domain-bound:

```
likes(john,bnd[X,dom[ann,mary,susan]]) :- likes(X,wine).
likes(dom[mary,peggy,susan],wine).
```

The query

```
likes(john,Whom)
```

here binds Whom to dom[mary,susan]. The query (indefinite even wrt john)

```
likes(dom[fred,john],bnd[Whom,dom[ann,susan,tina]])
```

binds Whom to susan (not selecting fred or john from the anonymous dom).

A 'negatively' typed version of the program again contains a rule with a non-single-occurrence variable X, whose head occurrence is exclusion-bound:

```
likes(john,bnd[X,exc[mary,claire,linda]]) :- likes(X,wine).
likes(exc[mary,peggy,susan],wine).
```

The query

```
likes(john,Whom)
```

now binds Whom to exc[peggy,susan,mary,claire,linda]. The query

```
likes(dom[fred,john],bnd[Whom,dom[ann,susan,tina]])
```

binds `Whom` to `dom[ann,tina]` (again leaving "`fred or john`" anonymous).

A binding construct $\text{bnd}[v, t]$ in a clause head can always be replaced by $v$ by introducing a new premise $v := t$. If $v := t$ is further transformed to $t'(v)$, applying a unary predicate $t'$ corresponding to $t$, the entire reduction is similar to the reduction of a sorted logic to an unsorted one.

Thus, the bnd/dom rule is equivalent to

```
likes(john,X) :- X .= dom[ann,mary,susan], likes(X,wine).
```

and, with $t' = $ `ann-mary-or-susan`, to

```
likes(john,X) :- ann-mary-or-susan(X), likes(X,wine).
ann-mary-or-susan(dom[ann,mary,susan]).
```

Also, the bnd/exc rule is equivalent to

```
likes(john,X) :- X .= exc[mary,claire,linda], likes(X,wine).
```

and, with $t' = $ `not-mary-claire-and-linda`, to

```
likes(john,X) :- not-mary-claire-and-linda(X), likes(X,wine).
not-mary-claire-and-linda(exc[mary,claire,linda]).
```

The reduced form can perform 'type' checking only **after** unification, once the former bnd variable is bound. Unlike the transformation (in section 4.4) of

```
bnd[X,dom[1,2,3]] .= dom[2,3,4,5]    % fact p(bnd[X,dom[1,2,3]]).
bnd[X,exc[1,2,3]] .= dom[2,3,4,5]    % fact p(bnd[X,exc[1,2,3]]).
```

to the 'pre-typing' (domain/exclusion-initializing, not possible for clause heads as indicated by the "%"-comments)

```
X .= dom[1,2,3], X .= dom[2,3,4,5]    % X .= dom[1,2,3] invisible
                                      %            for fact p(X).
X .= exc[1,2,3], X .= dom[2,3,4,5]    % X .= exc[1,2,3] invisible
                                      %            for fact p(X).
```

the above bnd-to-"`.=`" reduction thus performs 'post-typing' (domain/exclusion-specializing, generally applicable), as in

```
X .= dom[2,3,4,5], X .= dom[1,2,3]    % rule
                                      %    p(X) :- X .= dom[1,2,3].
X .= dom[2,3,4,5], X .= exc[1,2,3]    % rule
                                      %    p(X) :- X .= exc[1,2,3].
```

Unfortunately, post-typed clauses no longer permit the selectivity of typed (e.g. domain-constrained or sorted) unification and WAM-indexing and of typed anti-unification (for generalization, see section 4.7). Also, at least if compared with the ":"-infix syntax of bnd as usable for our versions of the PROLOG example,

```
likes(john,X:dom[ann,mary,susan]) :- likes(X,wine).
likes(john,X:exc[mary,claire,linda]) :- likes(X,wine).
```

the ".="-reduced formulations are less readable.

Combining post-typing with the reformulation of an ".="-assigned exclusion as a conjunction of solved disequalities (cf. (2) in section 4.3), we can repeatedly transform any $n$-ary-exc-head clause

$$p(..., X : \text{exc}[c_1, ..., c_n], ...) :- q_1(...), \ldots, q_z(...).$$

to an equivalent unary-exc-body clause

$$p(..., X, ...) :- X .= \text{exc}[c_1], \ldots, X .= \text{exc}[c_n], q_1(...), \ldots, q_z(...).$$

(for anonymous exclusions we choose a new variable for "$X$"),[7] representing

$$p(..., X, ...) :- X \neq c_1, \ldots, X \neq c_n, q_1(...), \ldots, q_z(...).$$

where the non-Horn-clause character engendered by the exc terms is revealed by the "$\neq$" constraints preceding the ordinary premises.

# 4.6 Finite-Domain/Exclusion Functional Programming

Having introduced finite domains and exclusions into relational programming as terms that can be values of logical variables, we now transfer them to functional programming as terms that can be arguments and values of functions. (Similarly, the binding construct can be employed in function arguments and values.)

Domains and exclusions thus become first-class citizens of relational-functional languages such as RELFUN.

---

[7]While we may also combine post-typing with the reformulation of an ".="-domain as a disjunction of solved equalities (cf. (1) in section 4.3), we can directly apply the *multout* algorithm (cf. section 4.5.1) to any $n$-ary-dom-head clause

$$p(..., X : \text{dom}[c_1, ..., c_n], ...) :- q_1(...), \ldots, q_z(...).$$

to obtain $n$ equivalent domless clauses

$$p(..., X : c_1, ...) :- q_1(...), \ldots, q_z(...). \quad \ldots \quad p(..., X : c_n, ...) :- q_1(...), \ldots, q_z(...).$$

(for anonymous domains we just omit "$X$:").

## 4.6.1 Domains/Exclusions as Function Arguments

The use of finite domains as *arguments* of functions works like their use in relations. For instance, the two directed equations (":&" is a left-to-right directed "=")

```
separates(dom[canada,mexico,usa],japan) :& pacific.
separates(dom[canada,mexico,usa],
 dom[denmark,france,germany,italy,spain,sweden,uk]) :& atlantic.
```

use 'anonymous' dom arguments for compactly defining a separates function.
(They could be multiplied out to 24 domless equations, analogous to the 24 facts in section 4.7.)

The query

```
separates(bnd[Source,dom[canada,usa,panama]],
          Destination)
```

binds Source to dom[canada,usa], Destination to japan, and returns pacific; on backtracking it rebinds Destination to the European subdomain and returns atlantic.

Analogously, finite exclusions act as function arguments as was shown for relation arguments. For instance, the safe-divide function

```
safe-divide(Nominator,bnd[Denominator,exc[0]]) :&
                      /(Nominator,Denominator).
```

or, using a post-typing function definition (":-" and "&" permit intervening relational premises),

```
safe-divide(Nominator,Denominator) :- Denominator .= exc[0] &
                      /(Nominator,Denominator).
```

'excludes' Denominator-named arguments which would lead to division by zero.

Thus, the query

```
safe-divide(8,4)
```

returns 2 because $4 \neq 0$ is true. On the other hand, the query

```
safe-divide(8,0)
```

yields unknown (rather than an error from the "/"-built-in) because $0 \neq 0$ is false.

Many function definitions, e.g. factorial and fibonacci (below) over the naturals, become more declarative than in PROLOG by excluding, in a defining clause, arguments of earlier clauses: the definition thus needs no cut and in fact has disjoint, order-independent ('OR-parallel') clauses. The fib definition can even be shortened to two clauses via complementary dom and exc arguments:

```
fib(dom[0,1])        :& 1.
fib(bnd[N,exc[0,1]]) :& +(fib(-(N,2)),fib(-(N,1))).
```

## 4.6.2 Functions with Domain/Exclusion Values

The use of finite domains as *values* of functions works as follows. Like any other term, a domain term can be specified as (part of) the returned value in a function definition. Such a function then returns the finite domain to its caller as a 'closed' term representing a finite number of non-deterministic values, which without domain terms available would typically be enumerated via backtracking.

For instance, the directed equations

```
direction(old) :& dom[east,west].
direction(new) :& dom[north,south].
direction(all) :& dom[north,west,south,east].
```

use dom values for compactly defining a direction function. The first clause, e.g., can be regarded as a 'closed' form of the non-deterministic, two-clause function definition produced by *multout* (section 4.5.1):

```
direction(old) :& east.
direction(old) :& west.
```

A main call unifies returned domain terms just like for anonymously specified domains. For instance, using the variable-length tup function for list building,

```
tup(direction(old),direction(new))
```

just like

```
tup(dom[east,west],dom[north,south])
```

returns [dom[east,west],dom[north,south]].

In particular, a domain functionally returned to the top-level gives the user a more compact representation of results than their enumeration, much like a domain assigned to a relational request variable.

We may also call domain-valued functions within ".="-calls. For example, while the query

```
D .= direction(old), D .= direction(new)
```

fails (the domains are disjoint), the query

```
D .= direction(all), D .= direction(new)
```

succeeds, temporally binding D to dom[north,west,south,east], but then specializing it to dom[north,south].

The ".="-embedded non-ground functional query

```
[new,dom[west,north]] .= tup(Which,direction(Which))
```

succeeds by binding, as its second attempt, Which to new and building the list [new,dom[north,south]], whose most general 'instantiation' in common with the ".="-lhs (left-hand side) is the domless ground list [new,north].

Analogously, an exclusion term can be (part of) the returned value of a function. For instance, the definition

```
admitted(butcher-shop) :& exc[dog].
admitted(pet-shop) :& exc[cat,dog].
```

prohibits certain entries to butcher and pet shops: the non-ground call

```
admitted(Where)
```

enumerates the exclusion values exc[dog], binding Where to butcher-shop, and exc[cat,dog], binding Where to pet-shop.

Two such admitted calls may be embedded into an ".="-call:

```
[cat,dom[kid,dog]] .= tup(admitted(Where),admitted(Where))
```

This succeeds by specializing the ".="-lhs to [cat,kid], consistently binding Where to butcher-shop.

Finally, a function can also return a mix of domains and exclusions. For example, the dishes (dis)liked by several people may be defined thus:

```
dish(john) :& dom[chilli,pizza,sushi,chop-suey].
dish(mary) :& exc[sushi].
dish(fred) :& exc[spaghetti,pizza].
dish(tina) :& dom[sushi,chop-suey,hamburger].
```

For constraining the set of candidate restaurants, they could perform intersection-difference operations equivalent to

```
[D,D,D,D] .= tup(dish(john),dish(mary),dish(fred),dish(tina))
```

binding D to the (fortunately unique) solution chop-suey.


## 4.7 Domain and Exclusion Anti-unification

In section 4.5.1 we have defined the *multout* algorithm for 'multiplying out' finite domains from clauses into an extensional form, and noted that the general reduction of finite exclusions would involve a strong form of negation.

Conversely, the automatic generation of intensional, domain/exclusion-using clauses from ordinary ones constitutes an interesting generalization task. In particular, a set of 'similar' clauses can often be generalized by individually generating a finite domain in each distinguishing argument position, thus 'compressing' the clauses' information. Generalizing more than one argument position at a time (giving rise to new combinations when multiplying out) amounts to 'inducing' new information from the clauses.

For instance, inverting two *multout* transformations, the 24 relational(ized) separates facts

```
separates(pacific,canada,japan).
separates(pacific,mexico,japan).
separates(pacific,usa,japan).
separates(atlantic,canada,denmark).
separates(atlantic,canada,france).
separates(atlantic,canada,germany).
separates(atlantic,canada,italy).
separates(atlantic,canada,spain).
separates(atlantic,canada,sweden).
separates(atlantic,canada,uk).
separates(atlantic,mexico,denmark).
separates(atlantic,mexico,france).
separates(atlantic,mexico,germany).
```

```
separates(atlantic,mexico,italy).
separates(atlantic,mexico,spain).
separates(atlantic,mexico,sweden).
separates(atlantic,mexico,uk).
separates(atlantic,usa,denmark).
separates(atlantic,usa,france).
separates(atlantic,usa,germany).
separates(atlantic,usa,italy).
separates(atlantic,usa,spain).
separates(atlantic,usa,sweden).
separates(atlantic,usa,uk).
```

can be generalized (compressed) to the two facts[8]

```
separates(pacific,dom[canada,mexico,usa],japan).
separates(atlantic,dom[canada,mexico,usa],
 dom[denmark,france,germany,italy,spain,sweden,uk]).
```

which are relationalized versions of the **separates** function in section 4.6.1.[9]

A simple method for this (least general) generalization is pairwise *domain anti-unification* of the input facts. For ease of presentation we will assume that clauses are represented as structures, e.g. regarding an atom (fact) as a structure whose constructor stands for the predicate. Domain anti-unification of two structures works like classic anti-unification [Plo70] (in our implementation, [Fis94], (nested) structures having different constructors or arities yield a new variable) with the following modifications. For a (named or anonymous) variable and a domain it yields a variable in the manner classic anti-unification handles variable/constant pairings. For different constants it yields a dom term containing these constants, not a (sometimes overly general) new variable. (For a constant and a structure it has to yield a new variable since currrent dom terms cannot contain structures.) Generally (constants can be treated as singleton domains),

---

[8]If some (interactive/automatic) analyzer notices that a certain domain such as dom[canada,mexico,usa] occurs repeatedly in a program, it may be useful to have it defined more globally as a predicate (with a user-provided name) such as america(dom[canada,mexico,usa]) and replace the domain by the predicate name used as a "$"-marked sort, e.g. in the clause separates(pacific,$america,japan). A comparison of the equivalent notations 'dom[. . .]' and '$...' reveals our convention that domains/exclusions do not carry a 'typing symbol' such as the "$" for sorts: their dom/exc-constructor marks them as types with 'built-in' unification behavior; on the other hand, "$"-less predicate names are just constants unifying with themselves. Domains/exclusions exhibit their built-in properties in all places they are permitted as first-class citizens. Making them passively passable data structures (without list-coding as in appendix 4.10), e.g. for amalgamated object/meta-level programming, is as hard as for logical variables, requiring a kind of quote operator.

[9]In RELFUN the relationalize algorithm can be used to make relational/functional knowledge more accessible to classical inductive-LP methods [Rae92], which could, however, also be transferred directly to functional knowledge representations.

domain anti-unification of two dom terms yields their union (unification: intersection). Identical dom (later: exc) terms can directly yield one copy unchanged, short-cutting spurious unions (later: intersections).

The complementary *exclusion anti-unification* for a (named or anonymous) variable and an exclusion yields a variable in the manner classic anti-unification handles variable/constant pairings. It yields the intersection (unification: union) of two exc terms. For an exclusion and a constant (singleton domain) it yields the exc term minus the constant. Generally, the *domain-exclusion anti-unification* of a dom and an exc term, in any order, yields the exc term with the elements of the dom term set-theoretically subtracted (unification: domain with exclusion subtracted). An empty-exclusion outcome, as usual, represents the always successful anonymous variable. Altogether, the domain/exclusion complementarity commutes nicely with the unification/anti-unification duality.

Let us start an example for domain anti-unification with, say, the first two input facts:

```
separates(pacific,canada,japan).
separates(pacific,mexico,japan).
```

Anti-unification generalizes them via a domain in the second argument:

```
separates(pacific,dom[canada,mexico],japan).
```

This intermediate result domain-anti-unified with the third input fact,

```
separates(pacific,usa,japan).          % usa = dom[usa]
```

leads to the completely generalized pacific fact above. Similarly, the remaining input facts, via three groups of textually ordered domain-anti-unification steps, generalize their third argument to a common domain:

```
separates(atlantic,canada,
 dom[denmark,france,germany,italy,spain,sweden,uk]).
separates(atlantic,mexico,
 dom[denmark,france,germany,italy,spain,sweden,uk]).
separates(atlantic,usa,
 dom[denmark,france,germany,italy,spain,sweden,uk]).
```

The completely generalized atlantic fact above is then obtained as for the pacific side. (Equivalently, the second argument could be generalized first.)

Suppose we have one additional input fact,[10]

---

[10]Such a **separates** enrichment was proposed by Manfred Meyer and Knut Hinkelmann. Thanks also to Otto Kühn, Michael Sintek, and Panagiotis Tsarchopoulos.

```
separates(atlantic,panama,denmark).
```

For group formation on the third argument, domain anti-unification would leave
this fact as a singleton group since denmark is the only European partner specified for panama. Now, the four resulting groups differ in two arguments, not just
in one. Still domain-anti-unifying them would generalize the second argument
and 'absorb' denmark into the domain of the third argument:

```
separates(atlantic,dom[canada,mexico,usa,panama],
 dom[denmark,france,germany,italy,spain,sweden,uk]).
```

This generalized atlantic fact expresses more information than the input facts,
namely an induction from Denmark to the other European countries (which
happens to be empirically true); again multiplying out the result makes these
induced facts explicit:

```
separates(atlantic,panama,france).
. . .
separates(atlantic,panama,uk).
```

However, since (domain) anti-unification can find a generalization for each pair
of structures, its use most be controlled. An example of overgeneralization would
result from further domain-anti-unifying the completely generalized pacific and
atlantic facts above, generating a single fact expressing much more than the 24
inputs via geographically vacuous Pacific/Atlantic and Japan/Europe domains.

An example for exclusion anti-unification can take two versions of a fact from
section 4.5.1 as input:

```
likes(X,exc[mary,claire,linda]).  % Everybody likes all except MCL
likes(john,exc[mary,tina]).    % John likes all except Mary & Tina
```

Anti-unification generalizes them via an intersection of the exclusions in the
second argument:

```
likes(X,exc[mary]).         % Everybody likes all except Mary
```

This is the least general generalization of the input facts since exactly the subex-
clusion common to both facts is kept. In cases where we have a closed universe,
say {ann, claire, john, linda, mary, peggy, susan, tina} of section 4.5.1, the inputs can be rewritten as complementary domain facts:

```
likes(X,dom[ann,john,peggy,susan,tina]).   %  (*)
likes(john,dom[ann,claire,john,linda,peggy,susan]).
```

Domain anti-unification via union generalizes them to

`likes(X,dom[ann,claire,john,linda,peggy,susan,tina]).`

which is the complement of the exclusion-anti-unification result above.

Finally, domain-exclusion anti-unification of the input facts

`likes(X,exc[mary,claire,linda]).`
`likes(john,dom[mary,tina]).   % (**)`

via subtraction generalizes them to

`likes(X,exc[claire,linda]).`

Here, the exclusion is minimally weakened (its extension being minimally enlarged) to accomodate what is specified by the domain. This can again be illustrated for the case of a closed universe: anti-unify (*) with (**) and re-complement the result. Such least general generalizations by domain-exclusion anti-unification thus remove dom-exc contradictions in a set of clauses, e.g. about John's liking of Mary in the above input facts; similarly, exclusion anti-unification removes the less obvious exc-exc contradictions concerning constants that occur in only one of the exclusions, e.g. about John's liking of, say Claire, in the previous input facts. This may be exploited for 'theory revision' [Rae92] of knowledge bases containing exclusion terms.

# 4.8   Operational Semantics

Since all user-defined relations and functions are invoked through unification, we were able to handle the relational-functional extensions for domains etc. in a uniform, efficient manner by building our first-class domain and exclusion notions, as well as the larger part of our bnds, into the (pure LISP) unification routine unify of the definitional interpreter of RELFUN. (A smaller, less interesting part of occurrence bindings is built into the term-instantiation routine, not treated here.) In appendix 4.10 we use a meta-interpreter approach for specifying the operational semantics of the extended unify via RELFUN clauses only relying on non-extended unification. This will contain enough detail both to document the actual RELFUN implementation and to permit transfers to other LP languages.

While constants will stand for themselves, non-constant terms will be coded as ground lists as shown by the table below, where *"'"* indicates recursive coding.

| constant | constant |
|---|---|
| $Identifier$ | $[\texttt{vari}, identifier]$ |
| $Identifier*level$ | $[\texttt{vari}, identifier, level]$ |
| $[a_1, \ldots, a_n]$ | $[\texttt{tup}, a_1', \ldots, a_n']$ |
| $constructor\,[a_1, \ldots, a_n]$ | $[constructor', a_1', \ldots, a_n']$ |
| $\texttt{dom}\,[c_1, \ldots, c_n]$ | $[\texttt{dom}, c_1, \ldots, c_n]$ |
| $\texttt{exc}\,[c_1, \ldots, c_n]$ | $[\texttt{exc}, c_1, \ldots, c_n]$ |
| $\texttt{bnd}\,[v, t]$ | $[\texttt{bnd}, v', t']$ |

Substitutions will be represented as lists of pair lists of variables and their values of the form $[[v_1', t_1'], \ldots, [v_n', t_n'], [\texttt{bottom}]]$, i.e. the empty substitution becomes $[[\texttt{bottom}]]$ (not $[]$, see below).

For instance, the call

```
unify( [bnd,[vari,x],[exc,a,b,c]], [dom,b,c,d,e], [ [bottom] ] )
```

successfully returns the substitution `[ [[vari,x],[dom,d,e]], [bottom] ]`.

In appendix 4.10, the unify function takes two terms X and Y and a substitution Environment (initially often empty), and returns the substitution extended by the mgu of X and Y in Environment (on success) or [] (on failure). It calls unify-ua with ultimate-assoc-dereferenced X/Y arguments for case analysis. This workhorse decomposes one or two bnds into their variable and expression parts for unify-bnd, where a missing bnd (variable) is indicated by []. Mixed dom/exc arguments are handed to dom-exc, performing (set-as-list) subtraction. Homogeneous doms are handed to dom-intersection for (set-as-list) intersection. In both cases (only) the non-emptiness of the result list is checked (so this can be optimized). Homogeneous excs are successful in any case. Plain partner arguments to doms and excs are checked via member calls simplifying earlier cases with singleton doms reduced to the plain argument. The last unify-ua clause does unify on constructors (incl. tup) and calls unify-args (not expanded here) for corecursive processing of their arguments. The unify-bnd function essentially parallels the dom and exc cases of unify-ua, but hands subtraction, intersection, and union results to unify-bnd-env for extension of the Environment argument, using the variable(s) of the bnd(s).[11] Such bnds for dom/exc-variable updates may be generated by the function ultimate-assoc: it returns the dereferenced value of a variable in Environment, except if the value is a dom or an exc, in which case it creates a bnd pair of the variable immediately preceding in the reference chain and of the dom or exc expression.

---

[11] Thus, while the update of non-ground structures in relational languages leads to bindings of free inner variables, the update of dom and exc structures leads to bindings shadowing previous ones, as known from function calls and let blocks in interpreters for functional languages. In a (WAM) compiler implementation we could get the efficiency of in-place assignment via real in-place deletion/addition of elements of dom/exc structures allocated on the heap.

While RELFUN's generalized is-primitive ".=" also automatically profits from the dom/exc-enhanced unification, for ordinary built-in relations and functions the actual arguments that are finite domains have to be 'multiplied out' (built-in calls cannot have exclusion arguments); for built-in (constant-valued) functions the values then have to be recollected into a new domain structure.

As we have seen in section 4.5.1, the *multout* transformation could be performed statically for user-defined operations, too, thus eliminating the domain extension for a non-enhanced LP implementation. However, this would lose the combinatorial efficiency advantage of finite domains. Also, their complementarity with finite exclusions, not allowing this treatment, would become occluded.

For a model-theoretic characterization [Llo87] of programs containing first-class finite domains, the *multout* transformation could also be exploited semantically. Of course, a characterization via a domain-extended Herbrand base would be more 'direct'. And again, leaving domains in the semantic kernel would allow to exploit the domain/exclusion complementarity.

## 4.9 Conclusions

Let us briefly summarize our notion of finite domains and exclusions:

- They are useful even without constraint (delay!) techniques because their backtracking-superseding 'closed' representation leads to

  - smaller proof trees (efficiency),
  - abstracted, intensional answers (readability).

- We have generalized them to first-class citizens (values of logical variables and of functions, usable anonymously as arguments and inside structures, no 'floundering' for non-singleton domain results).

- Their complementarity wrt unification (most general specialization) 'changes signs' wrt anti-unification (least general generalization).

- Their operational semantics and interpreter implementation is given by extensions of the unification routine of LP languages (specified here via meta-unification).

The examples presented here have indicated ways of employing our finite domain/exclusion concept for the compact representation of first-order knowledge. In RELFUN, domain/exclusion terms can also be used in the operator position, thus permitting a higher-order notation for knowledge like "Functions factorial, fibonacci, or exponential applied to 0 return 1" (domain anti-unification also generalizing operators/constructors could extract this from three multiplied out functional clauses):

```
dom[fac,fib,exp](0) :& 1.   % F:dom[exp,sin](0)  gives  1, F=exp
```

It will be instructive to observe which particular use of our domain/exclusion extension of LP is most profitable for a real-world representation task, e.g. in the areas of materials engineering [BBK94] or calendar management (e.g. just unify two agents' restrictions, "All dates except May 12 and 23" and "Only May 9-13": `exc[12-may,23-may] .= dom[9-may,...,13-may]`).

An area for further theoretical work would be the extension of Herbrand models for finite domains and, more demanding (perhaps via $T_P \downarrow \omega$ [Llo87]), finite exclusions. Concerning domain/exclusion anti-unification, it will be interesting to see how further inductive-LP or machine-learning methods based on classic anti-unification may profit from the domain/exclusion extension, using our recent LISP implementation [Fis94] of the rules introduced in section 4.7. On the unification side, an efficient WAM compiler/emulator extension for our (variable-length!) finite domains and exclusions should be written, building on the RELational/FUNctional machine (see chapter 5), FIDO III [Hei93, Ste93], and FLIP [Sin95], all in COMMON LISP: WAM instructions for unifying constants such as `get_constant` would need a membership/non-membership test case for `dom/exc` structures, new instructions `get_dom/get_exc` could unify `dom/exc` structures, performing, e.g., intersection/union for other `dom/exc` structures (perhaps maintaining canonically ordered elements), etc. Also, it could be studied how our specialized finite domains/exclusions could be fruitfully **characterized** as a CLP($\mathcal{FD}$)-like instance of the constraint-logic programming scheme [JL87], and if they could be usefully **combined** with our RELFUN-implemented finite-domain constraints FINDOM [Sin92] or those in FIDO III [Hei93, Ste93], or with concrete domains [Han93], or other, more general constraint formalisms.

Finally, let us explore a possible non-ground extension of the treatment of solved disequations, e.g. $X \neq 1$, as exclusion bindings, e.g. $X$ `.= exc[1]`, if only to confirm that ground exclusions in fact constitute the 'local optimum' suggested by section 4.3: Can we treat unsolved disequations, e.g. $X \neq Y$, as exclusion bindings with non-ground rhs's, e.g. $X$ `.= exc[Y]` and/or $Y$ `.= exc[X]`? Well, we could store both binding directions, but let us choose one direction, say $X$ `.= exc[Y]`, and put this into the substitution. If further computation instantiates $Y$ to a constant, say 1, perhaps via a binding chain, the disequation reduces to a solved form, $X$ `.= exc[1]`, treated as usual. If $X$ thus specializes to a constant, 1, we can 'swap' the disequation to a solved form, $Y$ `.= exc[1]`, within the substitution. For an added disequation, say the unsolved $X$ `.= exc[Z]`, the two bindings may be simplified to one, here $X$ `.= exc[Y,Z]`. For $Y$ `.= exc[Z]`, after swapping, they can be joined to $Y$ `.= exc[X,Z]`; this avoids (possibly circular) instantiations like $X$ `.= exc[exc[Z]]`, non-equivalent to $X$ `.= exc[Z]` because "$\neq$" is not transitive. If any variable of such a (generated) non-singleton, non-ground exclusion becomes instantiated, this exclusion becomes partially solved, now constraining unifiable values (e.g. ".="-lhs's). For example, X .= exc[Y,Z], Z .= 2 or X .= exc[Y,2] excludes the binding X .= 2. If such non-ground exclusions (generally, types) can treat a larger class of constraints as bindings directly put into the substitution, unlike constraints as delayed goals, they will thus require very careful substitution updates and uses.

# 4.10  Appendix: The RELFUN Meta-unify

Since this RELFUN unification meta-specification in RELFUN is deterministic (fortunately), there are many cuts (unfortunately), discussed in chapter 2, which are, however, not needed for obtaining the first (and only) solution, just for preventing (meaningless) attempts to search for more solutions. Using RELFUN's relationalize command, this unify function would become a relation, also runnable in PROLOG, binding an additional first argument to the result substitution.

```
unify(X,Y,Environment)  :&
        unify-ua(ultimate-assoc(X,Environment),
                 ultimate-assoc(Y,Environment),
                 Environment).

unify-ua([bnd,Xvar,Xexpr],[bnd,Yvar,Yexpr],Environment) !&
        unify-bnd(Xexpr,Yexpr,Xvar,Yvar,Environment).
unify-ua([bnd,Xvar,Xexpr],Y,Environment) !&
        unify-bnd(Xexpr,Y,Xvar,[],Environment).
unify-ua(X,[bnd,Yvar,Yexpr],Environment) !&
        unify-bnd(X,Yexpr,[],Yvar,Environment).
unify-ua(X,Y,Environment) :- equal(X,Y) !& Environment.
unify-ua([vari|Namel],Y,Environment) !&
        [[[vari|Namel],Y]|Environment].
unify-ua(X,[vari|Namel],Environment) !&
        [[[vari|Namel],X]|Environment].
unify-ua([dom|Delem],[exc|Eelem],Environment) !&
        conjn(dom-exc([dom|Delem],[exc|Eelem]),Environment).
unify-ua([exc|Eelem],[dom|Delem],Environment) !&
        conjn(dom-exc([dom|Delem],[exc|Eelem]),Environment).
unify-ua([dom|Xdelem],[dom|Ydelem],Environment) !&
        conjn(dom-intersection([dom|Xdelem],[dom|Ydelem]),
              Environment).
unify-ua([exc|Xeelem],[exc|Yeelem],Environment) !& Environment.
unify-ua([dom|Delem],Y,Environment) !&
        conjn(membern(Y,Delem),Environment).
unify-ua(X,[dom|Delem],Environment) !&
        conjn(membern(X,Delem),Environment).
unify-ua([exc|Eelem],Y,Environment) !&
        conjn(negn(membern(Y,Eelem)),Environment).
unify-ua(X,[exc|Eelem],Environment) !&
        conjn(negn(membern(X,Eelem)),Environment).
unify-ua(X,Y,Environment) :- atom(X) !& [].
unify-ua(X,Y,Environment) :- atom(Y) !& [].
unify-ua([Xfirst|Xrest],[Yfirst|Yrest],Environment) !-
        New-environment .= unify(Xfirst,Yfirst,Environment) &
        conjn(New-environment,unify-args(Xrest,Yrest,New-environment)).
```

```
unify-args([],[],Environment) !& Environment.
unify-args([],Y,Environment) !& [].
unify-args(X,[],Environment) !& [].
% vertical-bar treatment omitted: generate list from "|"-rest
unify-args([Xfirst|Xrest],[Yfirst|Yrest],Environment) !-
        New-environment .= unify(Xfirst,Yfirst,Environment) &
        conjn(New-environment,unify-args(Xrest,Yrest,New-environment)).

unify-bnd([dom|Delem],[exc|Eelem],Xvar,Yvar,Environment) !-
        Differ .= dom-exc([dom|Delem],[exc|Eelem]) &
        conjn(Differ,unify-bnd-env(Differ,Xvar,Yvar,Environment)).
unify-bnd([exc|Eelem],[dom|Delem],Xvar,Yvar,Environment) !-
        Differ .= dom-exc([dom|Delem],[exc|Eelem]) &
        conjn(Differ,unify-bnd-env(Differ,Xvar,Yvar,Environment)).
unify-bnd([dom|Xdelem],[dom|Ydelem],Xvar,Yvar,Environment) !-
        Inter .= dom-intersection([dom|Xdelem],[dom|Ydelem]) &
        conjn(Inter,unify-bnd-env(Inter,Xvar,Yvar,Environment)).
unify-bnd([exc|Xeelem],[exc|Yeelem],Xvar,Yvar,Environment) !&
        unify-bnd-env(exc-union([exc|Xeelem],[exc|Yeelem]),
                      Xvar,
                      Yvar,
                      Environment).
unify-bnd([dom|Delem],Y,Xvar,Yvar,Environment) :-
        neq([vari|Namel],Y) !&
        conjn(membern(Y,Delem),unify-bnd-env(Y,Xvar,Yvar,Environment)).
unify-bnd(X,[dom|Delem],Xvar,Yvar,Environment) :-
        neq([vari|Namel],X) !&
        conjn(membern(X,Delem),unify-bnd-env(X,Xvar,Yvar,Environment)).
unify-bnd([exc|Eelem],Y,Xvar,Yvar,Environment) :-
        neq([vari|Namel],Y) !&
        conjn(negn(membern(Y,Eelem)),
              unify-bnd-env(Y,Xvar,Yvar,Environment)).
unify-bnd(X,[exc|Eelem],Xvar,Yvar,Environment) :-
        neq([vari|Namel],X) !&
        conjn(negn(membern(X,Eelem)),
              unify-bnd-env(X,Xvar,Yvar,Environment)).
unify-bnd([vari|Namel],Y,Xvar,Yvar,Environment) !-
        New .= unify([vari|Namel],Y,Environment) &
        conjn(New,unify-bnd-env([vari|Namel],Xvar,Yvar,New)).
unify-bnd(X,Y,Xvar,Yvar,Environment) !-
        New .= unify(X,Y,Environment) &
        conjn(New,unify-bnd-env(Y,Xvar,Yvar,New)).

unify-bnd-env(Val,[vari|Xvarnamel],[vari|Yvarnamel],Environment) !&
        appfun(conjn(negn(equal([vari|Xvarnamel],[vari|Yvarnamel])),
                     [[[vari|Xvarnamel],[vari|Yvarnamel]]]),
               [[[vari|Yvarnamel],Val]|Environment]).
unify-bnd-env(Val,Xvar,Yvar,Environment) !&
        appfun(appfun(conjn(Xvar,[[Xvar,Val]]),
                      conjn(Yvar,[[Yvar,Val]])),
               Environment).
```

```
dom-intersection([dom|Xdelem],[dom|Ydelem]) :&
        mk-dom(intersection(Xdelem,Ydelem)).
exc-union([exc|Xeelem],[exc|Yeelem]) :& mk-exc(union(Xeelem,Yeelem)).
dom-exc([dom|Delem],[exc|Eelem]) :& mk-dom(set-difference(Delem,Eelem)).

ultimate-assoc([vari|Namel],Environment) !&
        ultimate-assoc-binding([vari|Namel],
                               assoc([vari|Namel],Environment),
                               Environment).
ultimate-assoc(X,Environment) !& X.

ultimate-assoc-binding([vari|Namel],[],Environment) !& [vari|Namel].
ultimate-assoc-binding([vari|Namel],
                       [[vari|Namel],[dom|Delem]],
                       Environment)
    !& [bnd,[vari|Namel],[dom|Delem]].
ultimate-assoc-binding([vari|Namel],
                       [[vari|Namel],[exc|Eelem]],
                       Environment)
    !& [bnd,[vari|Namel],[exc|Eelem]].
ultimate-assoc-binding([vari|Namel],[[vari|Namel],Y],Environment) !&
        ultimate-assoc(Y,Environment).

mk-dom([]) !& [].
mk-dom([D]) !& D.
mk-dom([D|Ds]) :& [dom,D|Ds].

mk-exc([]) !& _.
mk-exc(Eelem) :& [exc|Eelem].

neq(X,X) !& false.
neq(X,Y).

negn([])!.
negn(X) :& [].

membern(E,[]) !& [].
membern(E,[E|Rest]) !& [E|Rest].
membern(X,[Y|Rest]) :& membern(X,Rest).

assoc(N,[]) !& [].
assoc(N,[[N,V]|Ar]) !& [N,V].
assoc(N,[Af|Ar]) :& assoc(N,Ar).

% conjn(X,Y)   acts like   if neq([],X) then Y else []
% appfun    is the normal functional append
% equal, intersection, union, set-difference   are built-ins: ground args
```

# Chapter 5

# Multiple-Valued Horn Clauses and Their WAM Compilation

The first part discusses an extension of RELFUN on the basis of 'multiple-valued clauses'. These extend Horn clauses by multiple 'foot' premises, specifying the value sequence to be returned. Functions can thus, relation-like, succeed or fail, enumerate values non-deterministically, return multiple values, and have non-ground arguments and values. Relations act like characteristic functions, permit functionally nested call-by-value arguments, and, like functions, are definable as higher-order operators. Higher-order clauses are characterized by a structure or a (free) variable in some operator position.

The second part describes the WAM compilation of (multiple-valued) RELFUN. Multiple-valued functions are transformed to a 'denotative' form, eliminating foots that are active calls. Call-by-value nestings (possibly non-deterministic) are 'flattened'. Higher-order clauses are reduced to 'constant-operator' clauses. Finally, WAM code is generated by extending the use of X-registers and 'put'/'get' instructions: values are put into registers X1, ... just before a clause returns; from there, the caller can get them as arguments, as if loaded by top-level put instructions.

## 5.1 Introduction

The applicative (functional) and logic (relational) programming communities are still investing much effort in the development of independently standardized systems. While acceptable standards for languages like LISP and PROLOG will be of great practical utility, the separate growth of these software worlds also implies increasing duplication of effort. A possible alternative is to integrate the purely functional and relational language kernels, and then to develop a common impure language environment.

Various functional/relational amalgamation approaches have been proposed (see, e.g., the monograph [DL86] and the survey [Han94]). They can be studied with emphasis on *expressive power, semantic foundation, implementation method*, or *time/space efficiency*. Here we introduce a WAM implementation method [War83, GLLO85, AK91, VR94] of RELFUN (**r**elational/**fun**ctional language, chapter 2) extended by *multiple-valued functions*. First, however, the expressive power of RELFUN with multiple-valued functional clauses is discussed: RELFUN permits certain 'closed' (non-$\lambda$) higher-order relational/functional formulas while preserving both PROLOG's "non-ground (pattern) programming" style and, with multiple-valued clauses, its "I/O-argument" symmetry (by reformulating output arguments as returned values). It turns out that the multiple-valued extension of RELFUN permits elegant formulations of multiple-output algorithms, imposes little more demands on the implementation method, and, because of its I/O-symmetry, makes more effective use of the WAM's X-registers.

For illustration, let us define a half adder, $ha$, mapping two addend bits to their carry and sum bits (in that order):

$$ha : A{:}bit \times B{:}bit \quad \to \quad C{:}bit \times S{:}bit$$
$$ha(0,0) \quad = \quad 0,0$$
$$ha(0,1) \quad = \quad 0,1$$
$$ha(1,0) \quad = \quad 0,1$$
$$ha(1,1) \quad = \quad 1,0$$

The two outputs can be directly fed into the inputs of another function such as a (similarly definable) *or* gate: $or(ha(1,0)) \rightsquigarrow or(0,1) \rightsquigarrow 1$. Using two $ha$'s and an *or*, the 3-input, 2-output algorithm for a full adder (with an extra carry-input bit), $fa$, specified by the switching diagram

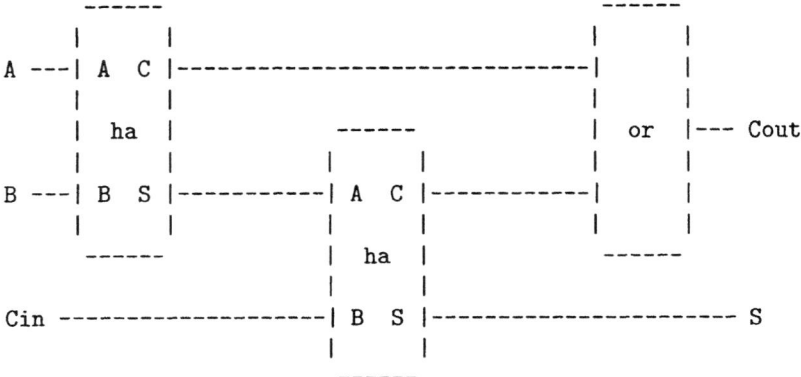

can be defined without intermediate variables in one line, using higher-order parallel combination [BL74, FW78] of functions ($\|$) with the identity ($id$) to represent wires that skip certain layers:

$$fa : A\!:\!bit \times B\!:\!bit \times C_{in}\!:\!bit \quad \to \quad C_{out}\!:\!bit \times S\!:\!bit$$
$$fa(A, B, Cin) \quad = \quad or\|id(id\|ha(ha(A, B), Cin))$$

Parallel function nestings can be reduced almost like ordinary ones, for instance obtaining the trace $fa(1, 0, 1) \rightsquigarrow or\|id(id\|ha(ha(1, 0), 1)) \rightsquigarrow or\|id(id\|ha(0, 1, 1)) \rightsquigarrow or\|id(id(0), ha(1, 1)) \rightsquigarrow or\|id(0, 1, 0) \rightsquigarrow or(0, 1), id(0) \rightsquigarrow 1, 0$. Such algorithms can be simulated by single-valued functions employing a tupling construct, "$[\ldots]$", for collecting multiple outputs into one. E.g., on the basis of an $ha : A\!:\!bit \times B\!:\!bit \to [C\!:\!bit \times S\!:\!bit]$ we could change the $fa$ definition as follows:

$$fa : A\!:\!bit \times B\!:\!bit \times C_{in}\!:\!bit \quad \to \quad [C_{out}\!:\!bit \times S\!:\!bit]$$
$$fa(A, B, Cin) \quad = \quad [Cout, S] \quad if$$
$$[C1, S1] = ha(A, B) \wedge$$
$$[\dot{C2}, S] = ha(S1, Cin) \wedge$$
$$Cout = or(C1, C2)$$

Note that instead of direct parallel function nesting, a flattened form with 'wiring variables' is now needed for decomposing intermediate tuples and feeding their elements into the correct input arguments.

In spite of its advantages, multiple-valuedness is a completely optional feature in RELFUN, unlike in COMMON LISP [SJ90], and is not presupposed in its kernel constructs. RELFUN's definitional pure-LISP interpreter, developed since [Bol86], and its model-theoretic semantics, described in chapter 3, could be easily extended by multiple-valuedness. However, for simplicity we preferred to implement a transformation algorithm `singlify`, reducing multiple-valued to single-valued functions; furthermore, in the following we show how WAM compilation can be tailored for implementing multiple-valuedness.

Generally, we use transformation and compilation techniques to explore the working hypothesis that the efficiency of relational/functional integrations will be able to catch up the efficiency of compiled PROLOG. RELFUN's functional features were conceived and implemented in the interpreter without concern for later compilation to WAM instructions. Nevertheless, after some preparatory transformations (mainly *flattening* and *constant-operator reduction*), functions (single-valued, and even more, multiple-valued) turn out to have a strong affinity to this standard relational implementation method: a functional clause can return values by just putting them, as its last action, into a WAM's "temporary (X-)registers", where a main function call can get them as its actual arguments. Several WAM-like X-register optimizations thus become also possible for functions. Alternatively, flattened, constant-operator-reduced RELFUN clauses can be further transformed to equivalent PROLOG clauses, which may then be compiled for high-efficiency PROLOG systems such as Aquarius Prolog [VR94]. The rationale for WAM compilation is discussed in chapter 1.

A COMMON LISP implementation of RELFUN is used at the University of Kaiserslautern and the DFKI Kaiserslautern. This relational/functional kernel language is enriched, e.g., by a hierarchical type system [Hal95] and augmented by a tailored programming environment. We have developed a RELFUN package of declarative operations on hypergraphs (semantic nets) [Bol92a] and further applications, discussed in chapter 1. One principal application area at the DFKI is the maintenance of/inferencing with engineering knowledge [ABH+95].

## 5.2 A Multiple-Valued Relational/Functional Language

This is a comprehensive description of multiple-valued RELFUN. We will distinguish first-order aspects (subsections 5.2.1 through 5.2.3) from higher-order aspects (subsection 5.2.4).

### 5.2.1 Amalgamating Relations and Functions

The basic idea of the relational/functional amalgamation can be understood in two steps:

1. PROLOG-like relations are augmented to *non-deterministic, non-ground functions*. A RELFUN function extends an n-ary relation by having it deliver a returned value along with possible variable bindings. Such values may be non-ground terms (e.g. unbound logical variables) and are enumerated using "don't-know" non-determinism (with failure being signaled by the special symbol unknown). Returned values thus correspond to variable values of an (n+1)-ary relation extended by a result argument. However, function calls can return values directly to a main function or relation call in pure LISP's *call-by-value* fashion absent from pure PROLOG.

2. RELFUN functions are specialized again to **true-***valued relations*. A RELFUN relation can either fail or succeed, as in PROLOG, but while it signals the special symbol unknown on failure, it actually **returns** the truth-value true on success. Thus, true and unknown can be regarded as the two outcomes of a characteristic function.[1]

---

[1] The interpreted RELFUN version has a third possible outcome, namely the (successful) truth-value false.

For example, roots is definable as a binary function such that the call roots(2,9) returns the positive square root 3 or, non-deterministically, the negative square root -3, of 9. Alternatively, it could be defined as a ternary relation such that the call roots(2,9,Res) returns true and binds the request variable Res to 3 or, non-deterministically, to -3. The non-ground function call roots(Nth,9) would, for both of the above returned values, bind Nth to 2, which corresponds to the solutions of the relation call roots(Nth,9,Res), now binding two request variables.

In summary, because both functions and relations can fail with unknown, their only remaining difference is that on success functions return arbitrary values while relations return true. More precisely, although a function may, like a relation, return true for certain argument sequences, it can be distinguished from a relation in that it must return a non-true value for at least one argument sequence.[2] Therefore, relations and functions have actually become unified to an abstract concept that we will refer to as *operators*.

Note that we deliberately did not call for *determinism* as a defining property of functions but used the more general notion of *non-deterministic functions*, for the following reasons:

- Non-deterministic functions permit the tight amalgamation with relations discussed above (non-determinism plus non-ground arguments enable function inversion).

- They are often useful for enumerating multiple solutions with the expressiveness of *generators* or *lazy lists*.

- They can be represented semantically as set-valued mappings from a domain to its power set (for roots, e.g., sending 9 to {3, -3}), with each set value representing zero or more enumerable solutions (the empty set represents unknown); their models are simple (see chapter 3).

- Since not only functions but also relations may be deterministic, the function/relation distinction does not coincide with the determinism/non-determinism distinction; explicit determinism specification should thus be regarded as an optional feature of all operators, either *call-time* (using something like PROLOG's once predicate) or *definition-time* (using cut/commit operators in clauses or determinism annotations for entire procedures).

- Non-deterministic functions can be nested with little overhead because of static flattening (cf. section 5.3.3); compilers can still optimize the important special case of determinism (either specified by the user or detected by static analysis) for both functions and relations.

---

[2]If three truth-values are used, on success (i.e., apart from unknown), all calls of a relation must return true or false, and some call of a function must return a non-true and non-false value. A relation palind and a function palinz assuming three possible truth-values will be considered in subsection 5.2.3.

The *single-valued* relational/functional amalgamation developed up to this point will now be extended by *multiple-valued* functions. For multiple-binding output, a relation call permits the use of more than one request variable; consequentially, a function call can be permitted to also return more than one value: in a fashion symmetric to the explicit argument sequence used for operator input, a value **sequence** can be used for function output, too. For example, in divide(9,5) $\leadsto$ 1,4 the nominator-denominator argument sequence 9,5 leads to the quotient-remainder value sequence 1,4.[3] This multiple-valuedness should not be confused with the non-deterministic enumeration of values discussed above. Indeed, the domain mapped to its power set now itself consists of sequences built from the base domain of terms: an extended RELFUN function can non-deterministically return several value sequences. In a final extension, the lengths not only of argument sequences but also of value sequences can be allowed to vary dynamically from zero to any number of elements, without upper bound.

The example below may help here, although detailed explanations of syntax etc. will have to await the next subsection. The RELFUN relation up is defined (deterministically) by three (non-overlapping) Horn-like clauses generalized to take a varying number of input arguments and to return true if the less relation over the naturals holds between adjacent arguments (literals permit a vertical bar acting much like in lists): up accepts the infinite set of argument sequences $\{(...,x,y,...) \mid \text{less}(x,y)\}$. The RELFUN function pa of zero arguments is defined by three grammar-like clauses generalizing a well-known context-free (CF) grammar for palindromes via **non-determinism** (the same clause head or grammar 'start symbol' pa() occurs three times), **multiple-valuedness** (the clauses represent palindromes as varying-length sequences of, respectively, zero, one, or more values), and **non-groundness** (the third clause generates a palindrome pattern whose free logical variables are renamed uniquely on each recursion): pa generates the infinite set of value sequences $\{(x_1, ..., x_{n-1}, x_{n-1}, ..., x_1)\} \bigcup \{(x_1, ..., x_{n-1}, x_n, x_{n-1}, ..., x_1)\}$. The RELFUN operator upa is defined by joining the argument testing of up with the value returning of pa: upa transforms each element $a_1, ..., a_{n-1}, a_n$ in up's accepted set to some elements $a_1, ..., a_{n-1}, a_n, a_{n-1}, ..., a_1$ or, non-deterministically, $a_1, ..., a_{n-1}, a_n, a_n, a_{n-1}, ..., a_1$ from pa's generated set. The informal mathematical notation in "%"-comments explains our syntax:

```
up().                           % up() holds
up(X).                          % up(X) holds (for all X)
up(X,Y|Z) :- less(X,Y), up(Y|Z).  % up(X,Y|Z) if less(X,Y)
                                %            and up(Y|Z)
```

---

[3]In certain syntactic contexts such as the result-checking, PROLOG-is-generalizing, multiple-lhs (-left-hand-side) ".="-primitive call (1,4) .= divide(9,5) **both** argument and value sequences have to be enclosed in parentheses; these are only needed for grouping or application, however, hence are not a proper part of sequences viewed as data structures, in contrast to, say, the term-forming brackets which are part of RELFUN's lists/tuples.

```
pa() :&.                          % pa() = void
pa() :& X.                        % pa() = X
pa() :& X,pa(),X.                 % pa() = X,pa(),X

upa() :&.                         % upa() = void
upa(X) :& X.                      % upa(X) = X
upa(X) :& X,X.                    % upa(X) = X,X
upa(X,Y|Z) :- less(X,Y) & X,upa(Y|Z),X.  % upa(X,Y|Z)=X,upa(Y|Z),X
                                  %             if less(X,Y)
```

Although up was described as a language acceptor, with a 'logical' definition of **less** it can also be used to generate ordered argument sequences; conversely, the language generator pa could be inverted using our multiple-lhs (-left-hand-side), consistent-assignment primitive ".="; finally, upa may generate ascending argument sequences and mirror them, returning 'up-down'-ordered odd- or even-length palindromes.

The last up and upa rules are prototypes of RELFUN's true- and multiple-valued (Horn) clauses, respectively. Multiple-valued RELFUN clauses can thus be perceived, among other possible views, as spanning the spectrum between (ordinary) Horn clauses and CF rules, exploiting several possibilities of cross-fertilization between both formalisms (such as the above grammar generalization by logical variables). Note, however, that the practical RELFUN implementation, developing that of PROLOG's WAM, employs depth-first search, while theoretical completeness (see chapter 3) of both Horn-clause and CF-rule derivations would call for breadth-first search. Comparing the representation of CF rules by multiple-valued functions (MVFs) and by definite clause grammars (DCGs) [PW80], we observe similarities (e.g., both avoid the chaining of additional argument pairs of the ordinary Horn-clause representation) and differences (e.g., while DCGs translate to explicitly chained predicates, MVFs keep implicit, left-to-right value concatenation).

## 5.2.2 Single-Valued and Multiple-Valued Clauses

Both a relation and a function is defined by a system of *valued clauses*, much like a pure-PROLOG procedure consisting of Horn clauses (the cut operator will be neglected in this subsection). The *head* of a valued clause corresponds to the conclusion of a Horn clause. Its *body* and *foot*, both arbitrary-length (possibly empty) conjunctions, generalize the premises of a Horn clause. Syntactically, the body and foot parts are separated by an ampersand (&) character:

$$head :- body_1, ..., body_B \ \& \ foot_1, ..., foot_F. \tag{5.1}$$

A *body* premise, like a Horn premise, contributes only success/fail and variable-binding information. A *foot* premise acts like a *body* premise but additionally delivers returned-value information. We call a valued clause *bodied* if it has at least one body premise, and call it *footed* if it has at least one foot premise.

Thus, besides the degenerate case of *empty-footed clauses* (F=0), our functional RELFUN extension proceeds from *single-footed clauses* (F=1), to *multiple-footed clauses* (F≥2): an empty-footed clause returns the empty sequence of values; a single-footed clause returns the value(s) of its foot, hence is guaranteed to be *single-valued* if also all other clauses of the program are single-footed; a multiple-footed clause returns the sequence left-to-right concatenated from the value(s) of each of its foots, hence is guaranteed to be *multiple-valued* if no clause of the program is empty-footed.

Generally, a valued clause acts as if the body/foot separator (&) were replaced by an ordinary conjunction separator (,) but also returns the $v_1 + \ldots + v_F$ values of $foot_1, \ldots, foot_F$ as a sequence $val_{1,1}, \ldots, val_{1,v_1}, \ldots, val_{F,1}, \ldots, val_{F,v_F}$. Thus, there is an important difference between the subconjunctions constituting the body and foot premises: since the foot premises construct a sequence of terms, different textual foot orders amount to declaratively different clauses; for body premises reordering can only amount to operationally different sequential behaviors.[4]

All operators can be called as both *body* and *foot* premises, where functional values are taken as mere success signals in the *body* part and relational (true) values become normal elements of the returned sequence in the *foot* part.

There are two extreme specializations of the general form (5.1) of valued clauses, symmetric apart from the role of the empty sequence.

1. **Valued clauses without any foot (F=0):** These *footless clauses* are further divided into two subclasses.

   If the ampersand is kept ("&", F=0), which denotes returning the empty sequence, i.e. the value void of the built-in call multid() (see below), one obtains *empty-footed clauses*:

$$head \; :\text{-} \; body_1, \ldots, body_B \; \& \; . \tag{5.2}$$

   If the ampersand is omitted (no "&", F=0), i.e. the top-level syntax coincides with that of PROLOG Horn clauses, one obtains *non-footed clauses*:

$$head \; :\text{-} \; body_1, \ldots, body_B. \tag{5.3}$$

   The complement set of footless clauses is footed clauses (F≥1). Note that both clause sets are **valued** in the sense that even footless clauses on success always either return void (empty-footed clauses) or true (non-footed

---

[4]Still, in a concurrent execution of premises, it would be possible to work on a certain $foot_j$ before working on a $foot_i$ with $j > i$, just as it is possible to work on a certain $body_j$ before working on a $body_i$ with $j > i$.

clauses). That is, empty-footed clauses of the form (5.2) are equivalent to void-footed clauses (F=1):

$$head \; :- \; body_1, ..., body_B \; \& \; \texttt{void}. \tag{5.4}$$

Similarly, non-footed clauses of the form (5.3) are equivalent to true-footed clauses (F=1):

$$head \; :- \; body_1, ..., body_B \; \& \; \texttt{true}. \tag{5.5}$$

A procedure consisting only of non-footed clauses is thus guaranteed to define a relation.

Non-footed clauses will be further classified like Horn clauses. *Non-footed bodied clauses* or *Hornish rules* have a non-empty body (B$\geq$1, no "&", F=0); unlike in Horn rules, the $body_i$'s may be/contain arbitrary operator calls. *Non-footed bodiless clauses* or *atomic clauses* or *facts* have no body (B=0, no "&", F=0), and are written without the ":-"-symbol:

$$head. \tag{5.6}$$

2. **Valued clauses without any body (B=0):** Here, ":- &" may be joined to ":&", i.e. these *bodiless clauses* can be seen as having the syntax of unconditional, context-free sequence-rewriting rules by reading ":&" as a right arrow ($\longrightarrow$):[5]

$$head \; :\& \; foot_1, ..., foot_F. \tag{5.7}$$

The complement set of bodiless clauses is bodied clauses (B$\geq$1). Note that both clause sets have a conditional-rewriting formulation since bodiless clauses can be transcribed using trivially successful body premises. That is, bodiless clauses of the form (5.7) are equivalent to void-bodied clauses (B=1)

$$head \; :- \; \texttt{void} \; \& \; foot_1, ..., foot_F. \tag{5.8}$$

as well as to true-bodied clauses (B=1)

$$head \; :- \; \texttt{true} \; \& \; foot_1, ..., foot_F. \tag{5.9}$$

and to infinitely many other term-bodied clauses (B$\geq$1)

$$head \; :- \; term_1, ..., term_B \; \& \; foot_1, ..., foot_F. \tag{5.10}$$

Bodiless clauses will again be further classified. *Bodiless footed clauses* or *replacement rules* have a non-empty foot (B=0, F$\geq$1). *Bodiless non-footed clauses* have no foot (B=0, no "&", F=0), and the remaining ":-"

---

[5]The semantics will allow a simulation of **conditional** rules by recasting the general clause form (5.1) as *head* $:\& \; body'_1, ..., body'_B, foot_1, ..., foot_F$, where $body'_i$ is a simple reformulation of $body_i$ which on success returns the empty sequence instead of other values truth-functionally equivalent to **true**. Also, of course, parameterization, non-groundness, etc. make bodiless clauses much more general than CF **grammar** rules.

is omitted, again obtaining the form (5.6) of facts or non-footed bodiless clauses. An intermediate specialization of bodiless clauses concerns the form of the foots themselves. *Molecular clauses* are replacement rules all of whose foots are terms:

$$head :\& \ term_1, ..., term_F. \qquad (5.11)$$

Facts, then, are equivalent to true-footed molecular clauses (B=0, F=1):

$$head :\& \ \text{true}. \qquad (5.12)$$

A procedure consisting only of footed clauses is thus not guaranteed to define a function: it may define a relation all of whose clauses have the form (5.12) [or, in general, (5.5)].[6]

The full name of our doubly derived, true-valued, fact specialization of valued clauses will be *valued facts* (B=0 **and** F=0); we will also employ the complementary notion of *valued rules* (B≥1 **or** F≥1), so that bodied or footed clauses are always bodied or footed rules.

Let us return to an earlier distinction for footed rules, namely *single-footed rules* (F=1) vs. *multiple-footed rules* (F≥2). This will be important for the following discussion of the use and implementation of **multiple-valued functions**, which can now be given a refined, recursive characterization (not generally decidable): a function is *multiple-valued* if for some argument constellation either at least two foots of a defining multiple-footed rule evaluate to non-empty values or the foot of a defining single-footed rule calls a multiple-valued function.

Since all the forms (5.2)-(5.12) above are special cases of the general form (5.1), valued clauses amalgamate the expressive power of relational and (multiple-valued) functional programming, permitting conditional, 'narrowing'-like non-ground rewrite rules (with multiple right-hand sides), whose conditions are PROLOG-like goals that can also accumulate partial results.

It is possible to encapsulate all multiple-valuedness into a single function, the multiple identity, definable by recursive clauses `multid() :&` and `multid(A|R) :& A,multid(|R)`. In fact, for fixed F, rules with up to F foots can be simulated by 1-footed rules using calls to a (0-to-F)-footed `multid` **built-in** WAM-coding F+1 molecular clauses that just return their ascending numbers of arguments. For $0 \le I \le$ F, each $I$-ary source clause (on the left) becomes a 'noop' WAM procedure `multid/`$I\!+\!I$ (as "%"-comments, on the right), which just returns, i.e., for $1 \le I \le$ F, leaves the arguments as values in the first to $I$th X-registers (since the "argument arity" $I$ and (equal) "return arity" $I$ of `multid/`$I\!+\!I$ is indicated by $I\!+\!I$ (cf. section 5.3.1), its callers know that the first $I$ values are relevant):

---

[6]While these relations are easily recognizable as such, for a clause with an arbitrary foot it cannot be decided in general whether it will return **true** as its only possible value.

```
multid() :&.                      %    multid/0+0:  proceed
multid(A1) :& A1.                 %    multid/1+1:  proceed
multid(A1,A2) :& A1,A2.           %    multid/2+2:  proceed
      . . .                                    . . .
multid(A1,...,AF) :& A1,...,AF.   %    multid/F+F:  proceed
```

The general form (5.1) is then simulated by

$$head :- body_1, ..., body_B \text{ \& } \texttt{multid}(foot_1, ..., foot_F). \tag{5.13}$$

While our multid function is quite similar to COMMON LISP's values function (but does not discard all but the first values of multiple-valued embeddings), we regard it only as a substitute for explicit sequences and F-footed clauses, which have no analogue in COMMON LISP.

Besides simulating arbitrary multiple-footed functions by (5.13), it is also possible to reduce them to single-(list-)valued functions by RELFUN's singlify transformation:[7] since the top-level elements of tuples (lists) can be regarded as constituting a sequence in the sense of multiple-valued RELFUN, it should be easy to translate between these linear data structures. In fact, because, unlike COMMON LISP, we permit multiple-valued argument passing, the inverse translators are accomplished by a 'tuple-sequencing' function elements (which uses multid, hence works up to fixed sequence/tuple length F), corresponding to COMMON LISP's values-list, and the already available 'sequence-tupling' function tuple, corresponding to LISP's list but also to an n-ary version of COMMON LISP's multiple-value-list:

```
elems([|Rest]) :& multid(|Rest).   % argument [|...] checks list
tup(|Rest) :& [|Rest].             % value [|...] emphasizes list
```

An important characteristics of our present sequence concept (in contrast to those of, say, FIT, RELFUN/X, and KIF [GF91]) is that for $F \neq 1$ an F-element sequence, perhaps returned by an F-footed rule, cannot be assigned to a single logical variable, because non-unit sequences conflict with the implicit single-term constraint of logical variables. Neither can multid change this since, although it permits to notate a single (active) call, it does not construct a single (passive) term but again a sequence of terms. However, we can call the above tup definition to construct one (list) term from a sequence, t1,...,tF, before assigning it to a logical variable, X, possibly combined with the inverse elems

---

[7]We will not go into details such as the issue of retaining the associativity of sequences also in their list representation via a concatenation function, related to imposition normalization in the FIT interpreter [Bol83] and smoothening in the RELFUN/X-to-PROLOG translator [SS91].

call after dereferencing the variable in order to restore the sequence from the list (this in a sense generalizes the internal list treatment of 'rest' parameters in LISP, PROLOG, and RELFUN):[8]

```
X .= tup(t1,...,tF) & elems(X)
```

Another, often better, possibility is using a "parallel assignment"-like *multiple-variable* ".="-primitive $(p_1, ..., p_v) .= q$, which unifies the value sequence $r_1, ..., r_v$ of $q$ with the variable sequence $p_1, ..., p_v$, as if there was a sequence of single-variable ".="-primitives $p_1 .= r_1$, ..., $p_v .= r_v$. In our case we would require $v$=F variables, $X1, ..., XF$, possibly recombining them to the sequence by simple juxtaposition:

```
(X1,...,XF) .= (t1,...,tF) & X1,...,XF
```

Let us close noting that the most general ".="-primitive has the multiple-lhs (-left-hand-side), multiple-rhs (-right-hand-side) form $(t_1, ..., t_v) .= (q_1, ..., q_w)$, with each $t_i$ an arbitrary term and each $q_j$ an arbitrary formula, which works analogously since the earlier $q$ could be defined via $q_1, ..., q_w$. (If $v$=1 and/or $w$=1, the ".="-parentheses around sequence $t_1, ..., t_v$ and/or $q_1, ..., q_w$ are normally omitted.)

### 5.2.3 An Example: Refining the `palindrome` Operator

While the `pa` function in subsection 5.2.1 was described as a non-deterministic 'generator' of palindrome sequences, we now describe deterministic 'acceptors' of palindrome lists (which will also be used as non-ground, non-deterministic generators): first, the basic RELFUN amalgamation via valued clauses will be illustrated by developing a palindrome relation into three functional versions. All four operators shall be defined on a list of arbitrary terms, possibly non-ground. The relational `palindrome` operator should succeed (with the value `true`) for palindrome lists and fail (with the signal `unknown`) for non-palindrome lists. The functional `palinclass` operator should refine `palindrome` by differentiating the success cases into palindromes of even and odd lengths, returning the values `even` and `odd`, respectively. Similarly, `palinzoom` should zero in on 'innermost palindromes', and `palinlength` should count palindrome elements. Table 5.1 contains I/O samples for these operators.

Note that RELFUN uses "[...]"-brackets not just for lists but also for *denotative* (record) structures such as the list-embedded `s[Y,b]`. "(...)"-parentheses are used only for *evaluative* (operator) calls such as the `palindrome`

---

[8]However, apart from 'rest' ("¦") variables, RELFUN patterns currently not only forbid sequence-tupling variables but also anonymous sequence-matching operators, since more than one occurrence of such varying-length pattern constructs would make unification non-deterministic (yielding more than one mgu).

| input argument | output value/signal | | output bindings |
|---|---|---|---|
| | palindrome | palinclass | |
| [] | true | even | |
| [a] | true | odd | |
| [a,b] | unknown | unknown | |
| [b,b] | true | even | |
| [a,d,a] | true | odd | |
| [a,n,n] | unknown | unknown | |
| [X,n,n] | true | odd | X=n |
| [n,X,b] | unknown | unknown | |
| [n,X,n] | true | odd | X=Center*4 |
| [s[Y,b],a,Y,X] | true | even | X=s[a,b], Y=a |
| [s[Y,b],a,Y,s[Z,Z]] | unknown | unknown | |
| [[m,Y],a,t[X,X,Y],a,[X,d]] | true | odd | X=m, Y=d |

| input argument | output value/signal | | output bindings |
|---|---|---|---|
| | palinzoom | palinlength | |
| [] | [] | 0 | |
| [a] | [a] | 1 | |
| [a,b] | unknown | unknown | |
| [b,b] | [] | 2 | |
| [a,d,a] | [d] | 3 | |
| [a,n,n] | unknown | unknown | |
| [X,n,n] | [n] | 3 | X=n |
| [n,X,b] | unknown | unknown | |
| [n,X,n] | [Center*4] | 3 | X=Center*4 |
| [s[Y,b],a,Y,X] | [] | 4 | X=s[a,b], Y=a |
| [s[Y,b],a,Y,s[Z,Z]] | unknown | unknown | |
| [[m,Y],a,t[X,X,Y],a,[X,d]] | [t[m,m,d]] | 5 | X=m, Y=d |

Table 5.1:  Palindrome variations

call palindrome([a,d,a]), producing the value true and no bindings. In the table, successful output consists of one returned value and zero to two variable bindings; failing output (i.e. the unknown signal) can never be accompanied by any bindings.

All palindrome versions shall build on the usual PROLOG *append* relation, here called apprel. The principal idea for their executable specification is apprel's inverted use to unify the last list element with the first one, and incidentally splitting out the middle list part for recursive calls. (For more efficient, lower-level palindrome implementations RELFUN's lth and thl built-ins could be employed to access the first and last list elements, which then could be unified, etc.) Fig. 5.1 contains our high-level definitions of the palindrome and palinclass operators, followed by those of palinzoom and palinlength.

```
palindrome([]).                              palinclass([]) :& even.
palindrome([Center]).                        palinclass([Center]) :& odd.
palindrome([First-and-Last|Rest]) :-         palinclass([First-and-Last|Rest]) :-
  apprel(Middle,[First-and-Last],Rest),        apprel(Middle,[First-and-Last],Rest) &
  palindrome(Middle).                          palinclass(Middle).

palinzoom([]) :& [].                         palinlength([]) :& 0.
palinzoom([Center]) :& [Center].             palinlength([Center]) :& 1.
palinzoom([First-and-Last|Rest]) :-          palinlength([First-and-Last|Rest]) :-
  apprel(Middle,[First-and-Last],Rest) &       apprel(Middle,[First-and-Last],Rest) &
  palinzoom(Middle).                           1+(1+(palinlength(Middle))).
```

Figure 5.1: Palindrome definitions

The palindrome clauses are non-footed but could be transcribed to the footed procedure

```
palindrome([]) :& true.
palindrome([Center]) :& true.
palindrome([First-and-Last|Rest]) :-
  apprel(Middle,[First-and-Last],Rest) &
  palindrome(Middle).
```

Here it gets explicit that the empty and singleton palindrome clauses discard their list-type information by both returning true. In palinclass this value becomes refined to the discriminative even and odd values.

The palinclass function can be further refined to the function palinzoom, which returns the listified central element of odd-length palindromes and, the empty list for even-length palindromes. Alternatively, palinclass can be refined to the palinlength function, returning the lengths of palindromes. Their sample I/O in Table 5.1 shows, e.g., the following: the non-ground call palinzoom([n,X,n]) returns the non-ground unit list [Center*4] and binds X to the renamed free variable Center*4; palinlength([n,X,n]) just returns the count 3. The bottom two definitions in Fig. 5.1 specify these behaviors.

Generalizing the relational translation of unconditionally defined, single-valued, deterministic functions in [Kow83], it is possible to represent each conditionally defined, multiple-valued, non-deterministic function by a flattened relation using $V$ extra arguments for binding the $V$ values that were returned by the function. This can be used for a RELFUN-to-PROLOG transformation of first-order functions to relations, which makes both PROLOG's model-theoretic semantics and compilation technology indirectly available for first-order REL-FUN. However, for non-invertible algorithms the additional arguments should carry an output-mode declaration, at variance with purely relational/functional programming. As a simple example, the unary, single-valued, deterministic, invertible, and already flat function palinclass, whose third defining clause is conditional, can be represented by the binary relation palinclass-r (the implemented `relationalize` transformation would introduce a new first rather than last argument):

```
palinclass-r([],even).
palinclass-r([Center],odd).
palinclass-r([First-and-Last|Rest],Class) :-
  apprel(Middle,[First-and-Last],Rest),
  palinclass-r(Middle,Class).
```

However, if the odd/even information is not often used its inclusion as an additional argument in a user relation `palinclass-r` would appear rather questionable, while its use as a returned function value of `palinclass` was quite natural:

1. `palinclass` can also be used as a unary **predicate** equivalent to `palindrome` by just ignoring the exact `true`-equivalent value in many contexts. The binary `palinclass-r` relation can only simulate this by 'absorbing' its second argument via an anonymous variable.

2. In the `palinclass` procedure only the two clauses actually returning additional information are affected by it; the third clause just "passes through" the recursively returned value without static (same source size) or dynamic (same WAM instructions) overhead over the third `palindrome` clause. In the `palinclass-r` procedure also the third clause requires a new argument, `Class` (a "permanent variable" occupying space in the local WAM stack), merely for handing on the recursively bound value.[9]

Even if the additional information is employed heavily, the normal use mode is from palindromes to their classes, not vice versa, which is best expressed by an explicit function. Should, however, the inverse use mode become necessary, the relational version can be called more naturally and efficiently, e.g. by `palinclass-r(Oddpalins,odd)`. The functional version would require REL-FUN's generalized is primitive ".=" (permitting arbitrary, non-arithmetic rhs calls) for inversion by fixing a lhs constant to be unified with the values enumerated via a non-ground rhs call, e.g. by `odd .= palinclass(Oddpalins)`. In general, RELFUN therefore offers both functional and relational styles of expression.

Both relations and functions may be defined such that they can also assume the truth-value `false`, e.g. to prevent a 'case exhaustion' unknown via a final 'catch-all' clause. For example, the original `palindrome` and `palinzoom` definitions may be modified and extended to the following `palind` and `palinz` operators:

---

[9]For a detailed comparison of value-returning and value-binding efficiency see [Hei89].

```
palind([]).
palind([Center]).
palind([First-and-Last|Rest]) :-
  apprel(Middle,[First-and-Last],Rest) !&
  palind(Middle).
palind([First,Second|Rest]) :& false.

palinz([]) :& [].              (alternatively  palinz([]).)
palinz([Center]) :& [Center].
palinz([First-and-Last|Rest]) :-
  apprel(Middle,[First-and-Last],Rest) !&
  palinz(Middle).
palinz([First,Second|Rest]) :& false.
```

The new fourth clauses return `false` for lists, perhaps found recursively, that are non-palindromes (non-list arguments still yield `unknown`). The third `palind` clause now also employs a "`&`", enforcing a `false` returned by the recursive call to become the value of the main call. The third clauses of both `palind` and `palinz` now use a cut operator "`!`", keeping the definitions deterministic, i.e. guarding lists with unifying first and last elements to fall into the fourth clauses should subsequent computation fail. In spite of this extra-logical aspect, such definitions provide a specification of an *operator-restricted closed-world assumption* (negative information is explicitly user-definable) for open-world systems like RELFUN, preferable to PROLOG's *global closed-world assumption* (negative information implicitly arises from each failure) (cf. chapter 2). Note that the empty list [] returned by the first `palinz` clause in RELFUN is truth-equivalent to `true`, hence distinct from the truth-value `false`, contrasting to the ambiguous `nil` in LISP. (The parenthesized alternative for even-length palindromes returns the truth-value `true` itself.)

While all palindrome versions are **defined** deterministically, it is possible to **call** them in a non-ground fashion giving rise to non-determinism. For example `palinzoom(X)` binds X to infinitely many palindrome-list patterns, alternatingly returning [] or a singleton-list pattern, whereas `palinz(X)`, because of the "`!`", stops this generation process after the non-ground palindrome [First-and-last*1, First-and-last*1].

Finally, suppose we wish to deterministically obtain both the lengths and centers of palindromes as sequences of two returned values. For this `palinlengthzoom` could be defined as a two-valued function that just applies `palinlength` as well as `palinzoom` to its argument:

```
palinlengthzoom(X) :& palinlength(X), palinzoom(X).
```

However, it is more efficient to recurse through the argument only once by merging the definitions of the above two foot-side calls:

```
palinlengthzoom([]) :& 0, [].
palinlengthzoom([Center]) :& 1, [Center].
palinlengthzoom([First-and-Last|Rest]) :-
  apprel(Middle,[First-and-Last],Rest) &
  addfrst2(palinlengthzoom(Middle)).
```

```
addfrst2(Frst,Scnd) :& 1+(1+(Frst)), Scnd.
```

Here, the first two `palinlengthzoom` clauses just denote the desired value sequences. The third clause applies an auxiliary **binary** function, `addfrst2`, to the **two** values returned from the recursion: the first `addfrst2` argument is incremented by 2 (cf. `palinlength`) and its second argument is left unchanged (cf. `palinzoom`).

Using the `multid` representation (5.13) of multiple-footed clauses in subsection 5.2.2, we can give the 1-footed simulation of the initial 2-footed `palinlengthzoom` version above (the refined version would call `multid` in its first two clauses):

```
palinlengthzoom(X) :& multid(palinlength(X),palinzoom(X)).
```

Instead of returning multiple values we might have defined a tuple-valued function `palinlengthzoomtup` equivalent to

```
palinlengthzoomtup(X) :& tup(palinlength(X),palinzoom(X)).
```

Using the `elements` function toward the end of subsection 5.2.2, we could still obtain our multiple-valued `palinlengthzoom` function:

```
palinlengthzoom(X) :& elems(palinlengthzoomtup(X)).
```

Conversely, for defining `palinlengthzoomtup`, we could employ tupling of returned `palinlengthzoom` sequences:

```
palinlengthzoomtup(X) :& tup(palinlengthzoom(X)).
```

Similarly, while a sequence like `[d],3`, returned by, say, `palinlengthzoom([a,d,a])` cannot be bound to a logical variable, say, `Res`, this variable can be `tup`-bound and later be `elems`-dereferenced, as in

```
Res .= tup(palinlengthzoom([a,d,a])) & elems(Res)
```

binding `Res` to `[[d],3]` and returning `[d],3`, or the sequence can be split into two single terms for variables `Res1,Res2` via the multiple-variable ".="-primitive at the end of subsection 5.2.2 and later be recombined, as in

```
(Res1,Res2) .= palinlengthzoom([a,d,a]) & Res1,Res2
```

binding Res1 and Res2 to [d] and 3, respectively, and again returning [d],3.

## 5.2.4  Higher-Order Functions and Relations

Some relational/functional higher-order operations can now be introduced on the basis of the palindrome examples. A more general explanation of higher-order clauses with the syntactic notion of *inconstant-operator clauses* will follow in section 5.3.4.

The four unary palindrome operators all follow a common recursion scheme that can be abstracted to a higher-order operator palin[...], where [...] contains three parameters denoting the value to be produced for the empty list, the function to be applied to a singleton list, and the function to be applied to recursive palindrome values:

```
palin[Emptyval,Singletonfun,Recursionfun]([]) :& Emptyval.
palin[Emptyval,Singletonfun,Recursionfun]([Center]) :&
    Singletonfun([Center]).
palin[Emptyval,Singletonfun,Recursionfun]([First-and-Last|Rest])
    :-
    apprel(Middle,[First-and-Last],Rest) &
    Recursionfun(palin[Emptyval,Singletonfun,Recursionfun](Middle)).
```

Suppose we also have defined the generally useful identity, constant, and twice (higher-order) functions by

```
id(A) :& A.
co[C](A) :& C.
twice[F](A) :& F(F(A)).
```

Now, instead of first-order operator calls such as palinclass([a,X,a]) we can parameterize palin for higher-order calls such as palin[even,co[odd],id]([a,X,a]), which via palin[even,co[odd],id]([X]) yields co[odd]([X]), i.e. returns odd.

Alternatively, we can define the original palindrome versions by four fixed palin parameterizations returned via function-valued clauses [palindrome etc. will be used as the short form of an argumentless call pattern palindrome() etc.]:

```
palindrome :& palin[true,co[true],id].
palinclass :& palin[even,co[odd],id].
```

```
palinzoom   :& palin[[],id,id].
palinlength :& palin[0,co[1],twice[1+]].
```

Here, e.g. palinclass([a,X,a]) or palinclass()([a,X,a]) first evaluates the operator, yielding palin[even,co[odd],id]([a,X,a]), which then evaluates as already shown.

Combining higher-orderness and multiple-valuedness, we can also define generally useful two-valued (higher-order) 'wiring' functions (for arbitrary single-valued, unary functions F, G), mapping values into sequences (fork) and sequences into sequences (juxtapose):[10]

```
fork[F,G](A) :& F(A), G(A).
jx[F,G](A,B) :& F(A), G(B).
```

These correspond to the operations $\langle F, G \rangle$ and $F \times G$ (written $F \| G$ in section 5.1) in [BL74], respectively, except that our sequences omit grouping parentheses. With the "parallel application" operator jx available, the variableless redefinition

```
addfrst2 :& jx[twice[1+],id].
```

of the auxiliary addfrst2 function in subsection 5.2.3 becomes possible, whose call in the third clause of the recursive palinlengthzoom definition may as well be unfolded, eliminating the need for a named addfrst2:

```
palinlengthzoom([First-and-Last|Rest]) :-
  apprel(Middle,[First-and-Last],Rest) &
  jx[twice[1+],id](palinlengthzoom(Middle)).
```

The higher-order palin operator can be generalized to multiple-valuedness by a new first clause, which expects a list in the Emptyval parameter, and, via elems (cf. subsection 5.2.2), transforms its elements into a sequence of values:

```
palin[Emptyval,Singletonfun,Recursionfun]([]) :& elems(Emptyval).
```

Employing the above fork function, the multiple-valued palinlengthzoom function itself can be redefined as a palin parameterization:

```
palinlengthzoom :& palin[[0,[]],fork[co[1],id],jx[twice[1+],id]].
```

---

[10] The direct application of any single-valued, binary function to its arguments, mapping sequences into values, can be regarded as the 'converse' to fork.

Note that the first and second `Emptyval` elements, `fork` parameters, and `jx` parameters exactly constitute the `palin` parameterization of `palinlength` and `palinzoom`, respectively.

Similarly, on the basis of a corresponding RELFUN half adder ha, the full adder depicted in section 5.1 can now be transcribed to RELFUN, writing $F\|G$ as `jx[F,G]`:

```
fa(A,B,Cin) :& jx[or,id](jx[id,ha](ha(A,B),Cin)).
```

The above higher-order clauses employ operators that are **structures** like `twice[F]` or **bound variables** like `F = 1+` in `F(F(A))`. In RELFUN it is also possible to employ operators that are **unbound variables** like `Property` in `Property([a,d,a])`. Given the clauses

```
femfirstname([a,d,a]).

langtrademark([a,d,a]).

palindrome([]).
palindrome([Center]).
palindrome(...) :- ...
```

this request can non-deterministically bind the *relation variable* `Property` three times, by 'extensionally', rather than $\lambda$-'intensionally', proving $(\exists Property)Property([a,d,a])$:

```
Property([a,d,a]).
↝
true
Property=femfirstname
↝
true
Property=langtrademark
↝
true
Property=palindrome
```

Similarly, with the clauses

```
femprogrammer([a,d,a]) :& lovelace.

langdeveloper([a,d,a]) :& [d,o,d].

palinlength([]) :& 0.
palinlength([Center]) :& 1.
palinlength(...) :- ...
```

a *function variable* Attribute can be non-deterministically bound three times, using corresponding proofs of $(\exists Attribute)(\exists Value)Attribute([a, d, a]) = Value$:

```
Attribute([a,d,a]).
```
⤳
```
lovelace
Attribute=femprogrammer
```
⤳
```
[d,o,d]
Attribute=langdeveloper
```
⤳
```
3
Attribute=palinlength
```

## 5.3 Relational/Functional WAM Compilation

A comparison of some of the specific problems in translating logic and functional as well as imperative languages can be found in [Wil89]. After a compilation overview, in the following subsection, we will discuss three transformational phases (subsections 5.3.2 through 5.3.4) and the final translation to WAM instructions (subsection 5.3.5).

### 5.3.1 A Compilation Strategy

Implementors of an amalgamated language like RELFUN could either extend functional compilation technology such as SECD and combinator machines toward relations or extend relational compilation technology such as the WAM toward functions. We chose the latter approach mainly because it nicely supports RELFUN's non-deterministic, non-ground, multiple-valued function concept discussed in section 5.2.1. (However, our extended WAM can be coupled with the functional LISP-light abstract machine for executing deterministic cases [Sin95].)

The main concern, then, was how to extend the WAM [War83] for functional value returning. Our initial approach was the introduction of one additional register, VALREG, as the "channel" for returning and fetching single values. WAM instructions for doing this have been implemented in LISP [Hei89]. Our second approach, the one being pursued here, is to use the existing temporary register X1 for the same purpose. Value returning and fetching can then be done by using existing put and get instructions. The reason why VALREG can be identified with X1 is that value returning occurs as the last action of clauses, at which time X1 is no longer needed for argument passing.[11] Using X1 for both the returned

---

[11]However, the last action can begin with the first instruction: in the optimization of

value and the first argument permits an important optimization of 1-argument nestings: the embedded function can directly put its value into the argument register of the main operator. Furthermore, X-register value returning can be generalized naturally to multiple-footed rules, whose $V$ values can be put into the consecutive registers $X1,...,XV$, again directly getable by a $V$-argument operator.

The next important issue was how to compile the nesting of an arbitrary number of function calls within a main call. For single-valued functions, this problem was already solved transformationally by *static flattening* with RELFUN's generalized is primitive [Bol86], now written ".=": a new variable replaces each nested call, associated with it by an ".="-primitive conjoined to the left of the main call. This solution was extended to nested multiple-valued functions.

Another preparatory compilation phase, akin to flattening, is *denotative normalization*, which initially transforms evaluative foots to variables and ".="-bodies.

The most involved part is how to compile RELFUN's higher-order clauses (e.g., with a variable or structure (e.g., a parameterized name) as head operator). We initially considered two approaches:

1. A transformer can reduce all (higher-order) operators to arguments by introducing a new operator ap, generalizing the relational apply in [War82].

2. The compiler can label all (higher-order) clauses of the same arity as an additional procedure, which for calls of matching arity gets the actual operator (before the actual arguments) via a new *operator register* X0 (before X1,...), put there prior to the calls.

We will elaborate approach 1. here, since this *constant-operator reduction* is much simpler than the direct "inconstant-operator WAM" approach 2., but still can be efficient if the underlying indexing mechanism exploits the first two arguments, as enabled, e.g., by RELFUN's command indexing :max-depth 2 [Sin93a]. Our current GWAM [Sin95] refinement of approach 1. introduces an apply primitive only for **variables** as operators, but also 'splices' **structures** as operators into the operand list such that a structure's constructor becomes the new operator and its arguments become extra initial operands.

Fig. 5.2 sequentializes the above phases into the compilation strategy elaborated in the following subsections. This is a didactic presentation simplifying certain aspects of the running compiler; e.g., the pure-LISP implementation of some transformation systems introduces further applicability restrictions or special-case treatments. Beyond that, the denotative normalizer, static flattener, and constant-operator reducer could be employed in different orders or,

---

'constructor-like' bodiless rules such as cns(H,T):&[H|T] a VALREG/X1 separation would allow to "put_list" the cell for [H|T] immediately to VALREG, unifying the arguments X1=H and X2=T into it, in order to save one transfer from an auxiliary X3 to the value register.

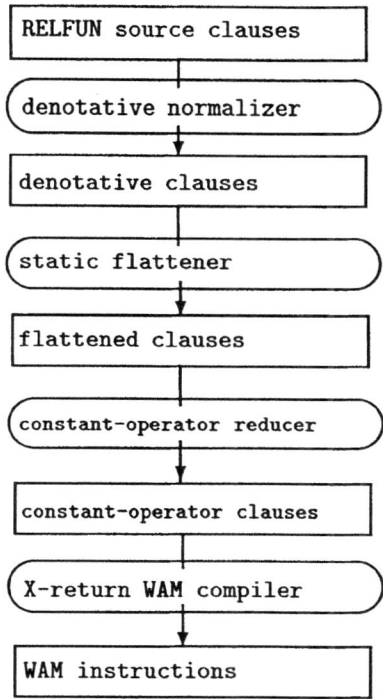

Figure 5.2: Compilation phases

indeed, be integrated to a single preprocessing phase, which itself could later be combined with the WAM compiler.

In the following subsections we will not detail on the compilation of multiple foots that generate varying-length value sequences as, e.g., exhibited by the introductory upa example or a multid without fixed arities. For WAM procedures the **fixed** "return arity" of multiple-footed clauses will be specified explicitly (after a "+" behind the PROLOG-usual "argument arity"). Thus, if f has one argument plus two values, e.g. f(W) :& b,c, and g has four arguments plus one value, then, as formalized in subsection 5.3.3, the 3-argument nesting g(a,f(b),d) expands to the 4-argument call g(a,b,c,d), as indicated by the arity specification g/4+1(a,f/1+2(b),d) or, omitting 1-return arities, g/4(a,f/1+2(b),d). Also, the ".="-call (K,L) .= f(a) expands to (K,L) .= (b,c), as indicated by (K,L) .= f/1+2(a). (The compiler could produce a static unknown for nestings or ".="-calls without such arity conformity.) Since fixed arities will continue to be inferable from the context, in the following we will provide arity specifications only when needed for formal or explanatory reasons. (**Varying** argument arity, as in the RELFUN interpreter, or even, return arity, as implemented, e.g., by our earlier FIT interpreter, RELFUN/X, and via REL-FUN's `singlify` reduction, in the WAM would require an additional register, `XMAX`, for passing the **actual** argument or return arity.)

## 5.3.2   Evaluative Foots and Denotative Normalization

Clauses can always be *(true-)footed* by appending the constant foot `true` to Hornish rules, so that they assume the explicitly `true`-footed form (5.5) of section 5.2.2 (leaving all other clauses unchanged). This leads to the *(true-)footened normal form* consisting of facts and footed rules, as used for uniformness in compilation or its presentation.

A formula is *denotative* iff it is a term, i.e. a constant (e.g. `john`), a variable (e.g. `Who` or `_1`), a structure (e.g. `children[john,Who]`), or a list (e.g. `[Who,[],Who]`). A formula is *evaluative* iff it is an application (e.g. `children(john,Who)`) or it is a setter, i.e. an ".="-primitive call (e.g. `_1 .= john`). An empty-/non-footed clause is always (implicitly `void`-/`true`-) denotative. A footed clause is denotative iff all its foots are denotative. (Thus, a molecular clause is denotative by definition; cf. section 5.2.2.) Any other clause is evaluative.

Clauses can always be made denotative by replacing evaluative foots of footed clauses by variables (leaving footless clauses unchanged). The resulting *denotative normal form* is an intermediate step for compiling multiple-footed rules (see below) and also simplifies the presentation of flattening (see subsection 5.3.3).

The *footened, denotative form*, then, is just the (disjoint) combination of the footened and denotative forms.

**Footening** is trivial: for instance, the (implicitly `true`-) denotative Hornish rule

```
parental(P) :- cares(P,child[P,Q]).
```

becomes normalized to the following (explicitly `true`-) denotative footed rule:[12]

```
parental(P) :- cares(P,child[P,Q]) & true.
```

---

[12] If performed indiscriminately, footening prevents the last-call optimization in the WAM (here, `parental` cannot just jump to, or `execute`, `cares` since it still has to put_constant true). In order to avoid this, footening should, in practice, only be performed on Hornish rules for which it cannot be assured that the last premise (here, `cares`) on success will itself return `true`. If, however, this 'true-return' property can be established for a Hornish rule, it should be 'foot-optimized', i.e. transformed into a footed rule reusing the last (relational) premise as its (functional) foot (here obtaining `parental(P) :& cares(P,child[P,Q])`). While in general this requires global analysis, for the important special case of tail-recursion optimization the analysis can be confined to individual procedures. Benchmark results for the latter case can be found in [Hei91].

**Denotative normalization** of footed clauses can be defined by a system of two rewrite rule schemata:

$$
\begin{aligned}
&\ldots \; \colon\!\!- \; \ldots \; \& \; \ldots, t_0/m{+}v\,(t_1,...,t_m),\ldots \qquad\qquad\qquad\qquad (5.1)\\
&\longrightarrow \quad \ldots \; \colon\!\!- \; \ldots, (\_\mathcal{G}_1,...,\_\mathcal{G}_v) \, .= t_0/m{+}v\,(t_1,...,t_m) \; \& \; \ldots, \_\mathcal{G}_1,...,\_\mathcal{G}_v,\ldots\\[4pt]
&\ldots \; \colon\!\!- \; \ldots \; \& \; \ldots, (p_1,...,p_v) \, .= q,\ldots \qquad\qquad\qquad\qquad\quad (5.2)\\
&\longrightarrow \quad \ldots \; \colon\!\!- \; \ldots, (p_1,...,p_v) \, .= q \; \& \; \ldots, p_1,...,p_v,\ldots
\end{aligned}
$$

Each pair of $\mathcal{G}_j$ occurrences in rewrite schema (1) stands for occurrences of an integer $1, 2, \ldots$ generated such that the variable $\_\mathcal{G}_j$ is not yet used in the clause. For $v=0$, $\_\mathcal{G}_1,...,\_\mathcal{G}_0$ denotes the empty sequence and the generated $()\,.= t_0/m+0\,(t_1,...,t_m)$ or $\texttt{void}\,.= t_0/m+0\,(t_1,...,t_m)$ can be simplified to $t_0/m+0\,(t_1,...,t_m)$.

Let us discuss our multiple-valued version of the well-known `divide` operator, whose form is similar to `palinlengthzoom` in section 5.2.3, but which is binary instead of unary: given single-valued functions `quotient/2+1` and `remainder/2+1`, the 2-valued function `divide/2+2` returning the quotient and remainder, in that order, could be defined by the following bodiless, 2-footed evaluative rule (both of whose foots are evaluative; more efficient versions will follow in subsection 5.3.3):[13]

```
divide(N,D) :& quotient(N,D), remainder(N,D).
```

Two applications of the above rewrite schema (1), with $v=1$ and $(\_\mathcal{G}_1)\,.= \ldots$ abbreviated to $\_\mathcal{G}_1\,.= \ldots$, give us an equivalent 2-bodied, 2-footed denotative rule:[14]

```
divide(N,D) :- _1 .= quotient(N,D), _2 .= remainder(N,D) & _1, _2.
```

If denotative normalization precedes WAM compilation, the code returning

---

[13]For two arguments `11,3` this again returns two values `3,2`; hence it can be self-nested as in `divide(divide(11,3))` $\rightsquigarrow$ `divide(3,2)` $\rightsquigarrow$ `1,1`. In the corresponding WAM instructions, the inner `divide` call would put the constant 3 into the temporary register X1 and 2 into X2; the outer call could directly get these register settings as its actual arguments.

[14]Such a denotative normal form of a multiple-footed function (with fixed return arity) could be easily further transformed to a relation without transforming subfunction definitions, which exhibits the relation-like I/O symmetry of functions once they permit multiple values: `divide-r(N,D,_1,_2) :- _1 .= quotient(N,D), _2 .= remainder(N,D).` With result variables inserted at the beginning rather than the end of argument sequences, this transformation would become part of a multiple-valued extension of RELFUN's `relationalize` algorithm, whose use was discussed in connection with the `palinclass-palinclass-r` transformation in section 5.2.3.

values (in the foot premises) can follow strictly after any (body) code containing `call` instructions, so in the example the `remainder` call cannot overwrite the `quotient` value in X1: the foots just put the `quotient` value from _1 to X1 and the `remainder` value from _2 to X2.

Since on `calling` the first foot no other foot values (that could become over-written) are returned yet, it is sufficient to use a *rest-denotative normal form* for returning multiple values, i.e. only replacing foots after the first one (which thus becomes the last one to be evaluated in the usual left-to-right order, a change that is irrelevant for the pure language considered here). In the example this leads to a 1-bodied, 2-footed evaluative rule:

```
divide(N,D) :- _1 .= remainder(N,D) & quotient(N,D), _1.
```

Here, the foot call of `quotient` would implicitly put the first `divide` value to X1, while the `remainder` value would be explicitly put from _1 to X2.[15]

If a foot is itself a call to a multiple-valued function, e.g. to `divide`, the above rewrite schema (1) replaces it by as many consecutive variables as required for this call's number of returned values. (The schema achieves this by 'transporting' $v$ from $t_0/m+v$ to $\_\mathcal{G}_v$.) Also, the corresponding ".="-body associates the entire variable sequence with the multiple-valued call, now needing the generality of the multiple-variable ".="-primitive of section 5.2.2.

For example, the `divide/2+2` function could be used to define a 5-valued `divtab/2+5` function for tabulating divisions in the form *nominator, denominator, yield, quotient, remainder*. Its bodiless, 4-footed evaluative rule

```
divtab(N,D) :& N, D, yield, divide(N,D).
```

via one application of rewrite schema (1), with $v=2$, is (denotatively and rest-denotatively) normalized to the 1-bodied, 5-footed denotative rule

```
divtab(N,D) :- (_1,_2) .= divide(N,D) & N, D, yield, _1, _2.
```

---

[15] Although the rest-denotative form of such a multiple-footed rule calls only one evaluative foot, this cannot be simply compiled as an **execute**, implementing the last-call optimization, because the rule still has to perform one or more puts. However, another optimization for arbitrary multiple-footed rules (not needing denotative normalization) may result from introducing a kind of relative addressing for the X-register sequence, administrating it analogously to the indented lines of a pretty printer: the first register for argument passing, internal processing, and value returning could be moved before subprocedure calls from X1 to some X*I*, with $I > 1$, by incrementing a base register such that each foot of a multiple-footed rule would write its value(s) to registers immediately to the right of the results of its predecessor (the contents of X1 through X*I-1* remaining intact); before returning (via **proceed**), the base register would be decremented by the sum of the rule's increments.

Note that denotative normalization is incompatible with the single-footed `multid` representation (5.13) in section 5.2.2, because `multid` makes clauses evaluative while the denotative form makes `multid` clauses multiple-footed:

```
divide(N,D)  :& multid(quotient(N,D),remainder(N,D)).                  % (a)

divide(N,D)  :- (_1, _2) .= multid(quotient(N,D),remainder(N,D)) &     % (b)
                                                          _1, _2.      %

divide(N,D)  :- _1 .= quotient(N,D), _2 .= remainder(N,D) & _1, _2.    % (c)

divide(N,D)  :- _1 .= quotient(N,D), _2 .= remainder(N,D) &            % (d)
                                                   multid(_1,_2).      %
```

If the `multid` form (a) of the original `divide` example is put into denotative form, the result is again multiple-footed (b). If this (b) or its single-variable ".="-equivalent (c), the original's denotative form, is (again) put into `multid` form, the result is (again) evaluative (d). The direct transformation from (a) to (d), however, can be regarded as a special case of flattening, our next issue.

## 5.3.3   Non-deterministic, Multiple-Valued Nestings and Static Flattening

A formula is *flat* iff it is denotative or it is evaluative and has only denotative subformulas. Otherwise it is *nested*. A clause is flat iff all its premises are flat. Otherwise it is nested. In particular, a denotative clause is flat iff its body is flat (since it can have only denotative foots, see subsection 5.3.2).

Clauses can always be flattened by recursively replacing evaluative subformulas by variables. In the resulting *flattened clauses* the subformulas to be evaluated become ".="-rhs formulas, which simplifies their call-by-value reduction. Since a nesting of evaluative subformulas leads to a conjunction of ".="-calls, *non-deterministic subformulas* can be managed by the WAM's standard backtracking techniques, thus avoiding the direct handling of non-deterministic nestings.

If we assume that clauses are in footened, denotative form (subsection 5.3.2), saving explicit treatment of nested Hornish rules and of foot-side nestings, static flattening can be defined by five rewrite rule schemata:

144

$$\ldots \; :- \; \ldots, s_0(s_1, \ldots, s_{i-1}, t_0/m{+}v\,(t_1, \ldots, t_m), s_{i+1}, \ldots, s_n), \ldots \; \& \; \ldots \qquad (5.1)$$
$$\longrightarrow \quad \ldots \; :- \; \ldots, (\_G_1, \ldots, \_G_v)\,.= t_0/m{+}v\,(t_1, \ldots, t_m),$$
$$s_0(s_1, \ldots, s_{i-1}, \_G_1, \ldots, \_G_v, s_{i+1}, \ldots, s_n), \ldots \; \& \; \ldots$$

$$\ldots \; :- \; \ldots, s_0(s_1, \ldots, s_{i-1}, (p_1, \ldots, p_v)\,.= q, s_{i+1}, \ldots, s_n), \ldots \; \& \; \ldots \qquad (5.2)$$
$$\longrightarrow \quad \ldots \; :- \; \ldots, (p_1, \ldots, p_v)\,.= q,\; s_0(s_1, \ldots, s_{i-1}, p_1, \ldots, p_v, s_{i+1}, \ldots, s_n), \ldots \; \& \; \ldots$$

$$\ldots \; :- \; \ldots, (r_1, \ldots, r_w)\,.= s_0(s_1, \ldots, s_{i-1}, t_0/m{+}v\,(t_1, \ldots, t_m), s_{i+1}, \ldots, s_n), \ldots \; \& \; \ldots$$
$$\longrightarrow \quad \ldots \; :- \; \ldots, (\_G_1, \ldots, \_G_v)\,.= t_0/m{+}v\,(t_1, \ldots, t_m), \qquad (5.3)$$
$$(r_1, \ldots, r_w)\,.= s_0(s_1, \ldots, s_{i-1}, \_G_1, \ldots, \_G_v, s_{i+1}, \ldots, s_n), \ldots \; \& \; \ldots$$

$$\ldots \; :- \; \ldots, (r_1, \ldots, r_w)\,.= s_0(s_1, \ldots, s_{i-1}, (p_1, \ldots, p_v)\,.= q, s_{i+1}, \ldots, s_n), \ldots \; \& \; \ldots \quad (5.4)$$
$$\longrightarrow \quad \ldots \; :- \; \ldots, (p_1, \ldots, p_v)\,.= q,$$
$$(r_1, \ldots, r_w)\,.= s_0(s_1, \ldots, s_{i-1}, p_1, \ldots, p_v, s_{i+1}, \ldots, s_n), \ldots \; \& \; \ldots$$

$$\ldots \; :- \; \ldots, (r_1, \ldots, r_w)\,.= ((p_1, \ldots, p_w)\,.= q), \ldots \; \& \; \ldots \qquad (5.5)$$
$$\longrightarrow \quad \ldots \; :- \; \ldots, (p_1, \ldots, p_w)\,.= q,\; (r_1, \ldots, r_w)\,.= (p_1, \ldots, p_w), \ldots \; \& \; \ldots$$

$\_G_j$ again stands for a new variable generated on each application of schemata (1) and (3). For $v=0$, the void-lhs ".="-call can again be simplified to its rhs. In schemata (1)-(4) the operator $s_0$ may itself be an evaluative formula because the position $i$ of subformula substitutions is understood to range from 0 to $n$.[16] The ".="-primitives transformed by schemata (3) and (4) may have been generated by applications of schemata (1) and (2), and later, of schemata (3) and (4) themselves; those transformed by schema (5) may have been generated by schemata (2) and (4), and later, (5).

To illustrate these concepts, we can employ child as an undefined binary functor or **constructor** in **structures** like child[P,Q], just **denoting** P and Q's children. An embedding of such a denotative formula into an evaluative formula leaves the main formula flat. Thus, the cares body of the footened form

```
parental(P) :- cares(P,child[P,Q]) & true.
```

in subsection 5.3.2 cannot be transformed by the above rewrite system. Instead, a request like parental(john) will directly evaluate the request cares(john,child[john,Q]), which may succeed using a monolithic fact like cares(john,child[john,mary]).

---

[16]This is important for operator evaluation in a higher-order call like palinclass()([a,X,a]) of section 5.2.4, which flattens to _1 .= palinclass(), _1([a,X,a]): _1 = palin[even,co[odd],id] is the actual operator value.

However, we can also employ `child` as a binary **operator** defined by

```
child(john,lucy) :& ann.
child(john,mary) :& bob.
```

in **calls** like `child(P,Q)`, **evaluating** to P and Q's children. An embedding of such an evaluative formula into another evaluative formula makes the main formula nested. Thus, the `cares` body of the footened form (cf. subsection 5.3.2)

```
parental(P) :- cares(P,child(P,Q)) & true.
```

will be flattened by one application of the above schema (1), with $v=1$ and single-variable ".="-syntax:

```
parental(P) :- _1 .= child(P,Q), cares(P,_1) & true.
```

Using the flat body, a request like `parental(john)` initially evaluates the ".="-rhs `child(john,Q)`, which may non-deterministically return the solutions `ann` or `bob` (binding Q to `lucy` or `mary`, respectively). Going through a _1-binding, the first value leads to the request `cares(john,ann)`. This request would fail if we suppose there is only a fact `cares(john,bob)`. But backtracking on the flat conjunction can easily reactivate the ".="-rhs. It now returns the second value, which finally leads to the successful request `cares(john,bob)`.

As an example of a deeper (yet deterministic) nesting consider the second clause of the factorial definition

```
fac(0) :& 1.
fac(N) :- >(N,0) & *(N,fac(1-(N))).
```

Its second clause's denotative form (cf. subsection 5.3.2)

```
fac(N) :- >(N,0), _1 .= *(N,fac(1-(N))) & _1.
```

can be flattened by two applications of rewrite schema (3), both again with $v=1$:

```
fac(N) :- >(N,0), _3 .= 1-(N), _2 .= fac(_3), _1 .= *(N,_2) & _1.
```

A flattened form of evaluative bodiless, 1-footed rules, e.g. of the original second `fac` clause, can be obtained easily (disregarding variable names) from their flattened denotative form by resubstituting the foot variable, here _1:

```
fac(N) :- >(N,0), _3 .= 1-(N), _2 .= fac(_3) & *(N,_2).
```

Since on WAM-calling[17] the first subformula of a formula no other subformula values (that could become overwritten) are returned yet, it is sufficient to use *rest-flattened clauses* in analogy to the rest-denotative normal form of subsection 5.3.2. Here, only the second and later subformulas are replaced by flattening variables. For example, this is a 1-footed, list-valued version of divide (using the tup function toward the end of section 5.2.2 to make one term from two values), along with its flattened and rest-flattened forms:

```
divide(N,D) :& tup(quotient(N,D),remainder(N,D)).
divide(N,D) :- _1 .= quotient(N,D), _2 .= remainder(N,D) &
                                                   tup(_1,_2).
divide(N,D) :- _1 .= remainder(N,D) & tup(quotient(N,D),_1).
```

In the last form, the call to the quotient subformula would implicitly put the first tup argument to X1, while the remainder value would be explicitly put from _1 to X2.

An important, degenerated case is the rest flattening of unary nestings: since there is only one subformula, they need not be flattened at all. The WAM register X1 thus acts as a fast "communication channel" from the subformula to the main formula of such an operator nesting, comparable to the top of the call stack in functional machines. In deeper nestings this leads to chains of consecutive calls, each expecting its argument in X1 and returning its value to X1. A simple example is the rest-flattened form of the second factorial clause, which needs only one new variable for a subformula of the binary * call, none for the subformula of the recursive unary fac call:

```
fac(N) :- >(N,0), _1 .= fac(1-(N)) & *(N,_1).
```

This form is perhaps better readable than the original form ("... let _1 be factorial of N-1 ...") and certainly more efficiently compiled than the flattened form ("...; invoke 1- on X1=N; call fac on X1=N-1; get _1 from X1=(N-1)!; ..."). Its actual WAM instructions (avoiding even _1) will be given in subsection 5.3.5.

As for multiple-valued foots, if an embedding is itself a call to a multiple-valued function, e.g. to divide, the flattening schemata (1) and (3) replace it by as many consecutive variables as needed for this call's number of returned values. Again, the corresponding ".="-body associates the entire variable sequence with the multiple-valued call, using the multiple-variable ".="-primitive (cf. section 5.2.2). For example, the divide/2+2 function may be given a direct 2-value-recursive definition (more efficient than calling quotient and remainder, assuming these are not built-ins) on the basis of an addfrst1/2+2 auxiliary inspired by palinlengthzoom/1+2 (cf. section 5.2.3):

---

[17]The term 'call' is employed here generically, encompassing the WAM instruction call and its optimized relatives **execute** (for last calls) and **invoke** (used here for built-in calls).

```
divide(N,D) :- <(N,D) & 0, N.
divide(N,D) :- >=(N,D) & addfrst1(divide(-(N,D),D)).

addfrst1(Frst,Scnd) :& 1+(Frst), Scnd.
```

We can put its second clause, with the 2-valued `divide` embedding, into denotative form (cf. subsection 5.3.2):

```
divide(N,D) :- >=(N,D), (_1,_2) .= addfrst1(divide(-(N,D),D)) &
                                                          _1, _2.
```

This can be initially flattened by one application of rewrite schema (3), with
$v=2$, via another 2-variable ".="-call:

```
divide(N,D) :- >=(N,D), (_3,_4) .= divide(-(N,D),D),
                        (_1,_2) .= addfrst1(_3,_4) & _1, _2.
```

Resubstituting the variable-sequence foot we obtain

```
divide(N,D) :- >=(N,D), (_3,_4) .= divide(-(N,D),D) &
                                              addfrst1(_3,_4).
```

It happens that the flat `addfrst1` premise can now be unfolded, leading (with
mnemonic ".="-variable names) to an even more elementary, rest-denotative
definition of `divide`, without utilizing `addfrst1` or its higher-order replacement
`jx[1+,id]` (cf. section 5.2.4):

```
divide(N,D) :- <(N,D) & 0, N.
divide(N,D) :- >=(N,D), (Q,R) .= divide(-(N,D),D) & 1+(Q), R.
```

Then, after complete flattening (also possible without unfolding) the second
clause becomes

```
divide(N,D) :- >=(N,D), _1 .= -(N,D), (Q,R) .= divide(_1,D) &
                                                          1+(Q), R.
```

Finally, non-deterministic and multiple-valued nesting can be orthogonally
combined without additional problems (backtracking can reactivate the rhs of a
multiple-variable ".=").

## 5.3.4  Higher-Order Clauses and Constant-Operator Reduction

A formula is *constant-operator* iff it is denotative or it is evaluative and uses a constant as operator and constant-operator subformulas as arguments. Otherwise, if some variable, structure, or evaluative formula is used in an operator position, the formula is *inconstant-operator*. A clause is constant-operator iff its head uses a constant operator[18] and all its premises are constant-operator. Otherwise the clause is inconstant-operator.

The notion of inconstant-operator clauses is a syntactic characterization of an (apply-reducible, $\lambda$-variableless) subset of relational/functional higher-order definitions: inconstant-operator clauses, unlike constant-operator clauses, call (bound or unbound) 'predicate' variables, structures (representing FP-like "program-forming operations" [Bac78]), or (values of) evaluative formulas in their premises, or are themselves defined with a variable or structure as their head operator.

Not included in the inconstant-operator subset are, e.g., simple higher-order relations like `transitive` as defined by constant-operator facts like `transitive(ancestor)`, whose second-order characteristics is dependent on ancestor's status as a first-order relation (as opposed to using it as an individual). On the other hand, the following two examples are inconstant-operator clauses:

The variable `Rel` can be defined as a higher-order relation, 'typed' to be `transitive`, by the variable-head-operator rule

```
Rel(A,C) :- transitive(Rel), Rel(A,B), Rel(B,C).
```

The structure `compose[Fun1,Fun2]` can be defined as a higher-order function by the structure-head-operator rule

```
compose[Fun1,Fun2](A) :& Fun1(Fun2(A)).
```

In general, RELFUN uses a term representation of operators, where each term (e.g. variable or structure) may play both the role of an operator and of an operand. This very much eases the higher-to-first-order transformation below.

Clauses can always be made constant-operator by introducing a new operator constant, which relegates all (non-primitive) operators to the first operand position. In the resulting *constant-operator-reduced clauses* evaluative formulas keep variables, structures, and embedded evaluative formulas only as arguments, which greatly simplifies their WAM compilation.

---

[18]Apart from `op :-...`, shortcutting `op() :-...`, clause heads cannot be denotative themselves but, because of RELFUN's "constructor discipline" [O'D85], clause-head arguments must always be denotative.

We assume that clauses are in footened, denotative form (subsection 5.3.2) and flattened (subsection 5.3.3), saving explicit treatment of Hornish rules, foot-side evaluative formulas, and body-side evaluative subformulas; constant-operator reduction can then be defined by four rewrite rule schemata:

$$h_0(h_1, ..., h_k). \tag{5.1}$$
$$\longrightarrow \quad \mathcal{A}(h_0, h_1, ..., h_k).$$

$$h_0(h_1, ..., h_k) \; :- \; ... \; \& \; .... \tag{5.2}$$
$$\longrightarrow \quad \mathcal{A}(h_0, h_1, ..., h_k) \; :- \; ... \; \& \; ....$$

$$... \; :- \; ..., t_0(t_1, ..., t_m), ... \; \& \; .... \tag{5.3}$$
$$\longrightarrow \quad ... \; :- \; ..., \mathcal{A}(t_0, t_1, ..., t_m), ... \; \& \; ....$$

$$... \; :- \; ..., (r_1, ..., r_v) \; . = t_0(t_1, ..., t_m), ... \; \& \; .... \tag{5.4}$$
$$\longrightarrow \quad ... \; :- \; ..., (r_1, ..., r_v) \; . = \mathcal{A}(t_0, t_1, ..., t_m), ... \; \& \; ....$$

$\mathcal{A}$ stands for an operator name (conventionally, ap) unique for the entire clause set to be transformed. The rewrite schemata are applied only under the following condition: the operator transformed into the first argument must not be $\mathcal{A}$ itself, i.e. $h_0 \neq \mathcal{A}$, in schemata (1) and (2), and $t_0 \neq \mathcal{A}$, in schemata (3) and (4).[19]

The above fact transitive(ancestor), second-order though constant-operator, is transformed to the apply form ap(transitive,ancestor) by schema (1), so that it can be called from the ap form of the above Rel rule.

This flat, footless (actually, Hornish), variable-head-operator rule, transcribed to footened form (denotativeness being preserved), yields a constant-operator version by one application of schema (2) and three applications of schema (3):

```
Rel(A,C) :- transitive(Rel), Rel(A,B), Rel(B,C) & true.
ap(Rel,A,C) :- ap(transitive,Rel), ap(Rel,A,B), ap(Rel,B,C) & true.
```

Similarly, the nested, bodiless, structure-head-operator rule, transformed to flattened, denotative form (footening being unnecessary), yields a constant-operator version by one application of schema (2) and two applications of schema (4):

---

[19]If the rewrite rules are reformulated in an algorithmic one-pass fashion, as done in the actual implementation, a single ap can be inserted where necessary, without need for any uniqueness or inequality checks.

150

```
compose[Fun1,Fun2](A) :- _2 .= Fun2(A), _1 .= Fun1(_2) & _1.
ap(compose[Fun1,Fun2],A) :- _2 .= ap(Fun2,A), _1 .= ap(Fun1,_2) &
                                                               _1.
```

In the constant-operator versions the operator variables Rel, Fun1, and Fun2 as well as the operator structure compose[Fun1,Fun2] are all relegated to first-operand positions.

Constant-operator forms not based on denotative normalization or even flattening can be obtained by resubstitution, starting, e.g., from the last compose version:

```
ap(compose[Fun1,Fun2],A) :- _2 .= ap(Fun2,A) & ap(Fun1,_2).
ap(compose[Fun1,Fun2],A) :& ap(Fun1,ap(Fun2,A)).
```

Finally, let us consider a constant-operator version of the palin example of section 5.2.4. It can be obtained by applying the schemata (2)-(4) to the usual preprocessed form and then keeping flattening but resubstituting denotative normalization. In this version of Fig. 5.3 the higher-order function palin is sufficiently prepared for translation to WAM instructions.[20]

```
ap(palin[Emptyval,Singletonfun,Recursionfun],[]) :& Emptyval.
ap(palin[Emptyval,Singletonfun,Recursionfun],[Center]) :&
  ap(Singletonfun,[Center]).
ap(palin[Emptyval,Singletonfun,Recursionfun],[First-and-Last|Rest])
  :-
  ap(apprel,Middle,[First-and-Last],Rest),
  _2 .= ap(palin[Emptyval,Singletonfun,Recursionfun],Middle) &
  ap(Recursionfun,_2).

ap(id,A) :& A.
ap(co[C],A) :& C.
ap(twice[F],A) :- _2 .= ap(F,A) & ap(F,_2).
```

Figure 5.3: The ap version of palin

---

[20]Constant-operator reduction also affects calls that already used a constant operator such as the transitive call in the Rel rule and the apprel call in Fig. 5.3. This works since the user definition of such operators is also ap-reduced by the rewrite schemata. Alternatively, we could consider all constant-operator procedures such as the usual apprel definition as 'elementals', whose definitions are not accessible to the ap transformation (as achievable by RELFUN's module system). Instead, for each elemental the constant-operator reducer must generate one new clause, here ap(apprel,L1,L2,L3) :& apprel(L1,L2,L3). It could then also leave constant-operator calls unchanged: the ap reduction of variable-operator calls would handle all higher-order uses of a constant operator (apprel may be passed as an argument and then be called via this bound variable), and only for such ap calls would an elemental need its newly generated ap clause. The efficiency advantage of this reducer variant increases with the percentage of pre-existing constant-operator clauses. To obtain still more efficiency, our implemented GWAM [Sin95] introduces an apply version only for variable-operator calls.

## 5.3.5 Translation to WAM Instructions

The WAM instructions employed here will abandon the distinguished naming of "argument (A) registers" in [War83], but refer to Warren's *temporary (X) registers* both for specifying argument passing and temporary processing. Indeed, we will extend the usage of the temporary registers (X1, X2, ..., X$V$) to a third task: permitting RELFUN clauses to return $V$ values. This generalization makes X-register use symmetrical with respect to input arguments, internal auxiliaries, and output values. However, for the single-valued clauses dealt with here, only X1 will be needed for value returning.

The instructions will be named as in [GLLO85], but with the regular X/Y-registers counted from 1, not 0 (X0 is reserved as an operator register, not yet needed here). For readability, *permanent (Y) registers* will be referred to by their source variable names, assuming a 'trimmable' name–Y$I$ association.

After the rest-denotative normalization presupposed here, the single (remaining) evaluative foot and the evaluative body-side premises can be compiled uniformly: we let **all** evaluative premises, from left to right, return their value(s) to X1,...,X$V_i$, so that the last one (the evaluative foot) overwrites X1,...,X$V$ for the final value(s). (Intermediate ".="-premises can communicate their value(s) to later premises in a similar manner: a compiled (multiple-variable) ".="-rhs returns its value(s) to X1,...,X$V_i$, subsequently fetchable there by its compiled lhs.) Since non-footed clauses can be rewritten as true-footed clauses we do not consider them here, with one exception: for facts the compiler inserts the final instruction proctrue as a short form of the two instructions put_constant true, X1; proceed.

All kinds of put instructions of the form put_$\mathcal{K}$ $k$, X1 except for $\mathcal{K}$ = y_variable can be reinterpreted as value-returning instructions; in particular, put_x_variable X1, X1 returns an anonymous (free) variable, and put_structure f/$N$, X1 returns a structure with constructor f/$N$, to be filled by $N$ subsequent unify instructions. Similarly, all kinds of get instructions of the form get_$\mathcal{K}$ $k$, X1 can be reinterpreted as value-fetching instructions; in particular, with get_y_variable and get_x_variable the value from X1 is fetched into permanent and temporary free variables.

Single-variable ".="-calls, $p$ .= $q$, can be translated by just translating $q$ and then using an instruction get_$\mathcal{K}$ $k$, X1 for $k$-fetching the value that $q$ returned to X1 ($k$ transcribes the source lhs $p$ and $\mathcal{K}$ represents the corresponding kind of get).

Let us now proceed to **functional WAM-register reuse** as the keystone of our extended WAM code generation for (non-ground, non-deterministic) functional programming.

Consider the transition from 'relational' instructions for a fact to corresponding 'functional' instructions for a 1-footed rule, taking the first factorial clause as an example. While the relational version **gets** two arguments and just `proctrue`s, the functional version only **gets** one argument but **puts** a non-trivial value:

```
fac(0,1).
```

```
fac/2: get_constant 0,X1
       get_constant 1,X2
       proctrue
```

```
fac(0) :& 1.
```

```
fac/1: get_constant 0,X1
       put_constant 1,X1
       proceed
```

The compilation of functional nestings can always be done using flattening variables and the ".="-primitive. For first-argument (incl. unary) nestings, however, a returned value can be left directly in the X1-argument of the main formula. Both situations can be illustrated with the rest-flattened form of the second functional factorial clause (cf. subsection 5.3.3), transferring the recursive (second-argument-embedded) `fac` value via a flattening variable, `_1`, and the (first-argument-embedded) `1-` value via the register X1 (the same X1 transfer would take place for the `call` value of a user-defined decrement function instead of the `invoke` value of the built-in `1-`):

```
fac(N) :- >(N,0), _1 .= fac(1-(N)) & *(N,_1).
```

```
fac/1: allocate
       get_y_variable N,X1
       put_constant 0,X2
       invoke >/2
       put_y_value N,X1
       invoke 1-/1
       call fac/1,2
       get_y_variable _1,X1
       put_y_value N,X1
       put_y_value _1,X2
       deallocate
       invoke */2
       proceed
```

While the above *first-nesting optimization* via X1 requires no value transport at all, a *last-nesting optimization* can at least avoid the use of a **permanent** flattening variable for one non-first position: if $t_0(...)$ is the last evaluative sub-formula of a call $s_0(..., t_0(...), s_{i+1}, ..., s_n)$, none of the subformulas $s_{i+1}$, ..., $s_n$ can destroy X-registers; hence the returned value of $t_0(...)$ can be put_x_valued directly from X1 to the main call's register X$i$. A simple example is the main * call of the second factorial clause, whose first argument is denotative but whose second argument is the last evaluative subformula[21] (this "temporary nesting" is made more explicit in the source line by resubstituting its flattening variable):

```
fac(N) :- >(N,0) & *(N,fac(1-(N))).
```

```
fac/1: allocate
       get_y_variable N,X1
       put_constant 0,X2
       invoke >/2
       put_y_value N,X1
       invoke 1-/1
       call fac/1,1
       put_x_value X1,X2
       put_y_value N,X1
       deallocate
       invoke */2
       proceed
```

Note that the first put_y_value instruction would not be necessary if built-in predicates such as > on success would return void (putting nothing into X1, like a >/2+0) instead of true (overwriting X1, like a >/2+1). However, we would then have to tolerate void-valuedness, i.e. degenerate multiple-valuedness, already in the built-in kernel of RELFUN. Actually, since RELFUN's built-in predicates on failure return the single value false, they would transmute into the (0-or-1)-valued or $^0_1$-valued (C-like) special case of operators such as >/2+$^0_1$ permitting different numbers of values or *heterogeneous return arity*.[22]

---

[21] Semantic properties such as the commutativity of * could lead to source-level transformations usable for further WAM optimizations: left-recursive nestings as in fac(N) :- >(N,0) & *(fac(1-(N)),N) can maximally exploit the first-nesting optimization, here rendering the put_x_value superfluous if the put_y_value is redirected to X2.

[22] When proceeding thus far toward "built-in $^0_1$-valuedness", one could also go the further step of **identifying** true with void, e.g. by regarding non-footed clauses as shorthands for void-footed rather than true-footed clauses, so that all successful relational computations would return void instead of true. The ensuing relational behavior would come closer to the "valueless success" of PROLOG's yes-printing queries, C's void-valued functions, operating systems' 'prompt-echoing' commands, etc. On the other hand, this would increase our distance from LISP's identification of another empty data structure with the complementary truth constant, namely (in our syntax) of nil = [] = [void] or (using the new identification) [true] with false. More seriously, it would become impossible to compute with true as an explicit boolean value in data structures, since, e.g., the boolean sequences false $\neq$ true,false $\neq$ false,true $\neq$ true,false,true $\neq$ ... became indistinguishable because void is the neutral element of sequences. Thus, with RELFUN's true being **truth-functionally** equivalent to all non-false and non-unknown values, including void, and the user being free to define void-

Non-deterministic functions pose no extra problems for WAM translation: values can be enumerated by setting and resetting X1 within the usual
try/retry/trust instructions. We give the flattened denotative normal form of
the parental example in subsection 5.3.3[23] together with its WAM instructions,
again compiling the flattening variable _1 as a temporary variable:

```
child(john,lucy) :& ann.
child(john,mary) :& bob.
parental(P) :- _1 .= child(P,Q) & cares(P,_1).
cares(john,bob).
```

```
child/2:    try_me_else c2,2
            get_constant john,X1
            get_constant lucy,X2
            put_constant ann,X1
            proceed
c2:         trust_me_else_fail
            get_constant john,X1
            get_constant mary,X2
            put_constant bob,X1
            proceed

parental/1: allocate
            get_y_variable P,X1
            put_x_variable X2,X2
            call child/2,1
            put_x_value X1,X2
            put_y_value P,X1
            deallocate
            execute cares/2

cares/2:    get_constant john,X1
            get_constant bob,X2
            proctrue
```

Similarly, non-ground functions are taken care by the WAM's variable-handling
instructions like get_constant. Actually, the child/2 WAM code above can be
called non-ground, e.g. when emulating the compiled form of the source-level
child(john,Q), explained in subsection 5.3.3.

Let us now discuss the WAM compilation of multiple-footed clauses, which
for the first time makes full, symmetric use of X-registers: just as $A$ arguments are
passed into procedures via X1,...,X$A$, $V$ values can be passed out of procedures

---

valued relations (even of the form mybuiltin(...) :- builtin(...) & void), we do not
pursue true-void identification here.

[23]Instead of using the naively footened form, parental is foot-optimized here to enable its
last-call optimization.

via X1,...,X V; often intermediate procedure calls need only be applied to the contents of an X1-headed register sequence found on procedure entry or as the multiple-valued result of some preceding intermediate call. For example, the rest-denotative normal form of the original 2-footed divide/2+2 function from subsection 5.3.2 can be translated to WAM instructions in a direct manner, where the X1 value is passed out through the quotient/2+1 call, and the X2 value, by the last put_y_value instruction:

```
divide(N,D) :- _1 .= remainder(N,D) & quotient(N,D), _1.
```

```
divide/2+2:  allocate
             get_y_variable N,X1
             get_y_variable D,X2
             call remainder/2,3
             get_y_variable _1,X1
             put_y_value N,X1
             put_y_value D,X2
             call quotient/2,1
             put_y_value _1,X2
             deallocate
             proceed
```

Coming to the more efficient divide versions in subsection 5.3.3, WAM translation permits the elimination of all flattening variables, corresponding to compiling a version that embeds a call to ⁻ into a divide call, which itself is nested into a 1+ call on divide's first returned value (the second being handed on unchanged). This top-most application is depicted here as if the source used the higher-order operator jx (cf. section 5.2.4) with the identity as its second parameter, while the corresponding instruction invoke 1+/1 just leaves X2 untouched when incrementing X1 (if the top-level called addfrst1 instead, the WAM linearization of the entire nesting would end with execute addfrst1/2+2):[24]

```
divide(N,D) :- <(N,D) & 0, N.
divide(N,D) :- >=(N,D) & jx[1+,id](divide(-(N,D),D)).
```

```
divide/2+2:  try_me_else d2,2
             put_x_value X1,X3
             invoke </2
             put_constant 0,X1
             put_x_value X3,X2
             proceed
```

---

[24]Note that no allocate instructions etc. are required since the variable N need only be saved temporarily in X3 before the invoke applications of the built-ins < and >= (arithmetical built-ins never affect any registers except X1). The put_x_value instructions employed for this purpose could also be omitted with empty-valued built-in predicates.

```
d2:          trust_me_else_fail
             put_x_value X1,X3
             invoke >=/2
             put_x_value X3,X1
             invoke -/2
             call divide/2+2,0
             invoke 1+/1
             proceed
```

Finally, constant-operator-reduced forms of higher-order clauses are compiled as procedures ap/$I$ (one for each arity $I$), 'non-deterministically' cascading through the original operators. Following are optimized WAM instructions for the palin example in Fig. 5.3 of subsection 5.3.4; they constitute a single procedure ap/2 because all ap clauses happen to have arity 2:

```
ap/2: try_me_else a2,2                        put_structure palin/3,X1
      get_structure palin/3,X1                unify_y_value Emptyval
      unify_x_variable X1                     unify_y_value Singletonfun
      get_nil X2                              unify_y_value Recursionfun
      proceed                                 put_unsafe_value Middle,X2
                                              call ap/2,1
a2:   retry_me_else a3                        put_x_value X1,X2
      get_structure palin/3,X1                put_y_value Recursionfun,X1
      unify_x_variable X3                     deallocate
      unify_x_variable X1                     execute ap/2
      get_list X2
      unify_x_variable X3               a4:   retry_me_else a5
      unify_nil                               get_constant id,X1
      execute ap/2                            put_x_value X2,X1
                                              proceed
a3:   retry_me_else a4
      allocate                         a5:   retry_me_else a6
      get_structure palin/3,X1                get_structure co/1,X1
      unify_y_variable Emptyval               unify_x_variable X1
      unify_y_variable Singletonfun           proceed
      unify_y_variable Recursionfun
      get_list X2                      a6:   trust_me_else_fail
      unify_x_variable X5                     allocate
      unify_x_variable X4                     get_structure twice/1,X1
      put_constant apprel,X1                  unify_y_variable F
      put_y_variable Middle,X2                put_y_value F,X1
      put_list X3                             call ap/2,1
      unify_x_value X5                        put_x_value X1,X2
      unify_nil                               put_y_value F,X1
      call ap/2,4                             deallocate
                                              execute ap/2
```

Of course, in practice, indexing instructions would be used to let the procedures ap/$I$ directly switch on their first arguments, the original operators: former constant-head-operator clauses and structure-head-operator clauses can be efficiently accessed with switch_on_constant and switch_on_structure. Second-argument switching does then achieve, for higher-order clauses, the efficiency of PROLOG's standard first-argument indexing [SS92, Ste92, Sin93a].

## 5.4   Conclusions

The multiple-valued extension of RELFUN presented here permits natural formulations of functions like roots, divide, palinlengthzoom, upa, fa, etc. whose number of values (or return arity, symmetrically to the usual argument arity) is unequal to one. It may even be advantageous to transcribe multiple-output relations such as partition/4 into multiple-valued functions such as partition/2+2, obtaining a purely functional duplicate-removing qsort/1+1, where multiple-variable ".="-calls are used like multiple-variable lets (appfun/2+1 being the usual functional form of apprel/3):

```
qsort([]) :& [].
qsort([X|Y]) :-
        (Sm,Gr) .= partition(X,Y) & appfun(qsort(Sm),tup(X|qsort(Gr))).

partition(X,[Y|Z]) :- <(Y,X), (Sm,Gr) .= partition(X,Z) & [Y|Sm], Gr.
partition(X,[Y|Z]) :- <(X,Y), (Sm,Gr) .= partition(X,Z) & Sm, [Y|Gr].
partition(X,[X|Z]) :& partition(X,Z).
partition(X,[]) :& [], [].
```

Note that the partition/2+2 and qsort/1+1 functions, unlike the usual partition/4 and the practically non-invertible qsort/2 relations, exhibit the intended direction of computation without requiring additional mode declarations.

For specification, high-level programming, and documentation multiple foots thus raise RELFUN's user expressiveness. For certain semantic, implementation, and interchange purposes multiple-valuedness may still be syntactically preprocessed to obtain single-valuedness via relationalize (replacing functions by relations), singlify (appending tupled value sequences), and structure-generating transformations (e.g. employing a single-valued, associatively "self-normalizing" (see chapter 2) sequence function, where seq(a,seq(b,c),d) returns the seq structure seq[a,b,c,d], while multid(a,multid(b,c),d) would return the sequence a,b,c,d); however, an important point of our discussion is that a **direct** WAM implementation of Horn logic with multiple-valued functions is both possible and preferable.

Higher-order notation can further raise the specification level, whose WAM implementation may employ apply reduction, such as in a compact qsort/1+1 definition on the basis of a generally useful parameterized list-construction function `constr[El]/1+1` (identity/1+1 and `juxtapose[F,G]/2+2` being reused here from section 5.2.4):

```
qsort([]) :& [].
qsort([X|Y]) :& appfun(jx[id,constr[X]](jx[qsort,qsort](partition(X,Y)))).

partition(X,[Y|Z]) :- <(Y,X) & jx[constr[Y],id](partition(X,Z)).
partition(X,[Y|Z]) :- <(X,Y) & jx[id,constr[Y]](partition(X,Z)).
partition(X,[X|Z]) :& partition(X,Z).
partition(X,[]) :& [], [].

constr[El](Lst) :& [El|Lst].
```

The embedding of the two-valued `partition` recursions into `jx[...]`-applications of (possibly parameterized) unary functions, `constr[Y]` and `id`, avoids the (NIL-)argument padding of [...]-applications of respective binary functions, `cons` and `second`, to the recursive two-list values of a LISP-style partition version modeled on the `lt-eq-gt` paradigm in [FW78]:

$$(\text{partition } x \ l) \ \equiv \ (\text{cond}$$
$$\quad if \ (\text{null } l) \ then \ [ \ [] \ [] \ ]$$
$$\quad elseif \ (\text{less? } (\text{car } l) \ x) \ then \ ([\text{cons second}] \ [(\text{car } l) \ \text{NIL}] \ (\text{partition } x \ (\text{cdr } l)))$$
$$\quad elseif \ (\text{less? } x \ (\text{car } l)) \ then \ ([\text{second cons}] \ [\text{NIL} \ (\text{car } l)] \ (\text{partition } x \ (\text{cdr } l)))$$
$$\quad else \ (\text{partition } x \ (\text{cdr } l)))$$

$$(\text{second } x \ y) \ \equiv \ y$$

The PROLOG-like RELFUN syntax adopted up to this point is very convenient for our multiple-footed extension (in fact, both were conceived together). Already the single-footed case of non-extended RELFUN employs the 'returns' infix "&" to separate any number of body premises from the single foot premise. In the case of foot numbers unequal to one a special separator such as "&" between multiple body and foot premises becomes unavoidable; body- and foot-internal separations, then, are accomplished by the usual 'conjoins' infix " , ".

We also use a LISP-like syntax for RELFUN's valued clauses. In it the multiple-footed (for F=0, empty-footed), single-footed, and hornish (non-footed) clause notations become (ft $head'$ $body'_1$ ... $body'_B$ & $foot'_1$ ... $foot'_F$), (ft $head'$ $body'_1$ ... $body'_B$ $foot'_1$), and (hn $head'$ $body'_1$ ... $body'_B$), respectively, where priming (') denotes further transformation, i.e. the formulas $head'$, $body'_I$, and $foot'_J$ also use Cambridge-Polish prefix notation: evaluative formulas like `child(P,Q)` become `(child _p _q)` and denotative formulas like `child[P,Q]` become `'(child _p _q)`. Single-footed clauses, not normally employing the 'returns' infix, and, as usual, true-footed clauses can be expressed equivalently, e.g. (ft (parental _p) (cares ...) & true)

$\Leftrightarrow$ (ft (parental _p) (cares ...) true) $\Leftrightarrow$ (hn (parental _p) (cares ...)). For multiple-lhs ".="-premises $(p_1, ..., p_v) . = q$ we obtain the equivalence (is $p'_1, ..., p'_v$ & $q'$) $\Leftrightarrow$ (is $p'_1, ..., p'_v$ $q'$).

In the present interpreter+compiler/emulator system [BAE+96, BEH+96], running in COMMON LISP, this radical prefix syntax is still employed internally,[25] for singlify-transforming multiple-footed clauses, and by LISP-acquainted users. However, in the long term the PROLOG-like syntax seems to become the uniformly preferred alternative for input reading and pretty printing [Her92]. The printing direction was also modified to become the back-end of a RELFUN-to-PROLOG translator, whose central transformation principle was illustrated in section 5.2.3.

Our general compilation approach stresses optimization of the WAM instructions, not speediness of the compiler. The RELFUN source transformation phases of sections 5.3.2-5.3.4, with optional simplifications by a *clause normalizer* [Kra91], are thus implemented as pure, recursive LISP functions (a version of the constant-operator reducer is even written in RELFUN itself).

The WAM translation phase of section 5.3.5 constitutes a much larger LISP program because it exploits many (register) optimizations already in the DATALOG and DATAFUN (structureless and listless RELFUN) subsets. We have defined *classified RELFUN* as an explicit representation language, intermediate between preprocessed RELFUN procedures and WAM instructions; e.g., the present RELFUN classifier extends clauses by *permanent/temporary, safe/unsafe*, and *first/non-first* declarations for variables, collects premises into *chunks* (in the sense of Debray), specifies the *argument sequence* for goal unification, etc. [Kra90]. The code generator thus has a platform from which it can almost read off the WAM instructions, but it also introduces additional low-level optimizations.

Starting mainly with a LISP-based WAM emulator from Sven-Olof Nyström, Uppsala University, we adapted it as the NYWAM [Hei89], evolved the NYWAM into the GWAM [Sin95], and reimplemented the GWAM through the RAWAM [Per98]. Using our X1-return compiler, only the printing of returned values had to be added to Nyström's original PROLOG emulator for obtaining our initial RELFUN emulator. After the described compilation to X1,...,X V-returning WAM instructions, multiple-valued RELFUN can similarly reuse existing WAM emulators. Later, our emulators were enriched for RELFUN features such as higher-order operators and sorted variables. We confirmed a small emulator-performance increase proceeding from relational to equivalent functional definitions of the palinclass-r/palinclass type. In order to quantify the LISP overhead, we transcribed the unification parts of the NYWAM to C, extrapolating a speed-up factor of six for this whole emulator [Els90]. Building on the experience with a successful LISP-to-C translation of the entire RELFUN in-

---

[25] The original interpreter [Bol86] used only single-footed clauses (ft *head' body'*$_1$ ... *body'*$_B$ *foot'*$_1$) and facts (hn *head'*), leaving out the ft and hn tags.

terpreter [GBH+96], by the CLiCC group of Friedemann Simon [BCF+94], a CLiCC-supported C translation of the LISP-based GWAM would seem to be possible. However, Markus Perling meanwhile reimplemented and optimized the GWAM in C, using [AK91] but no translation assistance, and measured a speed-up factor of up to thirty for this new RAWAM (350 KLIPS on an UltraS-PARC) [Per98]. As the next efficiency step after emulation in C, the WAM-implementation techniques for RELFUN's (multiple-)valued PROLOG extensions presented here could be developed into a RELFUN-to-C translator (relying on C compilers for native-code generation) on the basis of PROLOG-to-C translators, our RAWAM, our native-like functional system LLAMA [Sin95], and native-code relational systems such as Parma or Aquarius [VR94].

# Bibliography

[ABH+95]    Andreas Abecker, Harold Boley, Knut Hinkelmann, Holger Wa-
            che, and Franz Schmalhofer. An Environment for Exploring and
            Validating Declarative Knowledge. DFKI Technical Memo TM-
            95-03, DFKI GmbH, November 1995. Also in: Proc. Workshop
            on Logic Programming Environments at ILPS'95, Portland, Ore-
            gon, Dec. 1995.

[AK91]      Hassan Aït-Kaci. *Warren's Abstract Machine: A Tutorial Re-
            construction*. The MIT Press, Cambridge, Massachusetts, 1991.

[AKP93]     Hassan Aït-Kaci and Andreas Podelski. Logic Programming with
            Functions over Order-Sorted Feature Terms. In Evelina Lamma
            and Paola Mello, editors, *Proceedings of the 3rd International
            Workshop on Extensions of Logic Programming, ELP '92, Bolo-
            gna 1992*, volume 660 of *LNAI*. Springer, 1993.

[Bac78]     John Backus. Can programming be liberated from the von Neu-
            mann style? A functional style and its algebra of programs.
            *CACM*, 21(8):613–641, August 1978.

[BAE+96]    Harold Boley, Simone Andel, Klaus Elsbernd, Michael Herfert,
            Michael Sintek, and Werner Stein. RELFUN Guide: Program-
            ming with Relations and Functions Made Easy. Document D-
            93-12, DFKI GmbH, July 1996. Second, Revised Edition.

[BBK94]     Harold Boley, Ulrich Buhrmann, and Christof Kremer. Towards
            a sharable knowledge base on recyclable plastics. In James K.
            McDowell and Kenneth J. Meltsner, editors, *Knowledge-Based
            Applications in Materials Science and Engineering*, pages 29–42.
            TMS, 1994.

[BCF+94]    Harry Bretthauer, Thomas Christaller, Horst Friedrich, Wolf-
            gang Goerigk, Winfried Heicking, Ulrich Hoffmann, Andreas
            Kind, Bert Klude, Heinz Knutzen, Jürgen Kopp, E. Ulrich Krie-
            gel, Ingo Mohr, Rainer Rosenmüller, and Friedemann Simon.

162

Von der APPLY-Methodik zum System. Technical Report AP-PLY/XIII/10, CAU, GMD, ISST, VW-GEDAS, June 1994. Abschlußbericht Verbundvorhaben APPLY.

[BEH+96]   Harold Boley, Klaus Elsbernd, Hans-Günther Hein, Thomas Krause, Markus Perling, Michael Sintek, and Werner Stein. RFM Manual: Compiling RELFUN into the Relational/Functional Machine. Document D-91-03, DFKI GmbH, July 1996. Third, Revised Edition.

[BGM88]   P.G. Bosco, E. Giovannetti, and C. Moiso. Narrowing vs. SLD-resolution. *Theoretical Computer Science*, 59:3–23, 1988.

[BHH+91]   Harold Boley, Philipp Hanschke, Martin Harm, Knut Hinkelmann, Thomas Labisch, Manfred Meyer, Joerg Mueller, Thomas Oltzen, Michael Sintek, Werner Stein, and Frank Steinle. $\mu$CAD2NC: A declarative lathe-workplanning model transforming CAD-like geometries into abstract NC programs. Document D-91-15, University of Kaiserslautern, DFKI, November 1991.

[BHHM95]   H. Boley, P. Hanschke, K. Hinkelmann, and M. Meyer. COLAB: A hybrid knowledge representation and compilation laboratory. *Annals of Operations Research*, 55:11–79, 1995. Preprinted as: DFKI Research Report RR-93-08, Jan. 1993.

[BL74]   W. S. Brainerd and L. H. Landweber. *Theory of Computation*. Wiley, New York, 1974.

[BL86]   M. Bellia and G. Levi. The relation between logic and functional languages: A survey. *Journal of Logic Programming*, 3:217–236, 1986.

[Bol83]   Harold Boley. FIT - PROLOG: A functional/relational language comparison. Interner Bericht 95/83, MEMO SEKI-83-14, Univ. Kaiserslautern, FB Informatik, December 1983.

[Bol86]   Harold Boley. RELFUN: A relational/functional integration with valued clauses. *SIGPLAN Notices*, 21(12):87–98, December 1986.

[Bol90]   Harold Boley. A relational/functional language and its compilation into the WAM. Technical Report SEKI SR-90-05, University of Kaiserslautern, Department of Computer Science, April 1990.

[Bol92a]   Harold Boley. Declarative operations on nets. In Fritz Lehmann, editor, *Semantic Networks in Artificial Intelligence*, volume 23, pages 601–637. Special Issue of Computers & Mathematics with Applications, Pergamon Press, 1992. Preprinted as: DFKI Research Report RR-90-12, Oct. 1990.

[Bol92b]    Harold Boley. Extended Logic-plus-Functional Programming. In Lars-Henrik Eriksson, Lars Hallnäs, and Peter Schroeder-Heister, editors, *Proceedings of the 2nd International Workshop on Extensions of Logic Programming, ELP '91, Stockholm 1991*, volume 596 of *LNAI*. Springer, 1992.

[Bol93a]    Harold Boley, editor. *A Sampler of Relational/Functional Definitions*, Technical Memo TM-91-04, March 1991, Second, Revised Edition July 1993. DFKI Kaiserslautern.

[Bol93b]    Harold Boley. A Direct Semantic Characterization of RELFUN. In Evelina Lamma and Paola Mello, editors, *Proceedings of the 3rd International Workshop on Extensions of Logic Programming, ELP '92, Bologna 1992*, volume 660 of *LNAI*. Springer, 1993.

[Bol94]     Harold Boley. Finite Domains and Exclusions as First-Class Citizens. In Roy Dyckhoff, editor, *Proceedings of the 4th International Workshop on Extensions of Logic Programming, ELP '93, St. Andrews, Scotland, 1993*, volume 798 of *LNAI*. Springer, 1994.

[Bol96]     Harold Boley. Knowledge Bases in the World Wide Web: A Challenge for Logic Programming. In Paul Tarau, Andrew Davison, Koen De Bosschere, and Manuel Hermenegildo, editors, *Proc. JICSLP'96 Post-Conference Workshop on Logic Programming Tools for INTERNET Applications*, pages 139–147. COMPULOG-NET, Bonn, Sept. 1996. Revised versions in: International Workshop "Intelligent Information Integration", KI-97, Freiburg, Sept. 1997; DFKI Technical Memo TM-96-02, Oct. 1997.

[Bol97]     Harold Boley. Coordinates for Declarative-Programming Education. 6th International Workshop on Functional and Logic Programming, Schwarzenberg, Germany, January 1997.

[Bol99a]    Harold Boley. Functional-Logic Integration via Minimal Reciprocal Extensions. *Theoretical Computer Science*, 212:77–99, 1999.

[Bol99b]    Harold Boley. ONTOFILE: Exterior and Interior Ontologies of File/HTTP URLs. In Hannu Jaakkola, Hannu Kangassalo, and Eiji Kawaguchi, editors, *Information Modelling and Knowledge Bases X*. IOS Press, Amsterdam, "Frontiers in Artificial Intelligence and Applications", Spring 1999.

[BPS97]     Harold Boley, Markus Perling, and Michael Sintek. Transforming Workpiece Geometries into Lathe-NC Programs by Qualitative Simulation. In Ulrich Geske, editor, *Session on Simulation with*

*Knowledge-Based Systems of the 15th IMACS World Congress on Scientific Computation, Modelling and Applied Mathematics.* Wissenschaft und Technik Verlag, Berlin, August 1997.

[BR91]    Harold Boley and Michael M. Richter, editors. *Proceedings of the International Workshop on Processing Declarative Knowledge (PDK'91)*, number 567 in Lecture Notes in Artificial Intelligence (LNAI). Springer-Verlag, Berlin, Heidelberg, 1991.

[Buh94]   Ulrich Buhrmann. Erstellung einer deklarativen Wissensbasis über recyclingrelevante Materialien. Diplomarbeit, Universität Kaiserslautern, FB Informatik, Postfach 3049, 67608 Kaiserslautern, Februar 1994.

[CK85]    Mats Carlsson and Kenneth M. Kahn. LM-Prolog user manual. Technical Report UPMAIL 24, Uppsala University, Department of Computer Science, Revised April 1985.

[CKW93]   Weidong Chen, Michael Kifer, and David S. Warren. HiLog: A Foundation for Higher-Order Logic Programming. *Journal of Logic Programming*, 15:187–230, 1993.

[Col87]   Alain Colmerauer. Introduction to Prolog III. In *ESPRIT '87*, pages 611–629. North Holland, 1987.

[Der95]   Nachum Dershowitz. Goal Solving as Operational Semantics. In John Lloyd, editor, *Proceedings of the International Symposium on Logic Programming*, pages 3–17, Cambridge, December 1995. MIT Press.

[DL86]    D. DeGroot and G. Lindstrom, editors. *Logic Programming: Functions, Relations, and Equations*. Prentice-Hall, 1986.

[Els90]   Klaus Elsbernd. Effizienzvergleiche zwischen einer LISP- und C-codierten WAM. Technical Report SWP–90–03, University of Kaiserslautern, Department of Computer Science, June 1990.

[FHPJW92] J. H. Fasel, P. Hudak, S. Peyton-Jones, and P. Wadler. Special Issue on the Functional Programming Language Haskell. *SIGPLAN Notices*, 27(5), 1992.

[Fis94]   Cornelia Fischer. PAntUDE — An Anti-Unification Algorithm for Expressing Refined Generalizations. Technical Report TM-94-04, DFKI Kaiserslautern, May 1994.

[Fri84]   Laurent Fribourg. Oriented equational clauses as a programming language. *J. Logic Programming*, 1(2):165–177, 1984.

[Fri85]      Laurent Fribourg. SLOG: A logic programming language inter-
             preter based on clausal superposition and rewriting. In *1985
             Symposium on Logic Programming*, pages 172–184. IEEE Com-
             puter Society Press, 1985.

[FW78]       Daniel P. Friedman and David S. Wise. Functional Combination.
             *Computer Languages*, 3:31–35, 1978.

[GBH+96]     Wolfgang Goerigk, Harold Boley, Ulrich Hoffmann, Markus Per-
             ling, and Michael Sintek. Komplettkompilation von Lisp: Eine
             Studie zur Übersetzung von Lisp-Software für C-Umgebungen.
             *KI*, (2), Juni 1996.

[GF91]       Michael R. Genesereth and Richard Fikes in collaboration with
             Danny Bobrow, Piero Bonissone, Ron Brachman, Ramana-
             than Guha, Reed Letsinger, Valdimir Lifschitz, Bob MacGre-
             gor, John McCarthy, Peter Norvig, Ramesh Patil, and Len Schu-
             bert. Knowledge Interchange Format Version 2.2 Reference Ma-
             nual. Technical Report Logic-90-4, Stanford University, Compu-
             ter Science Department, Logic Group, March 1991.

[GLLO85]     John Gabriel, Tim Lindholm, E.L. Lusk, and R.A. Overbeek. A
             tutorial on the Warren abstract machine for computational lo-
             gic. Technical Report ANL-84-84, Argonne National Laboratory,
             Illinois, June 1985.

[GLMP91]     E. Giovannetti, G. Levi, C. Moiso, and C. Palamidessi. Kernel-
             LEAF: A logic plus functional language. *Journal of Computer
             and System Sciences*, 42:139–185, 1991.

[GM84]       Joseph A. Goguen and José Meseguer. Equality, types, modu-
             les, and (why not?) generics for logic programming. *J. Logic
             Programming*, 1(2):179–210, 1984.

[GMHGRA97]   J.C.   Gonzalez-Moreno,    M.T.   Hortala-Gonzalez,    and
             M. Rodríguez-Artalejo.   A Higher Order Rewriting Logic
             for Functional Logic Programming. In *The Fourteenth Inter-
             national Conference on Logic Programming*, ICLP'97, Leuven,
             July 1997.

[Hal95]      Victoria Hall. Integration von Sorten als ausgezeichnete taxono-
             mische Prädikate in eine relational-funktionale Sprache. Docu-
             ment D-95-04, DFKI GmbH, March 1995.

[Han91]      Michael Hanus. Efficient Implementation of Narrowing and Re-
             writing. In Boley and Richter [BR91].

[Han93]      Philipp Hanschke.  A Declarative Integration of Terminologi-
             cal, Constraint-based, Data-driven, and Goal-directed Reaso-
             ning. Research Report RR-93-46, DFKI Kaiserslautern, October
             1993.

[Han94]      Michael Hanus.  The Integration of Functions into Logic Pro-
             gramming: From Theory to Practice. *Journal of Logic Program-
             ming*, 19,20:583–628, 1994.

[Han97]      Michael Hanus.  A Unified Computation Model for Functional
             and Logic Programming. In *POPL'97*, Paris 1997.

[Hei89]      Hans-Günther Hein.  Adding WAM instructions to support va-
             lued clauses for the relational/functional integration language
             RELFUN. Technical Report SWP–90–02, University of Kaisers-
             lautern, Department of Computer Science, December 1989.

[Hei91]      Hans-Günther Hein. WAM indexing and footening techniques for
             RELFUN — a case study on the DNF benchmark. ARC-TEC
             Discussion Paper 91-11, DFKI Kaiserslautern, August 1991.

[Hei93]      Hans-Günther Hein. Propagation Techniques in WAM-based Ar-
             chitectures — The FIDO-III Approach. DFKI Technical Memo
             TM-93-04, DFKI Kaiserslautern, October 1993.

[Hen80]      Peter Henderson.  *Functional Programming – Application and
             Implementation.*  Series in Computer Science. Prentice-Hall,
             Englewood Cliffs, NJ, 1980.

[Her92]      Michael Herfert.  Parsen und Generieren der PROLOG-artigen
             Syntax von RELFUN. Technical Report D-92-23, DFKI GmbH,
             October 1992.

[Her95]      Michael Herfert.  Deklarative statische und dynamische Softwa-
             remodule.  Diplomarbeit, Universität Kaiserslautern, February
             1995.

[HL94]       P. M. Hill and J. W. Lloyd. *The Gödel Programming Language.*
             Logic Programming Series. MIT Press, 1994.

[HLW92]      Werner Hans, Rita Loogen, and Stephan Winkler. On the Inter-
             action of Lazy Evaluation and Backtracking. In *Proceedings of
             the Symposium on Programming Language Implementation and
             Logic Programming, PLILP '92*, LNCS. Springer, 1992.

[JL87]       Joxan Jaffar and Jean-Louis Lassez. Constraint Logic Program-
             ming. In *Proceedings of the 14th ACM Symposium on Principles
             of Programming Languages (POPL), Munich, Germany*, pages
             111–119. ACM, January 1987.

[Kow83]      Robert Kowalski. Logic programming. In *INFORMATION PROCESSING 83, Proc. IFIP 9th World Computer Congress*, pages 133–145, Paris, 1983.

[Kra90]      Thomas Krause. Klassifizierte relational/funktionale Klauseln: Eine deklarative Zwischensprache zur Generierung von Register-optimierten WAM-Instruktionen. Technical Report SWP–90–04, University of Kaiserslautern, Department of Computer Science, May 1990.

[Kra91]      Thomas Krause. Globale Datenflußanalyse und horizontale Compilation der relational-funktionalen Sprache RELFUN. Diplomarbeit, DFKI D-91-08, Universität Kaiserslautern, FB Informatik, Postfach 3049, D-6750 Kaiserslautern, March 1991.

[Llo87]      John W. Lloyd. *Foundations of Logic Programming.* Springer-Verlag, Berlin, Heidelberg, New York, 1987.

[Llo94]      John W. Lloyd. Combining Functional and Logic Programming Languages. In *1994 International Logic Programming Symposium*, ILPS'94.

[MAE+62]     John McCarthy, Paul W. Abrahams, Daniel J. Edwards, Timothy P. Hart, and Michael I. Levin. *LISP 1.5 programmer's manual.* MIT Press, Cambridge, Mass., 1962.

[MNRA92]     J.J. Moreno-Navarro and M. Rodriguez-Artalejo. Logic programming with functions and predicates: The language BABEL. *Journal of Logic Programming*, 12:191–223, 1992.

[NM90]       Gopalan Nadathur and Dale Miller. Higher-order Horn clauses. *JACM*, 37(4):777–814, October 1990.

[O'D85]      M. J. O'Donnell. *Equational Logic as a Programming Language.* MIT Press, Cambridge, Mass., 1985.

[Per97]      Markus Perling. GeneTS: A Relational-Functional Genetic Algorithm for the Traveling Salesman Problem. Technical Report TM-97-01, DFKI GmbH, August 1997.

[Per98]      Markus Perling. The RAWAM: Relfun-Adapted WAM Emulation in C. Technical Report TM-98-07, DFKI GmbH, December 1998.

[Plo70]      Gordon D. Plotkin. A Note on Inductive Generalization. In B. Meltzer and D. Michie, editors, *Machine Intelligence*, volume 5, pages 153–163. Elsevier North-Holland, New York, 1970.

[PP82]       Luís Moniz Pereira and António Porto. Pure Lisp in pure Prolog. Logic Programming Newsletter 3, Summer 1982. Universidade Nova de Lisboa, Departamento de Informática.

168

[PS91]       Lawrence C. Paulson and Andrew W. Smith. Logic program-
             ming, functional programming, and inductive definitions. In
             P. Schroeder-Heister, editor, *Extensions of Logic Programming*,
             pages 283–309, Berlin, Heidelberg, New York, 1991. Springer-
             Verlag. LNCS 475.

[PW80]       Fernando C. N. Pereira and David H. D. Warren. Definite clause
             grammars for language analysis—a survey of the formalism and
             a comparison with augmented transition networks. *Artificial In-
             telligence*, 13(3):231–278, 1980.

[Rae92]      Luc De Raedt. *Interactive Theory Revision – An Inductive Logic
             Programming Approach*. Academic Press, London, 1992.

[Ric93]      Michael M. Richter. Some Recent Developments in the Represen-
             tation and Processing of Knowledge. *Fundamenta Informaticae*,
             18:233–248, 1993.

[Sin91]      Michael Sintek. Monolinguistic $\mu$CAD2NC: A Deterministic
             RELFUN Application Generating Abstract NC Programs from
             CAD-like Geometries. DFKI Kaiserslautern, September 1991.

[Sin92]      Michael Sintek. FINDOM — Finite Domains in RELFUN Via
             Simulated Reassignment Variables. DFKI Kaiserslautern, June
             1992.

[Sin93a]     Michael Sintek. Indexing PROLOG procedures into DAGs
             by heuristic classification. Technical Memo TM-93-05, DFKI
             GmbH, 1993.

[Sin93b]     Michael Sintek. ORF — Object-Centered RELFUN. DFKI Kai-
             serslautern, November 1993.

[Sin95]      Michael Sintek. FLIP: Functional-plus-logic programming on an
             integrated platform. Technical Memo TM-95-02, DFKI GmbH,
             May 1995.

[SJ90]       Guy L. Steele Jr. *COMMON LISP: The Language, Second Edi-
             tion*. Digital Press, 1990.

[SS91]       W. Stein and M. Sintek. RELFUN/X: An Experimental PRO-
             LOG Implementation of RELFUN. ARC-TEC Document 91-1,
             DFKI GmbH, March 1991.

[SS92]       Werner Stein and Michael Sintek. A generalized intelligent in-
             dexing method. In H. Boley, U. Furbach, and W.-M. Lippe,
             editors, *Workshop "Sprachen für KI-Anwendungen, Konzepte -
             Methoden - Implementierungen" in Bad Honnef, 12/92-1*. Insti-
             tute of Applied Mathematics and Computer Science, University
             of Münster, May 1992.

[SSB93]     Michael Sintek, Werner Stein, and Ulrich Buhrmann. Validation and Exploration of the Period System of the Elements: A Relfun Knowledge Base. In Boley [Bol93a].

[Ste92]     Werner Stein. Indexing Principles for Relational Languages Applied to PROLOG Code Generation. Document D-92-22, DFKI GmbH, 1992.

[Ste93]     Werner Stein. Nutzung globaler Analysetechniken in einem optimierenden Compiler für die Constraint-Logic-Programming-Sprache FIDO III. Diplomarbeit, Universität Kaiserslautern, FB Informatik, Juli 1993.

[Van89]     Pascal Van Hentenryck. *Constraint Satisfaction in Logic Programming*. MIT Press, Cambridge, Ma., 1989.

[VR94]      Peter Van Roy. 1983-1993: The Wonder Years of Sequential Prolog Implementation. *The Journal of Logic Programming*, 19,20:385–441, 1994.

[War82]     David H. D. Warren. Higher-order extensions to PROLOG: Are they needed? *Machine Intelligence*, 10:441–454, 1982.

[War83]     David H. D. Warren. An abstract PROLOG instruction set. Technical Report 309, SRI International, AI Center, 1983.

[Wil89]     Reinhard Wilhelm. Übersetzer für imperative, funktionale und logische Programmiersprachen: Ein Vergleich. In W.-M. Lippe, editor, *Software-Entwicklung — Konzepte, Erfahrungen, Perspektiven*, pages 156–165. Springer-Verlag, 1989. Proc. Fachtagung, veranstaltet vom Fachausschuß 2.1 der GI, Marburg, Juni 1989.

[WPP77]     David H. D. Warren, Luis M. Pereira, and Fernando Pereira. Prolog - the language and its implementation compared with Lisp. *SIGPLAN Notices*, 12(8):109–115, August 1977. Special Issue.

# Lecture Notes in Artificial Intelligence (LNAI)

# Lecture Notes in Computer Science